THE VIETNAM WAR
OPPOSING VIEWPOINTS®

Other Books of Related Interest:

American History Series

Opposing Viewpoints in American History

THE VIETNAM WAR

O P P O S I N G   V I E W P O I N T S®

David L. Bender, *Publisher*
Bruno Leone, *Executive Editor*

William Dudley, *Series Editor*
John C. Chalberg, Ph.D., professor of history,
   Normandale Community College, *Consulting Editor*

William Dudley, *Book Editor*

Greenhaven Press, Inc.
San Diego, California

Cover photographs, clockwise from top: 1) Vietnamese children fleeing after accidental aerial napalm strike, June 8, 1972 (AP/Wide World Photos); 2) Members of the US 173rd Airborne Brigade patrolling in Phuoc Tuy Province, South Vietnam, June 1966 (Archive Photos); 3) President Lyndon B. Johnson and Secretary of Defense Robert S. McNamara conferring in the White House, December 1, 1964 (Archive Photos); 4) Peace demonstration in Central Park, New York, April 1968 (Archive Photos).

Library of Congress Cataloging-in-Publication Data

The Vietnam war : opposing viewpoints / William Dudley,
    book editor.
        p.   cm. — (American history series)
    Includes bibliographical references and index.
    ISBN 1-56510-701-2 (lib. : alk. paper) —
ISBN 1-56510-700-4 (pbk. : alk. paper)
        1. Vietnamese Conflict, 1961–1975—United States.
    2. Vietnamese Conflict—Protest movements—United States.
    3. Vietnamese Conflict, 1961–1975—Public opinion. 4. Public
    opinion—United States. 5. United States—Foreign relations—
    1963–1969. 6. United States—Foreign relations—1969–1974.
    I. Dudley, William, 1964–   . II. Series: American history series
    (San Diego, Calif.)
    DS558.V59   1998   97-9448
    959.704'3373—dc21   CIP

©1998 by Greenhaven Press, Inc., PO Box 289009,
San Diego, CA 92198-9009

Printed in the U.S.A.

"America was born of revolt, flourished in dissent, became great through experimentation."

Henry Steele Commager, American Historian

Contents

Chapter 5: Protesters and Soldiers

Chapter 6: A Debate over the Media's Role in Vietnam

Foreword

Aboard the *Arbella* as it lurched across the cold, gray Atlantic, John Winthrop was as calm as the waters surrounding him were wild. With the confidence of a leader, Winthrop gathered his Puritan companions around him. It was time to offer a sermon. England lay behind them, and years of strife and persecution for their religious beliefs were over, he said. But the Puritan abandonment of England, he reminded his followers, did not mean that England was beyond redemption. Winthrop wanted his followers to remember England even as they were leaving it behind. Their goal should be to create a new England, one far removed from the authority of the Anglican church and King Charles I. In Winthrop's words, their settlement in the New World ought to be "a city upon a hill," a just society for corrupt England to emulate.

A Chance to Start Over

One June 8, 1630, John Winthrop and his company of refugees had their first glimpse of what they came to call New England. High on the surrounding hills stood a welcoming band of fir trees whose fragrance drifted to the *Arbella* on a morning breeze. To Winthrop, the "smell off the shore [was] like the smell of a garden." This new world would, in fact, often be compared to the Garden of Eden. Here, John Winthrop would have his opportunity to start life over again. So would his family and his shipmates. So would all those who came after them. These victims of conflict in old England hoped to find peace in New England.

Winthrop, for one, had experienced much conflict in his life. As a Puritan, he was opposed to Catholicism and Anglicanism, both of which, he believed, were burdened by distracting rituals and distant hierarchies. A parliamentarian by conviction, he despised Charles I, who had spurned Parliament and created a private army to do his bidding. Winthrop believed in individual responsibility and fought against the loss of religious and political freedom. A gentleman landowner, he feared the rising economic power of a merchant class that seemed to value only money. Once Winthrop stepped aboard the *Arbella*, he hoped, these conflicts would not be a part of his American future.

Yet his Puritan religion told Winthrop that human beings are fallen creatures and that perfection, whether communal or individual, is unachievable on this earth. Therefore, he faced a paradox: On the one hand, his religion demanded that he attempt to live a perfect life in an imperfect world. On the other hand, it told him that he was destined to fail.

Soon after Winthrop disembarked from the *Arbella*, he came face-to-face with this maddening dilemma. He found himself presiding not over a utopia but over a colony caught up in disputes as troubling as any he had confronted in his English past. John Winthrop, it seems, was not the only Puritan with a dream of a heaven on earth. But others in the community saw the dream differently. They wanted greater political and religious freedom than their leader was prepared to grant. Often, Winthrop was able to handle this conflict diplomatically. For example, he expanded participation in elections and allowed the voters of Massachusetts Bay greater power.

But religious conflict was another matter because it was grounded in competing visions of the Puritan utopia. In Roger Williams and Anne Hutchinson, two of his fellow colonists, John Winthrop faced rivals unprepared to accept his definition of the perfect community. To Williams, perfection demanded that he separate himself from the Puritan institutions in his community and create an even "purer" church. Winthrop, however, disagreed and exiled Williams to Rhode Island. Hutchinson presumed that she could interpret God's will without a minister. Again, Winthrop did not agree. Hutchinson was tried on charges of heresy, convicted, and banished from Massachusetts.

John Winthrop's Massachusetts colony was the first but far from the last American attempt to build a unified, peaceful community that, in the end, only provoked a discord. This glimpse at its history reveals what Winthrop confronted: the unavoidable presence of conflict in American life.

American Assumptions

From America's origins in the early seventeenth century, Americans have often held several interrelated assumptions about their country. First, people believe that to be American is to be free. Second, because Americans did not have to free themselves from feudal lords or an entrenched aristocracy, America has been seen as a perpetual haven from the troubles and disputes that are found in the Old World.

John Winthrop lived his life as though these assumptions were true. But the opposing viewpoints presented in the American History Series should reveal that for many Americans, these assumptions were and are myths. Indeed, for numerous Americans, liberty has not always been guaranteed, and disputes have been an integral, sometimes welcome part of their life.

The American landscape has been torn apart again and again by a great variety of clashes—theological, ideological, political, economic, geographical, and social. But such a landscape is not necessarily a hopelessly divided country. If the editors hope to prove anything during the course of this series, it is not that the United States has been destroyed by conflict but rather that it has been enlivened, enriched, and even strengthened by Americans who have disagreed with one another.

Thomas Jefferson was one of the least confrontational of Americans, but he boldly and irrevocably enriched American life with his individualistic views. Like John Winthrop before him, he had a notion of an American Eden. Like Winthrop, he offered a vision of a harmonious society. And like Winthrop, he not only became enmeshed in conflict but eventually presided over a people beset by it. But unlike Winthrop, Jefferson believed this Eden was not located in a specific community but in each individual American. His Declaration of Independence from Great Britain could also be read as a declaration of independence for each individual in American society.

Jefferson's Ideal

Jefferson's ideal world was composed of "yeoman farmers," each of whom was roughly equal to the others in society's eyes, each of whom was free from the restrictions of both government and fellow citizens. Throughout his life, Jefferson offered a continuing challenge to Americans: Advance individualism and equality or see the death of the American experiment. Jefferson believed that the strength of this experiment depended upon a society of autonomous individuals and a society without great gaps between rich and poor. His challenge to his fellow Americans to create—and sustain—such a society has itself produced both economic and political conflict.

A society whose guiding document is the Declaration of Independence is a society assured of the freedom to dream—and to disagree. We know that Jefferson hated conflict, both personal and political. His tendency was to avoid confrontations of any sort, to squirrel himself away and write rather than to stand up and speak his mind. It is only through his written words that we can grasp Jefferson's utopian dream of a society of independent farmers, all pursuing their private dreams and all leading lives of middling prosperity.

Jefferson, this man of wealth and intellect, lived an essentially happy private life. But his public life was much more troublesome. From the first rumblings of the American Revolution in the 1760s to the North-South skirmishes of the 1820s that ultimately produced the Civil War, Jefferson was at or near the center of American political history. The issues were almost too many—and too crucial—for one lifetime: Jefferson had to choose between supporting or rejecting the path of revolution. During and after the ensuing war, he was at the forefront of the battle for religious liberty. After endorsing the Constitution, he opposed the economic plans of Alexander Hamilton. At the end of the century, he fought the infamous Alien and Sedition Acts, which limited civil liberties. As president, he opposed the Federalist court, conspiracies to divide the union, and calls for a new war against England. Throughout his life, Thomas Jefferson, slaveholder, pondered the conflict between American freedom and American slavery. And from retirement at his Monticello retreat, he frowned at the rising spirit of commercialism he feared was dividing Americans and destroying his dream of American harmony.

No matter the issue, however, Thomas Jefferson invariably supported the rights of the individual. Worried as he was about the excesses of commercialism, he accepted them because his main concern was to live in a society where liberty and individualism could flourish. To Jefferson, Americans had to be free to worship as they desired. They also deserved to be free from an over-reaching government. To Jefferson, Americans should also be free to possess slaves.

Harmony, an Elusive Goal

Before reading the articles in this anthology, the editors ask readers to ponder the lives of John Winthrop and Thomas Jefferson. Each held a utopian vision, one based upon the demands of community and the other on the autonomy of the individual. Each dreamed of a country of perpetual new beginnings. Each found himself thrust into a position of leadership and found that conflict could not be avoided. Harmony, whether communal or individual, was a forever elusive goal.

The opposing visions of Winthrop and Jefferson have been at the heart of many differences among Americans from many backgrounds through the whole of American history. Moreover, their visions have provoked important responses that have helped shape American society, the American character, and many an American battle.

The editors of the American History Series have done extensive research to find representative opinions on the issues included in these volumes. They have found numerous outstanding opposing viewpoints from people of all times, classes, and genders in American history. From those, they have selected commentaries that best fit the nature and flavor of the period and topic under consideration. Every attempt was made to include the most important and relevant viewpoints in each chapter. Obviously, not every notable viewpoint could be included. Therefore, a selective, annotated bibliography has been provided at the end of each book to aid readers in seeking additional information.

The editors are confident that as this series reveals past conflicts, it will help revitalize the reader's views of the American present. In that spirit, the American History Series is dedicated to the proposition that American history is more complicated, more fascinating, and more troubling than John Winthrop or Thomas Jefferson ever dared to imagine.

John C. Chalberg
Consulting Editor

Greenhaven Press anthologies primarily consist of previously published material taken from a variety of sources, including periodicals, books, scholarly journals, newspapers, government documents, and position papers from private and public organizations. These original sources are often edited for length and to ensure their accessibility for a young adult audience. The anthology editors also change the original titles of these works in order to clearly present the main thesis of each viewpoint and to explicitly indicate the opinion presented in the viewpoint. These alterations are made in consideration of both the reading and comprehension levels of a young adult audience. Every effort is made to ensure that Greenhaven Press accurately reflects the original intent of the authors included in this anthology.

Indochina During the Vietnam War

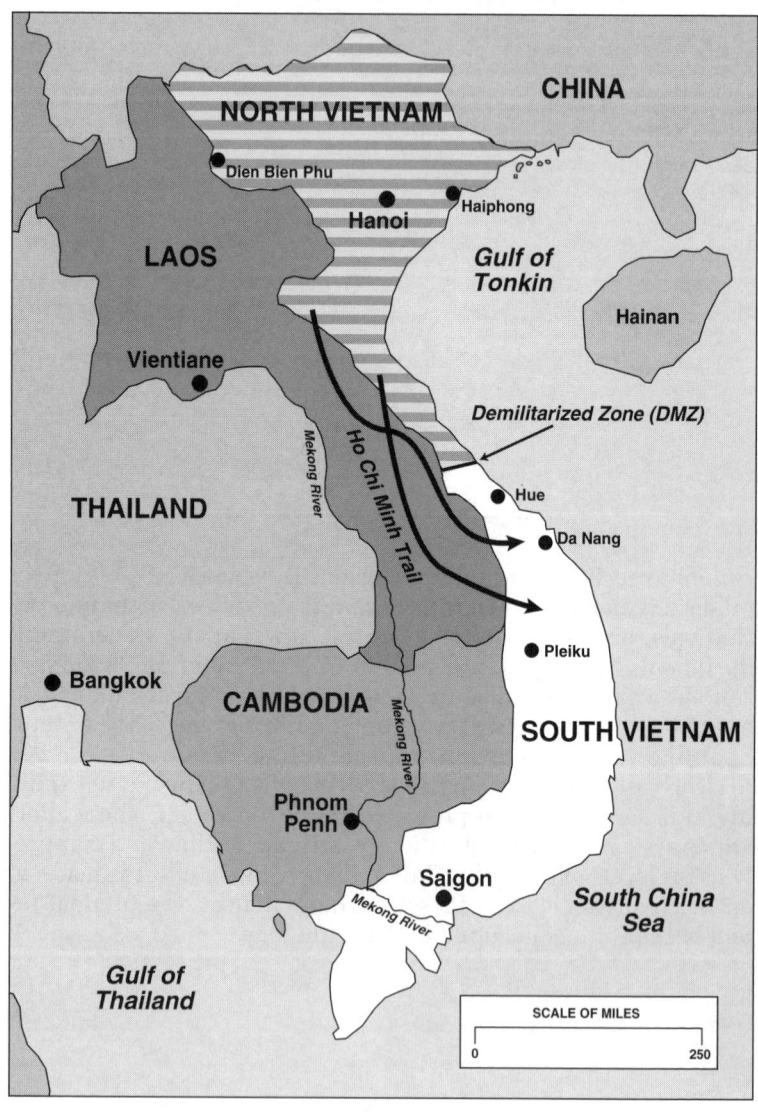

Introduction

"Whether the preservation of South Vietnam was worth the actions of the United States and the human and financial costs such actions incurred is but one of many questions concerning the Vietnam War that is still debated."

On September 2, 1945, a gaunt man in a plain khaki tunic spoke before a crowd of half a million people at Ba Dinh square in Hanoi, Vietnam. Shops, offices, and schools had been closed for the occasion; red flags and banners bearing nationalist slogans hung from city buildings. As the crowd listened, the speaker—a revolutionary Communist leader who had taken the name Ho Chi Minh ("he who enlightens")—declared Vietnam to be independent both of Japan, which had occupied Vietnam during World War II, and of France, which had ruled Vietnam as a colony since the nineteenth century. His declaration began with the words, "We hold truths that all men are created equal, that they are endowed by their Creator with certain unalienable rights, among these are Life, Liberty, and the pursuit of Happiness."

These phrases borrowed from America's 1776 Declaration of Independence were but one of several references to the United States on that day. The band providing music for the festivities played "The Star-Spangled Banner." Several Americans—members of the Office of Strategic Services (OSS) who had cooperated with Ho Chi Minh and his forces in fighting the Japanese—stood on the reviewing stand with General Vo Nguyen Giap, the head of the army of the League for the Independence of Vietnam (known as the Vietminh). In an address following Ho's pronouncement, Giap said, "We regard the U.S. as a good friend."

This celebration, the culmination of the "August Revolution" in which the Vietminh had seized power in most of Vietnam's provinces, was part of a long history of independence efforts in

15

Vietnam. Roughly one thousand years before, Vietnam had first won independence from China after centuries of foreign rule. Ho himself had been involved in independence struggles for most of his life. In the early 1930s, his Indochinese Communist Party (ICP) had unsuccessfully rebelled against French rule. From 1941 to 1945, the Vietminh, a coalition of nationalist groups created by Ho and led by members of the ICP, had waged guerrilla warfare against the Japanese, who had displaced the French during World War II. The Vietminh had also created a network of political associations and organizations in Vietnamese cities and villages. The success of the 1945 revolution was a result of the work of the Vietminh and the popular support it had attracted, but it was also a product of timing. Japan had been defeated in World War II, and France had yet to send soldiers and personnel back to Vietnam to retake its lost colony.

Most people in the United States were unaware of these developments in Vietnam, a country more than eight thousand miles away on the other side of the world. On the day Ho Chi Minh declared Vietnamese independence, Americans were instead celebrating the news that the Japanese had formally signed surrender terms, finally bringing World War II to a close.

The End of a War

Three decades later, on April 30, 1975, a different scene unfolded. The division of Vietnam into two separate states was coming to an end as 150,000 North Vietnamese troops closed in on Saigon, the capital of South Vietnam. Order had collapsed—mobs roamed the streets and looted residences and businesses. Thousands of Vietnamese people converged outside the American embassy. Some of the unruly crowd jeered at the Americans, but many others attempted to enter the embassy, hoping that the Americans would evacuate them from Vietnam. U.S. Marines stood on the walls of the embassy compound and beat members of the crowd back with their boots and rifle butts. Inside the embassy two thousand people—Americans and South Vietnamese refugees, including those who had worked for the Americans and their families—waited to be picked up by helicopters that landed on the rooftop of the embassy building. Over an eighteen-hour period, 1,375 Americans and 5,595 Vietnamese were evacuated by helicopter from the embassy and several other sites. After Graham Martin, the U.S. ambassador, departed the embassy clutching the American flag, the final flight of U.S. Marines lifted off. Looking down, Sergeant Juan Valdez, a U.S. Marine embassy guard on that last flight, saw Vietnamese evacuees still trying to enter the barricaded embassy grounds, waving papers to the sky showing that they, too, should be taken.

A few hours later North Vietnamese troops in Soviet-made tanks drove by the U.S. embassy on their way to the presidential palace, where they arrested what remained of South Vietnam's political leadership. Radio announcers proclaimed that Saigon had been liberated and renamed Ho Chi Minh City in honor of the late leader (who had died in 1969). Ho Chi Minh's 1945 vision of a unified and independent Vietnam had become reality despite the determined opposition of the United States, which had long sought to prevent just such a development.

A Tragic Episode

The decades between these two scenes encompassed one of the most violent and tragic episodes in the histories of both Vietnam and the United States. For Vietnam, the end result was a costly victory for Ho Chi Minh and his supporters and a bitter defeat for those who opposed him. Before Ho Chi Minh's 1945 proclamation would be realized, Vietnam would find itself divided in two and situated at the front lines of the Cold War between the global superpowers. Achieving Ho's vision would require three decades of nearly constant warfare in which four million of the country's inhabitants (10 percent of the population) would be killed or wounded and millions of acres of its land would be bombed, destroyed, or defoliated by chemical toxins. The post-1975 legacy of the conflict would include the mass exodus of over one million refugees fleeing both from poverty and from Communist rule in Vietnam.

For the United States, the events in Vietnam between 1945 and 1975 added up to a costly and divisive failure. America spent $150 billion on the war—more than on any previous war save World War II—and in the process wreaked havoc on its economy. The country also suffered large-scale human losses; of the approximately 2.7 million American men and women who served in Vietnam, 58,000 were killed and 300,000 were wounded. America dropped 7 million tons of bombs on North Vietnam and South Vietnam—more than three times the amount of bombs dropped in Europe and Asia during World War II. U.S. actions in Vietnam brought about a divisive national debate that culminated in street demonstrations, civil unrest, and feelings of disillusionment among many Americans who believed that they had been betrayed by their leaders. A 1975 editorial in *Newsweek*, one of America's leading newsmagazines, stated that the Vietnam War

> has been the saddest chapter in the past century of American history, and it will take years for the United States to come to grips with what it did to Vietnam—and what Vietnam did to America. The faith of Americans in their leadership was practically destroyed and many were left convinced that they had been both seduced and deceived by their government.

All of this came about because of an effort to prevent the realization of Ho Chi Minh's vision of a unified Vietnam under a Communist government.

Rationale for Intervention

America's intervention in Vietnam was not the result of a single decision but of a series of many choices made by five successive U.S. presidents (the exclusion of Congress from these decisions became a controversy in itself). In 1950, Harry S. Truman decided to provide France, which sought to retain colonial control of Vietnam, with financial and military aid in its war against Ho Chi Minh's independence movement. This commitment was continued by Dwight D. Eisenhower. Following France's defeat in 1954 and the division of Vietnam into a Communist-dominated North and an anti-Communist South, Eisenhower committed American diplomatic and economic support—and several hundred military advisers—to build up and protect South Vietnam. John F. Kennedy increased the number of advisers and support troops in Vietnam to sixteen thousand by 1963 to aid South Vietnam in its war against Communist insurgents supported by North Vietnam. When South Vietnam appeared to be on the verge of collapse, Lyndon B. Johnson increased the deployment of American troops (the number ultimately reached half a million), officially changed their role from advisory to combat, and ordered daily air strikes against North Vietnam. Richard M. Nixon gradually reduced the number of American troops in Vietnam but expanded the use of American air power.

These various decisions were made with the same general goal: the prevention of a Ho Chi Minh–led Communist unification of Vietnam. Johnson summed up this goal in 1965: "Our objective is the independence of South Viet-Nam, and its freedom from attack." Although these five presidents were different in many respects, they all possessed similar views on the state of the world and America's place in it. This general consensus, which was shared by most of America's political leadership at the time, regarded Vietnam's fate as a matter of vital American interest.

According to this worldview, the United States was engaged in a "Cold War" against the Communist countries of the Soviet Union and the People's Republic of China. America's national survival, it was believed, was threatened by these two countries and their attempts to spread Communist governments around the world by supporting various insurgent movements. Thus, that Ho Chi Minh had borrowed from America's Declaration of Independence and had cooperated with Americans during World War II meant less to American leaders than the fact that he was a longtime Communist who had lived in the Soviet Union, had worked with the Soviet government, and (by 1950) had received diplomatic recognition and military aid from both the Soviet Union and China.

The American intervention in Vietnam had its grounding in the "Truman Doctrine" enunciated by Truman and the "domino theory" promulgated by Eisenhower. In 1947 Truman declared that, to counter the threat of global Communism and its support of insurgent movements, the United States should "support free peoples who are resisting attempted subjugation by armed minorities or by outside pressures." The Truman Doctrine was first applied to Greece and Turkey but was later extended to Vietnam. American leaders maintained that the Vietnamese needed American intervention to prevent their "attempted subjugation" by "armed minorities" (Vietnamese Communists) and "outside pressures" (Soviet and Chinese aid). According to the domino theory, first publicly voiced by Eisenhower in a 1954 press conference, Vietnam was not the only nation threatened by Communism. Eisenhower argued that if Vietnam were to come under Communist rule, other neighboring states would soon follow suit; the "possible consequences of the loss are just incalculable to the free world," he stated. Eisenhower's warning was frequently repeated by subsequent presidents; in a typical example, Kennedy asserted in 1963 that if South Vietnam fell, "Thailand, Cambodia, Laos, . . . would go and all of Southeast Asia would be under the control of the Communists and under the domination of the Chinese."

In addition to fears of the spread of Communism, America's leaders were also concerned that once the United States was committed to supporting South Vietnam, a withdrawal from that region would have international repercussions because it would cause America's allies around the world to doubt the value of U.S. alliances and security commitments. A defeat in Vietnam, Johnson declared in 1965, "would shake the confidence of all these people in the value of an American commitment." Similarly, in defending his opposition to immediate U.S. withdrawal in 1969, Nixon stressed that it could result not only in the loss of South Vietnam, but "in a collapse of confidence in American leadership, not only in America, but throughout the world." Thus, the continuation of America's commitment to Vietnam was justified as a means of preserving U.S. credibility in the international community.

Critics of Intervention

The series of presidential decisions on intervening in Vietnam, and the Cold War rationale behind such intervention, were not made without debate or criticism. In the 1950s and early 1960s, such criticism was mostly confined to arguments within the executive branch of government. As the 1960s progressed, however, congressional opposition grew and a large and influential anti-war movement emerged in the form of mass protest marches and various acts of civil disobedience. Public support for the war in Vietnam fell after 1964 as casualties mounted with no apparent end in sight.

Critics of the Vietnam War were far from unified in their views and goals. However, it is possible to categorize these critics into three broad groups: "hawks," who advocated greater military escalation; liberal, antiwar "doves," who questioned whether the war in Vietnam was worth its cost to America; and radical dissenters, who rejected the entire Cold War framework under which the war was being fought.

The first group of critics believed wholeheartedly in the Cold War and the goal of preventing a Communist victory in Vietnam but found fault with the way the war was being pursued. Many criticized the decisions of American presidents to gradually increase U.S. involvement in Vietnam, calling instead for a massive and quick deployment of U.S. troops. Others attacked the limits American political leaders imposed on the American military. For example, American troops engaged in combat in Vietnam were restricted (except during one 1970 operation) from pursuing enemy soldiers into the bordering countries of Cambodia and Laos. Within these officially neutral countries, enemy forces were able to rest, resupply themselves, and prepare for their return to South Vietnam. U.S. military leaders repeatedly asked that the rules of engagement be modified in order to allow the pursuit of enemy forces into Cambodia and Laos. Republican senator Barry Goldwater, while running for president against Johnson in 1964, articulated the view held by many Americans:

> We are at war in Vietnam and we must have the will to win that war. . . . We must not . . . tolerate a so-called "privileged sanctuary" from which Communism feeds its military aggression in Vietnam. America cannot again afford the tragedy of sending our boys into a war we will not permit them to win.

Goldwater and others believed that such restrictions on the U.S. military frustrated U.S. efforts to protect South Vietnam.

The second group of dissenters generally held that the preservation of a non-Communist South Vietnam, although a laudable goal, was neither essential to American Cold War policy nor attainable at acceptable costs to the United States. They disputed several of the reasons used to justify the escalating American intervention in Vietnam. Some criticized the domino theory, arguing that it was simplistic to maintain that the loss of Vietnam would lead to an inexorable spread of Communism throughout Asia. In addition, many critics rejected the theory that the credibility of American policy was at stake in Vietnam. In 1966, J. William Fulbright stated, "I do not believe that there is much evidence that this is the kind of a test in which it would follow that, if we should make a compromise, then all the world will collapse because we have been defeated." Fulbright and others believed that, rather than a Cold War test, the war in Vietnam was primarily an internal matter for the Vietnamese people to decide.

Many in this second group of critics insisted that the war's central goal of an independent non-Communist South Vietnam was virtually unachievable. They maintained that success in Vietnam was not simply a matter of imposing American "will" and "permitting" American soldiers to win. Victory would remain elusive, they argued, as long as the government of South Vietnam remained unable to gain the popular support of its people. Political scientist Hans J. Morgenthau wrote in 1964 that

> the problem is political and not military, and it is impossible to win the war in Vietnam without the political support of at least a very substantial segment of the population.

> Popular support can be strengthened from the outside where it exists, but it cannot be created from the outside.

Some of these critics asserted that the South Vietnamese government was a client regime beholden to the United States for its existence—"a government without a country or a people," in the words of historian Stephen Ambrose—and was thus ultimately unsalvageable regardless of the amount of American military intervention.

The third group of Vietnam War opponents went much further in questioning the basic Cold War rationale for sending American soldiers and bombs to Vietnam. They rejected both the goal of an independent non-Communist South Vietnam and the morality of U.S. intervention in the country. Many openly supported Ho Chi Minh as the legitimate nationalist leader of all Vietnam (the chanting of pro–Ho Chi Minh slogans was a cause of division within the antiwar movement, however). Members of this group considered the United States, rather than North Vietnam or Communists in general, to be the leading aggressor in Southeast Asia. Noam Chomsky, a professor and noted antiwar activist, wrote in 1969 that

> the Vietnam War is the most obscene example of a frightening phenomenon of contemporary history—the attempt by our country to impose its particular concept of order and stability throughout much of the world. By any objective standard, the United States has become the most aggressive power in the world, the greatest threat to peace, to national self-determination, and to international cooperation.

Chomsky and other radical critics held the United States directly responsible for the Vietnam War and the devastation it wrought on Vietnam and its people. To them, the war served as a damning indictment of American foreign policy.

Enduring Questions

Whether the preservation of South Vietnam was worth the actions of the United States and the human and financial costs such actions incurred is but one of many questions concerning the Vietnam War that is still debated. Among other controversies surrounding the conflict are whether American presidents were correct in escalating American involvement in Vietnam without a congressional declaration of war, whether the antiwar movement was responsible for America's withdrawal, whether the American people were lied to by their presidents concerning the reasons for American intervention and the prospects for victory, and whether fears of "another Vietnam" have paralyzed subsequent U.S. foreign policy. However, the issue of whether American intervention was fundamentally justified is central in determining whether the Vietnam War was a "noble cause," as Ronald Reagan has argued, or "the greatest military, political, economic, and moral blunder in our national history," as George S. McGovern has maintained.

In his inaugural address in 1989, President George Bush stated that "the final lesson of Vietnam is that no great nation can long afford to be sundered by memory." Despite his plea for Americans to put to rest lingering conflicts about Vietnam, the war has remained an emotionally charged and controversial topic. Furthermore, some commentators contend that rather than putting the Vietnam conflict behind them, Americans should take pains to remember and reexamine the war and the rifts it caused. In response to Bush's 1989 statement, Robert Drinan, a Jesuit priest and former congressman, wrote, "On the contrary, a truly great nation would ask itself why it is divided and 'sundered' by Vietnam." The collection of opinions found in *The Vietnam War: Opposing Viewpoints* examines the controversies created by that war and may help to illuminate why the conflict still divides the nation more than twenty years after America departed Vietnam in the helicopter airlift of 1975.

CHAPTER 1

Early Decisions

Chapter Preface

In 1858, France, seeking to protect the lives of Roman Catholic missionaries and to enlarge its colonial empire, began a military campaign against Vietnam. In 1861 it seized Saigon (now Ho Chi Minh City). Six years later France held the rest of southern Vietnam, and by 1883 it controlled northern Vietnam as well. France divided the country into three regions—Cochinchina in the south, Annam in the center, and Tonkin in the north—and governed these areas as separate parts of French Indochina (which also included the neighboring countries of Laos and Cambodia).

Throughout its colonial rule of Vietnam, France had to contend with sporadic outbreaks of nationalist resistance. It was able to put down such attempts at revolution and maintain control of Vietnam until World War II, when France itself was occupied by Germany and its Indochinese colonies were occupied by Japan. American military involvement in Vietnam began at this time, when American operatives provided assistance to Vietnamese guerrillas fighting the Japanese. The operations in Indochina were a relatively insignificant part of America's worldwide efforts during the war. However, for the Vietnamese, World War II presented an opportunity to win independence from French colonial rule. After the war ended, the United States faced the decision of whether or not to support France's efforts to regain its colonies in Indochina.

The leading nationalist faction in Vietnam was the Vietminh, a Communist-dominated coalition led by Ho Chi Minh. On September 2, 1945, Ho Chi Minh declared the existence of the independent Democratic Republic of Vietnam (DRV). He established a provisional government in Hanoi, the former French capital of Tonkin. The Vietminh were less successful in winning political control in southern Vietnam, and France was able to reestablish colonial rule in Cochinchina. In December 1946, war broke out between France and the Vietminh; the fighting would last until 1954.

French army units wrested control of Vietnam's large cities, including Hanoi, and the country's major roads. But they made little headway in rural areas, where Vietminh guerrillas had won the support of much of the peasant population. In 1949 France created the State of Vietnam, a nominally independent national government headed by Vietnam's former emperor Bao Dai, who

24

had reigned in Annam in cooperation with the French in the 1930s and had also collaborated with the Japanese in 1945. His government attracted some Vietnamese nationalists who opposed the Communist control of the Vietminh, but others viewed the emperor (who spent most of his time in France) as little more than a figurehead for continued French rule.

The United States, however, saw the so-called "Bao Dai solution" as providing a way for it to support France without endorsing colonialism. In February 1950 America granted formal recognition to the State of Vietnam and soon thereafter began furnishing the French with military and economic assistance for their conflict in Indochina, including arms, ammunition, aircraft, and other equipment. American aid continued after Dwight D. Eisenhower replaced Harry S. Truman as president in 1953; by 1954 the United States was funding 78 percent of the French war effort and had stationed military advisers in Vietnam.

This commitment was made in the context of the Cold War. The determination to prevent the spread of Communism in Europe, Asia, and other parts of the world had become America's primary foreign policy focus in the years after World War II. In 1949 America was shaken by several developments, including the Soviet testing of an atomic bomb, a standoff between the Soviet Union and the United States over the fate of Berlin in Germany, and the fall of China to Communism. Furthermore, many Americans considered the Korean War (1950–1953) to be confirmation of their fears that the Soviet Union and China were trying to spread Communism around the world by force. Historian George Moss writes in *Vietnam: An American Ordeal* that these global concerns transformed American perceptions of the war in Vietnam:

> What Washington perceived to be at stake by 1950 was no longer merely the outcome of a regional colonial war. Indochina had become one of the front lines in the global Cold War between Communism and Freedom. In American eyes, the French were no longer merely fighting to reimpose colonialism on the Vietnamese, they were part of the Western world's concerted effort to contain Chinese and Soviet Communism in Europe and Asia.

Despite significant American support, the French were unable to defeat the Vietminh in what was becoming an increasingly unpopular war back in France. Ho Chi Minh's forces, which in late 1949 began to receive considerable assistance and weaponry from China, gained control of much of Vietnam, especially in the north. In March 1954 Vietminh forces succeeded in trapping ten thousand French troops at Dien Bien Phu in the northwestern corner of Vietnam. France's surrender at Dien Bien Phu on May 7, 1954, signaled the end of what would be called the First Indochina War. It did not, however, mark the end of American involvement in Vietnam.

VIEWPOINT 1

"Our goal is full independence and full cooperation with the UNITED STATES."

The United States Should Support an Independent Vietnam

Ho Chi Minh (1890–1969)

Ho Chi Minh was the leader of what came to be known as North Vietnam. To some, he was a nationalist hero who led his country of Vietnam to independence from French colonial rule. To others, he was a ruthless totalitarian who betrayed the hopes of many Vietnamese by attempting to make Vietnam into a Communist state. The question of whether Ho was predominantly a Communist or predominantly a Vietnamese nationalist underlies most debates about American involvement in the Vietnam War.

Born in 1890 as Nguyen That Than, Ho left Vietnam in 1911 and did not return for thirty years. During this period he traveled and lived under a variety of names in France, Great Britain, the United States, the Soviet Union, and China. He organized the Communist Party of Indochina in 1930, writing the party's founding statement in which he decried France's "barbarous oppression and ruthless exploitation" of Vietnam and praised the Soviet Union for being the "vanguard force" of world revolution against capitalism and imperialism. He adopted the name "Ho Chi Minh" (He Who Enlightens) in 1943.

World War II brought new hope for Ho and other Vietnamese revolutionaries. France, which had been the colonial ruler of Vietnam since 1883, surrendered to Germany in June 1940. In September 1940, France granted Japan virtual control over its colonial possessions in Indochina (the French colonial regime officially re-

Ho Chi Minh, letter to Harry S. Truman, February 16, 1946.

mained in place until March 1945, when Japan installed a puppet regime headed by Vietnamese emperor Bao Dai, who had previously reigned under French tutelage). On February 8, 1941, Ho finally returned to Vietnam. In May of that year he helped create and became leader of the Vietnam Doc Lap Dong Minh Hoi (Vietnamese League for Independence), or the Vietminh. Historian George Moss writes in *Vietnam: An American Ordeal* that "Ho and his associates created the Vietminh as a national-front association controlled by the Indochinese Communist Party to attract Vietnamese patriots of all political persuasions to a common cause, the struggle to rid their country of Japanese and French rule." During World War II Ho and his organization collaborated with American operatives of the Office of Strategic Services (OSS, a precursor of the CIA) in war activities against the Japanese. In August 1945 Ho Chi Minh led a general uprising in Vietnam; he proclaimed the existence of an independent Democratic Republic of Vietnam (DRV) on September 2, 1945, using phrases lifted directly from America's Declaration of Independence.

The following viewpoint is taken from the last of several letters Ho wrote to U.S. president Harry S. Truman seeking U.S. recognition and support of the DRV and calling for the United States to oppose the reimposition of French colonial rule. Ho argues that the French are violating the principles of international law and of the United Nations. To bolster his position, Ho also points out that the Vietnamese cooperated with the Allies (including the United States) during World War II, he refers to statements made by the Allies during World War II in support of national self-determination, and he mentions that the United States has stated its intention to grant independence to its own Asian colony, the Philippines. Ho's letters to Truman were never answered.

I avail myself of this opportunity to thank you and the people of United States for the interest shown by your representatives at the United Nations Organization in favour of the dependent peoples.

Our VIETNAM people, as early as 1941, stood by the Allies' side and fought against the Japanese and their associates, the French colonialists.

From 1941 to 1945 we fought bitterly, sustained by the patriotism of our fellow-countrymen and by the promises made by the Allies at [the summits in] YALTA, SAN FRANCISCO AND POTSDAM.

When the Japanese were defeated in August 1945, the whole Vietnam territory was united under a Provisional Republican

The Only Realistic Alternative

In 1949 France attempted to maintain control over Vietnam by installing a regime under the nominal leadership of Vietnamese emperor Bao Dai. Bao Dai, who resided for much of his life in France, had previously cooperated with French colonialists and, during World War II, with the Japanese. Raymond Fosdick, a consultant to the State Department, writes in a November 4, 1949, memorandum that the Bao Dai government is not truly independent, that it lacks the support of the Vietnamese people, and that therefore the United States might have no choice but to support Ho Chi Minh.

My belief is that the Bao Dai regime is doomed. The compromises which the French are so reluctantly making cannot possibly save it. The Indochinese are pressing toward complete nationalism and nothing is going to stop them. They see all too clearly that France is offering them a kind of semi-colonialism; and to think that they will be content to settle for less than Indonesia has gained from the Dutch or India from the British is to underestimate the power of the forces that are sweeping Asia today. . . .

Ho Chi Minh as an alternative is decidedly unpleasant, but . . . there may be unpredictable and unseen factors in this situation which in the end will be more favorable to us than now seems probable. The fundamental antipathy of the Indochinese to China is one of the factors. Faced with a dilemma like this the best possible course is to wait for the breaks. Certainly we should not play our cards in such a way that once again, as in China, we seem to be allied with reaction. Whether the French like it or not, independence is coming to Indochina. Why, therefore, do we tie ourselves to the tail of their battered kite?

Government which immediately set out to work. In five months, peace and order were restored, a democratic republic was established on legal bases, and adequate help was given to the Allies in the carrying out of their disarmament mission.

French Aggression

But the French colonialists, who had betrayed in war-time both the Allies and the Vietnamese, have come back and are waging on us a murderous and pitiless war in order to reestablish their domination. Their invasion has extended to South Vietnam and is menacing us in North Vietnam. It would take volumes to give even an abbreviated report of the crimes and assassinations they are committing every day in the fighting area.

This aggression is contrary to all principles of international law and to the pledges made by the Allies during the World War. It is a challenge to the noble attitude shown before, during and after the war by the United States Government and People. It violently contrasts with the firm stand you have taken in your twelve point [January 1, 1942, United Nations] declaration, and with the idealistic loftiness and generosity expressed by your delegates to the United Nations Assembly, MM [James] BYRNES, [Edward] STETTINIUS and J.F. DULLES.

The French aggression on a peace-loving people is a direct menace to world security. It implies the complicity, or at least, the connivance of the Great Democracies. The United Nations ought to keep their words. They ought to interfere to stop this unjust war, and to show that they mean to carry out in peace-time the principles for which they fought in war-time.

Our Vietnam people, after so many years of spoliation and devastation, is just beginning its building-up work. It needs security and freedom, first to achieve internal prosperity and welfare, and later to bring its small contribution to world-reconstruction.

These securities and freedoms can only be guaranteed by our independence from any colonial power, and our free cooperation with all other powers. It is with this firm conviction that we request of the United States as guardians and champions of World Justice to take a decisive step in support of our independence.

What we ask has been graciously granted to the Philippines. Like the Philippines our goal is full independence and full cooperation with the UNITED STATES. We will do our best to make this independence and cooperation profitable to the whole world.

VIEWPOINT 2

"We have not urged the French to negotiate with Ho Chi Minh, even though he probably is now supported by a considerable majority of the Vietnamese people, because of his record as a Communist."

The United States Cannot Support an Independent Vietnam Led by Communists

U.S. State Department

In December 1946, war broke out between French forces attempting to maintain colonial control of Vietnam and Vietnamese nationalists led by Ho Chi Minh. The conflict posed a dilemma for U.S. policymakers. On the one hand, the United States was generally on record as being against colonialism; the Atlantic Charter, a statement of World War II aims by the United States and Great Britain, spoke of "the right of all peoples to choose the form of government under which they will live." The United States, through its Office of Strategic Services (OSS), had also cooperated with Ho during World War II against the Japanese (during the war a small group of OSS operatives were sent from China to Vietnam to give Ho and his Vietminh organization military arms, training, and assistance). However, the U.S. government was unwilling to support Ho after the war due to his Communist background and beliefs. In addition, the United States placed a high priority on maintaining good relations with France. The United States therefore recognized French sovereignty over

U.S. State Department, policy statement on Indochina, September 27, 1948.

Indochina, but urged France to eventually grant independence to Vietnam and its neighbors, Laos and Cambodia.

The American government's stance toward Vietnam and the rest of Indochina during this period is found in the following viewpoint, which is taken from the first lengthy statement of U.S. policy toward the region written by the U.S. State Department. The government officials who wrote the September 27, 1948, document argue for eventual Vietnamese independence, but not for a Communist regime led by Ho Chi Minh. The authors acknowledge that the United States has been indirectly involved in the conflict by shipping arms and supplies to France. By 1950 the United States was directly supplying the French military effort in Vietnam.

The immediate objective of US policy in Indochina is to assist in a solution of the present impasse which will be mutually satisfactory to the French and the Vietnamese peoples, which will result in the termination of the present hostilities, and which will be within the framework of US security.

Our long-term objectives are: (1) to eliminate so far as possible Communist influence in Indochina and to see installed a self-governing nationalist state which will be friendly to the US and which, commensurate with the capacity of the peoples involved, will be patterned upon our conception of a democratic state as opposed to the totalitarian state which would evolve inevitably from Communist domination; (2) to foster the association of the peoples of Indochina with the western powers, particularly with France with whose customs, language and laws they are familiar, to the end that those peoples will prefer freely to cooperate with the western powers culturally, economically and politically; (3) to raise the standard of living so that the peoples of Indochina will be less receptive to totalitarian influences and will have an incentive to work productively and thus contribute to a better balanced world economy; and (4) to prevent undue Chinese penetration and subsequent influence in Indochina so that the peoples of Indochina will not be hampered in their natural developments by the pressure of an alien people and alien interests.

Recognizing French Sovereignty

To attain our immediate objective, we should continue to press the French to accommodate the basic aspirations of the Vietnamese: (1) unity of Cochinchina [southern Vietnam], Annam [central Vietnam], and Tonkin [northern Vietnam], (2) complete internal autonomy, and (3) the right to choose freely regarding participation in the French Union. We have recognized French sovereignty over Indochina but have maintained that such recognition does not imply any commitment on our part to assist France to exert its authority over the Indochinese peoples. Since V-J day, the majority people of the area, the Vietnamese, have stubbornly resisted the reestablishment of French authority, a struggle in which we have tried to maintain insofar as possible a position of non-support of either party.

While the nationalist movement in Vietnam (Cochinchina, Annam, and Tonkin) is strong, and though the great majority of the Vietnamese are not fundamentally Communist, the most active element in the resistance of the local peoples to the French has been a Communist group headed by Ho Chi Minh. This group has successfully extended its influence to include practically all armed forces now fighting the French, thus in effect capturing control of the nationalist movement.

The French on two occasions during 1946 attempted to resolve the problem by negotiation with the government established and dominated by Ho Chi Minh. The general agreements reached were not, however, successfully implemented and widescale fighting subsequently broke out. Since early in 1947, the French have employed about 115,000 troops in Indochina, with little result, since the countryside except in Laos and Cambodia remains under the firm control of the Ho Chi Minh government. A series of French-established puppet governments have tended to enhance the prestige of Ho's government and to call into question, on the part of the Vietnamese, the sincerity of French intentions to accord an independent status to Vietnam.

We have regarded these hostilities in a colonial area as detrimental not only to our own long-term interests which require as a minimum a stable Southeast Asia but also detrimental to the interest of France, since the hatred engendered by continuing hostilities may render impossible peaceful collaboration and cooperation of the French and the Vietnamese peoples. This hatred of the Vietnamese people toward the French is keeping alive antiwestern feeling among oriental peoples, to the advantage of the USSR and the detriment of the US.

Alternatives to Ho Chi Minh

We have not urged the French to negotiate with Ho Chi Minh, even though he probably is now supported by a considerable majority of the Vietnamese people, because of his record as a Communist and the Communist background of many of the influential figures in and about his government.

Postwar French governments have never understood, or have chosen to underestimate, the strength of the nationalist movement with which they must deal in Indochina. It remains possible that the nationalist movement can be subverted from Communist

Acceptance of Communism
Would Be a Disastrous Mistake

On March 8, 1949, President Vincent Auriol of France and former emperor Bao Dai (who had previously reigned in collaboration with both the French and, during World War II, with the Japanese) signed the Elysee Agreement establishing the "State of Vietnam." The U.S. State Department, in a memorandum to the French Foreign Office excerpted below, argues that France must give the new state true independence if the Vietnamese people are to avoid the "mistake" of supporting Ho Chi Minh's Democratic Republic of Vietnam. The United States extended diplomatic recognition to Bao Dai's government in February 1950. Most Vietnamese, however, viewed Bao Dai's government as a facade for continued French control.

Because of its conviction that concession by France to the Nationalist movement commensurate with the strength of that movement can alone provide the basis for a resolution of the Indochinese situation and the creation of a stable, representative Vietnamese Government, the United States Government welcomes the step taken by the President of France in arriving at an agreement with ex-Emperor Bao Dai whereby the territorial unity of Vietnam, comprising Tonkin, Annam, and Cochinchina, may be realized and the Vietnamese State enjoy far reaching powers of internal autonomy. It may be stated at once that in the opinion of the United States Government the Vietnamese people would be guilty of a mistake disastrous to their future should they reject this solution and give their support not to the Vietnamese Government formed under the March 8 agreement but to the so-called Democratic Republic of Vietnam. For those in command of this Republic are men trained in the methods and doctrine of international communism, and regardless of their present espousal of the nationalist cause, it cannot be ignored that they have never disavowed their Kremlin connections or repudiated the techniques and objectives of communism, which are the cause of so much suffering in the world today. It must be assumed, therefore, that should their government succeed in its aims with the support or through the acquiescence of the Vietnamese people, the pattern of a foreign totalitarianism will be clamped upon Vietnam under which all liberties, national and personal, will be lost. Such an outcome would not only be fatal to the welfare and hopes of the Vietnamese but would be most detrimental to the interests of all free peoples, particularly those of southern Asia who stand in most immediate danger of further Communist aggression.

control but this will require granting to a non-Communist group of nationalists at least the same concessions demanded by Ho Chi Minh. The failure of French governments to deal successfully with the Indochinese question has been due, in large measure, to the overwhelming internal issues facing France and the French Union, and to foreign policy considerations in Europe. These factors have combined with the slim parliamentary majorities of postwar governments in France to militate against the bold moves necessary to divert allegiance of the Vietnamese nationalists to non-Communist leadership.

In accord with our policy of regarding with favor the efforts of dependent peoples to attain their legitimate political aspirations, we have been anxious to see the French accord to the Vietnamese the largest possible degree of political and economic independence consistent with legitimate French interests. We have therefore declined to permit the export to the French in Indochina of arms and munitions for the prosecution of the war against the Vietnamese. This policy has been limited in its effect as we have allowed the free export of arms to France, such exports thereby being available for re-shipment to Indochina or for releasing stocks from reserves to be forwarded to Indochina. . . .

Evaluating US Policy

The objectives of US policy towards Indochina have not been realized. Three years after the termination of war a friendly ally, France, is fighting a desperate and apparently losing struggle in Indochina. The economic drain of this warfare on French recovery, while difficult to estimate, is unquestionably large. The Communist control in the nationalist movement has been increased during this period. US influence in Indochina and Southeast Asia has suffered as a result.

The objectives of US policy can only be attained by such French action as will satisfy the nationalist aspirations of the peoples of Indochina. We have repeatedly pointed out to the French the desirability of their giving such satisfaction and thus terminating the present open conflict. Our greatest difficulty in talking with the French and in stressing what should and what should not be done has been our inability to suggest any practicable solution of the Indochina problem, as we are all too well aware of the unpleasant fact that Communist Ho Chi Minh is the strongest and perhaps the ablest figure in Indochina and that any suggested solution which excluded him is an expedient of uncertain outcome. We are naturally hesitant to press the French too strongly or to become deeply involved so long as we are not in a position to suggest a solution or until we are prepared to accept the onus of intervention. The above considerations are further complicated by the fact that we have an immediate interest in maintaining in power a friendly French Government, to assist in the furtherance of our aims in Europe. This immediate and vital interest has in consequence taken precedence over active steps looking toward the realization of our objectives in Indochina.

We are prepared, however, to support the French in every way possible in the establishment of a truly nationalist government in Indochina which, by giving satisfaction to the aspirations of the peoples of Indochina, will serve as a rallying point for the nationalists and will weaken the Communist elements. By such support and by active participation in a peaceful and constructive solution in Indochina we stand to regain influence and prestige.

Some solution must be found which will strike a balance between the aspirations of the peoples of Indochina and the interests of the French. Solution by French military reconquest of Indochina is not desirable. Neither would the complete withdrawal of the French from Indochina effect a solution. The first alternative would delay indefinitely the attainment of our objectives, as we would share inevitably in the hatred engendered by an attempted military reconquest and the denial of aspirations for self-government. The second solution would be equally unfortunate as in all likelihood Indochina would then be taken over by the militant Communist group. At best, there might follow a transition period, marked by chaos and terroristic activities, creating a political vacuum into which the Chinese inevitably would be drawn or would push. The absence of stabilization in China will continue to have an important influence upon the objective of a permanent and peaceable solution in Indochina.

We have not been particularly successful in our information and education program in orienting the Vietnamese toward the western democracies and the US. The program has been hampered by the failure of the French to understand that such informational activities as we conduct in Indochina are not inimical to their own long-term interests and by administrative and financial considerations which have prevented the development to the maximum extent of contacts with the Vietnamese. An increased effort should be made to explain democratic institutions, especially American institutions and American policy, to the Indochinese by direct personal contact, by the distribution of information about the US, and the encouraging of educational exchange.

Viewpoint 3

"The imposition in Southeast Asia of the political system of Communist Russia and its Chinese Communist ally . . . would be a grave threat to the whole free community."

America Should Consider Direct Military Intervention in Indochina

John Foster Dulles (1888–1959)

From 1946 to 1954, France and the Vietnamese independence forces led by Ho Chi Minh were at war. Both sides received outside support. The Vietnamese received artillery, weapons, and training from neighboring China after that country was taken over by Communists in 1949. In response, in early 1950 the U.S. government under President Harry S. Truman decided to funnel financial and military aid to the French war effort.

By 1954 the United States was paying up to 78 percent of France's costs in Vietnam, but France was unable to defeat Ho Chi Minh's forces. An attempt by France to inflict a decisive victory by massing its forces at Dien Bien Phu (close to the border with Laos) backfired when Vietnamese forces, supplied with artillery from China, were able to besiege the French troops; by the end of March it was clear that France was on the verge of a crushing defeat. President Dwight D. Eisenhower and his subordinates, including Secretary of State John Foster Dulles and Admiral Arthur W. Radford, chairman of the Joint Chiefs of Staff, seriously considered various forms of direct military intervention, including air strikes and the use of U.S. troops.

On March 29, 1954, while military action was being considered

John Foster Dulles, speech to Overseas Press Club (New York, March 29, 1954), *Department of State Bulletin*, April 12, 1954.

in Washington, Dulles gave a speech to the Overseas Press Club. In the speech, reprinted here, he argues that the war in Indochina is part of a larger pattern of Communist expansion in the world. Dulles argues that the region of Southeast Asia is strategically important to the United States and asserts that the threat of communist takeover of the region should be met with a strong U.S. response ("united action").

On April 3, 1954, Dulles and Radford met with eight congressional leaders (including Lyndon B. Johnson) to discuss the possibility of launching air strikes and sending troops to Vietnam. Eisenhower ultimately decided against all plans of U.S. military intervention that did not have the support of Congress and of other nations, especially Great Britain—support that did not materialize.

This provides a timely occasion for outlining the administration's thinking about two related matters—Indochina and the Chinese Communist regime.

Indochina is important for many reasons. First, and always first, are the human values. About 30 million people are seeking for themselves the dignity of self-government. Until a few years ago, they formed merely a French dependency. Now, their three political units—Viet-Nam, Laos, and Cambodia—are exercising a considerable measure of independent political authority within the French Union. Each of the three is now recognized by the United States and by more than 30 other nations. They signed the Japanese peace treaty with us. Their independence is not yet complete. But the French Government last July [1953] declared its intention to complete that independence, and negotiations to consummate that pledge are actively under way.

The United States is watching this development with close attention and great sympathy. We do not forget that we were a colony that won its freedom. We have sponsored in the Philippines a conspicuously successful development of political independence. We feel a sense of kinship with those everywhere who yearn for freedom.

The Communists are attempting to prevent the orderly development of independence and to confuse the issue before the world. The Communists have, in these matters, a regular line which [Joseph] Stalin laid down in 1924.

The scheme is to whip up the spirit of nationalism so that it becomes violent. That is done by professional agitators. Then the violence is enlarged by Communist military and technical leadership and the provision of military supplies. In these ways, international communism gets a stranglehold on the people and it uses that power to "amalgamate" the peoples into the Soviet orbit.

"Amalgamation" is [Vladimir] Lenin's and Stalin's word to describe their process.

Communist Imperialism in Indochina

"Amalgamation" is now being attempted in Indochina under the ostensible leadership of Ho Chi Minh. He was indoctrinated in Moscow. He became an associate of the Russian, [Mikhail] Borodin, when the latter was organizing the Chinese Communist Party which was to bring China into the Soviet orbit. Then Ho transferred his activities to Indochina.

Those fighting under the banner of Ho Chi Minh have largely been trained and equipped in Communist China. They are supplied with artillery and ammunition through the Soviet-Chinese Communist bloc. Captured materiel shows that much of it was fabricated by the Skoda Munition Works in Czechoslovakia and transported across Russia and Siberia and then sent through China into Viet-Nam. Military supplies for the Communist armies have been pouring into Viet-Nam at a steadily increasing rate.

Military and technical guidance is supplied by an estimated 2,000 Communist Chinese. They function with the forces of Ho Chi Minh in key positions—in staff sections of the High Command, at the division level, and in specialized units such as signal, engineer, artillery, and transportation.

In the present stage, the Communists in Indochina use nationalistic anti-French slogans to win local support. But if they achieved military or political success, it is certain that they would subject the people to a cruel Communist dictatorship taking its orders from Peiping [Peking] and Moscow.

The tragedy would not stop there. If the Communist forces won uncontested control over Indochina or any substantial part thereof, they would surely resume the same pattern of aggression against other free peoples in the area.

The propagandists of Red China and Russia make it apparent that the purpose is to dominate all of Southeast Asia.

Southeast Asia is the so-called "rice bowl" which helps to feed the densely populated region that extends from India to Japan. It is rich in many raw materials, such as tin, oil, rubber, and iron ore. It offers industrial Japan potentially important markets and sources of raw materials.

The area has great strategic value. Southeast Asia is astride the most direct and best-developed sea and air routes between the Pacific and South Asia. It has major naval and air bases. Communist control of Southeast Asia would carry a grave threat to the

The Domino Theory

The "domino theory"—the idea that if Vietnam were to fall to communism, other countries would soon follow—was first enunciated by President Dwight D. Eisenhower at an April 7, 1954, news conference. The following is excerpted from his reply to a question about the "strategic importance of Indochina to the free world."

First of all, you have the specific value of a locality in its production of materials that the world needs.

Then you have the possibility that many human beings pass under a dictatorship that is inimical to the free world.

Finally, you have broader considerations that might follow what you would call the "falling domino" principle. You have a row of dominoes set up, you knock over the first one, and what will happen to the last one is the certainty that it will go over very quickly. So you could have a beginning of a disintegration that would have the most profound influences.

Now, with respect to the first one, two of the items from this particular area that the world uses are tin and tungsten. They are very important. There are others, of course, the rubber plantations and so on.

Then with respect to more people passing under this domination, Asia, after all, has already lost some 450 million of its peoples to the Communist dictatorship, and we simply can't afford greater losses.

But when we come to the possible sequence of events, the loss of Indochina, of Burma, of Thailand, of the Peninsula, and Indonesia following, now you begin to talk about areas that not only multiply the disadvantages that you would suffer through loss of materials, sources of materials, but now you are talking about millions and millions and millions of people.

Finally, the geographical position achieved thereby does many things. It turns the so-called island defensive chain of Japan, Formosa, of the Philippines and to the southward; it moves in to threaten Australia and New Zealand. . . .

So, the possible consequences of the loss are just incalculable to the free world.

Philippines, Australia, and New Zealand, with whom we have treaties of mutual assistance. The entire Western Pacific area, including the so-called "offshore island chain," would be strategically endangered.

President Eisenhower appraised the situation last Wednesday [March 24] when he said that the area is of "transcendent importance."

The United States Position

The United States has shown in many ways its sympathy for the gallant struggle being waged in Indochina by French forces and those of the Associated States. Congress has enabled us to provide material aid to the established governments and their peoples. Also, our diplomacy has sought to deter Communist China from open aggression in that area.

President Eisenhower, in his address of April 16, 1953, explained that a Korean armistice would be a fraud if it merely released aggressive armies for attack elsewhere. I said last September that if Red China sent its own army into Indochina, that would result in grave consequences which might not be confined to Indochina.

Recent statements have been designed to impress upon potential aggressors that aggression might lead to action at places and by means of free-world choosing, so that aggression would cost more than it could gain.

The Chinese Communists have, in fact, avoided the direct use of their own Red armies in open aggression against Indochina. They have, however, largely stepped up their support of the aggression in that area. Indeed, they promote that aggression by all means short of open invasion.

Under all circumstances it seems desirable to clarify further the United States position.

Under the conditions of today, the imposition in Southeast Asia of the political system of Communist Russia and its Chinese Communist ally, by whatever means, would be a grave threat to the whole free community. The United States feels that that possibility should not be passively accepted but should be met by united action. This might involve serious risks. But these risks are far less than those that will face us a few years from now if we dare not be resolute today.

The free nations want peace. However, peace is not had merely by wanting it. Peace has to be worked for and planned for. Sometimes it is necessary to take risks to win peace just as it is necessary in war to take risks to win victory. The chances for peace are usually bettered by letting a potential aggressor know in advance where his aggression could lead him.

I hope that these statements which I make here tonight will serve the cause of peace.

"To pour money, material, and men into the jungles of Indochina without at least a remote prospect of victory would be dangerously futile and self-destructive."

America Should Be Cautious About Direct Military Intervention in Indochina

John F. Kennedy (1917–1963)

John Foster Dulles's March 29, 1954, speech, in which he called for "united action" in response to the communist aggression in Southeast Asia, stirred much debate within the United States. Among those who responded was a young Massachusetts senator, John F. Kennedy, who later, as president, would expand U.S. commitments in Vietnam.

By April 6, 1954, when Kennedy addressed the Senate, France had been fighting in Vietnam for eight years and was on the verge of a disastrous defeat at Dien Bien Phu. Meanwhile, an international peace conference in Geneva, Switzerland, was about to begin discussions in an attempt to come to a political solution to the conflict.

In his speech, excerpted here, Kennedy responds to Dulles's "united action" speech as well as to the upcoming Geneva conference by strongly arguing against direct U.S. military intervention in Vietnam. Kennedy, who had visited Southeast Asia in 1951 for several weeks, argues that many U.S. government offi-

From John F. Kennedy, speech before U.S. Senate, *Congressional Record*, 83rd Cong., 2nd sess. (April 6, 1954).

cials have been wrong in predicting a French victory in Vietnam. He asserts that no amount of military intervention can change the fact that the Vietnamese are fighting for independence from French colonial rule.

Mr. President [of the Senate], the time has come for the American people to be told the blunt truth about Indochina.

I am reluctant to make any statement which may be misinterpreted as unappreciative of the gallant French struggle at Dien Bien Phu and elsewhere; or as partisan criticism of our Secretary of State just prior to his participation in the delicate deliberations in Geneva. Nor, as one who is not a member of those committees of the Congress which have been briefed—if not consulted—on this matter, do I wish to appear impetuous or an alarmist in my evaluation of the situation. But the speeches of President [Dwight] Eisenhower, Secretary [John Foster] Dulles, and others have left too much unsaid, in my opinion—and what has been left unsaid is the heart of the problem that should concern every citizen. For if the American people are, for the fourth time in this century, to travel the long and tortuous road of war—particularly a war which we now realize would threaten the survival of civilization—then I believe we have a right—a right which we should have hitherto exercised—to inquire in detail into the nature of the struggle in which we may become engaged, and the alternative to such struggle. Without such clarification the general support and success of our policy is endangered.

The Geneva Negotiations

In as much as Secretary Dulles has rejected, with finality, any suggestion of bargaining on Indochina in exchange for recognition of Red China, those discussions in Geneva which concern that war may center around two basic alternatives:

The first is a negotiated peace, based either upon partition of the area between the forces of the Viet Minh and the French Union, possibly along the 16th parallel; or based upon a coalition government in which Ho Chi Minh is represented. Despite any wishful thinking to the contrary, it should be apparent that the popularity and prevalence of Ho Chi Minh and his following throughout Indochina would cause either partition or a coalition government to result in eventual domination by the Communists.

The second alternative is for the United States to persuade the French to continue their valiant and costly struggle; an alternative which, considering the current state of opinion in France, will be adopted only if the United States pledges increasing support. Secretary Dulles' statement that the "imposition in southeast Asia of the political system of Communist Russia and its Chinese Communist ally . . . should be met by united action" indicates that it is our policy to give such support; that we will, as observed by the *New York Times*, "fight if necessary to keep southeast Asia out of their hands"; and that we hope to win the support of the free countries of Asia for united action against communism in Indochina, in spite of the fact that such nations have pursued since the war's inception a policy of cold neutrality. . . .

This editorial cartoon by Daniel Fitzgerald expressed the fear that America might repeat France's experiences in Vietnam.

Certainly, I, for one, favor a policy of a "united action" by many nations whenever necessary to achieve a military and political victory for the free world in that area, realizing full well that it may eventually require some commitment of our manpower. . . .

But to pour money, material, and men into the jungles of Indochina without at least a remote prospect of victory would be dangerously futile and self-destructive. Of course, all discussion of "united action" assumes the inevitability of such victory; but such assumptions are not unlike similar predictions of confidence which have lulled the American people for many years and which, if continued, would present an improper basis for determining the extent of American participation. . . .

In February 1954, Defense Secretary Charles Erwin Wilson said that a French victory was "both possible and probable" and that the war was going "fully as well as we expected it to at this stage. I see no reason to think Indochina would be another Korea." Also in February, Under Secretary of State [Walter Bedell] Smith stated that:

> The military situation in Indochina is favorable. . . . Contrary to some reports, the recent advances made by the Viet Minh are largely "real estate" operations. . . . Tactically, the French position is solid and the officers in the field seem confident of their ability to deal with the situation.

In later March, Admiral Arthur Radford, Chairman of the Joint Chiefs of Staff, stated that "the French are going to win." And finally, in a press conference some days prior to his speech to the Overseas Press Club in New York, Secretary of State Dulles stated that he did not "expect that there is going to be a Communist victory in Indochina"; that "in terms of Communist domination of Indochina, I do not accept that as a probability.". . .

Despite this series of optimistic reports about eventual victory, every member of the Senate knows that such victory today appears to be desperately remote, to say the least, despite tremendous amounts of economic and materiel aid from the United States, and despite a deplorable loss of French Union manpower. The call for either negotiations or additional participation by other nations underscores the remoteness of such a final victory today, regardless of the outcome at Dien Bien Phu. It is, of course, for these reasons that many French are reluctant to continue the struggle without greater assistance; for to record the sapping effect which time and the enemy have had on their will and strength in that area is not to disparage their valor. If "united action" can achieve the necessary victory over the forces of communism, and thus preserve the security and freedom of all Southeast Asia, then such united action is clearly called for. But if, on the other hand, the increase in our aid and the utilization of our troops would only result in further statements of confidence without ultimate victory over aggression, then now is the time when we must evaluate the conditions under which that pledge is made.

I am frankly of the belief that no amount of American military assistance in Indochina can conquer an enemy which is everywhere and at the same time nowhere, "an enemy of the people" which has the sympathy and covert support of the people. . . .

Moreover, without political independence for the Associated States [of French Indochina], the other Asiatic nations have made it clear that they regard this as a war of colonialism; and the "united action" which is said to be so desperately needed for victory in that area is likely to end up as unilateral action by our own country. Such intervention, without participation by the armed forces of the other nations of Asia, without the support of the great masses of the people of the Associated States, with increasing reluctance and discouragement on the part of the French—and, I might add, with hordes of Chinese Communist troops poised just across the border in anticipation of our unilateral entry into their kind of battleground—such intervention, Mr. President, would be virtually impossible in the type of military situation which prevails in Indochina.

Asia for Asians

John F. Kennedy was not the only future U.S. president to oppose U.S. military intervention in Vietnam in 1954. In an April 20 speech, Texas senator Lyndon B. Johnson strongly objected to the idea of sending American soldiers to Asia.

I am against sending American G.I.'s into the mud and muck of Indochina on a bloodletting spree to perpetuate colonialism and white man's exploitation in Asia. The Monroe Doctrine and Asia for Asians should be the foundation of our foreign policy.

This is not a new point, of course. In November of 1951, I reported upon my return from the Far East as follows:

> In Indochina we have allied ourselves to the desperate effort of a French regime to hang on to the remnants of empire. There is no broad, general support of the native Vietnam government among the people of that area. To check the southern drive of communism makes sense but not only through reliance on the force of arms. The task is rather to build strong native non-Communist sentiment within these areas and rely on that as a spearhead of defense rather than upon the legions of General de Lattre. To do this apart from and in defiance of innately nationalistic aims spells foredoomed failure.

In June of last year, I sought an amendment to the Mutual Security Act which would have provided for the distribution of American aid, to the extent feasible, in such a way as to encourage the freedom and independence desired by the people of the Associated States. My amendment was soundly defeated on the grounds that we should not pressure France into taking action on this delicate situation; and that the new French government could be expected to make "a decision which would obviate the necessity of this kind of amendment or resolution." The distinguished majority leader [William Knowland] assured us that "We will all work, in conjunction with our great ally, France, toward the freedom of the people of those states."

Every year we are given three sets of assurances: First, that the independence of the Associated States is now complete; second, that the independence of the Associated States will soon be completed under steps "now" being undertaken; and, third, that military victory for the French Union forces in Indochina is assured, or is just around the corner, or lies two years off. But the stringent limitations upon the status of the Associated States as sovereign states remain; and the fact that military victory has not yet been achieved is largely the result of these limitations. Repeated failure of these prophecies has, however, in no way diminished the frequency of their reiteration, and they have caused this nation to delay definitive action until now the opportunity for any desirable solution may well be past.

It is time, therefore, for us to face the stark reality of the difficult situation before us without the false hopes which predictions of military victory and assurances of complete independence have given us in the past. The hard truth of the matter is, first, that without the wholehearted support of the peoples of the Associated States, without a reliable and crusading native army with a dependable officer corps, a military victory, even with American support, in that area is difficult if not impossible, of achievement; and, second, that the support of the people of that area cannot be obtained without a change in the contractual relationships which presently exist between the Associated States and the French Union.

If the French persist in their refusal to grant the legitimate independence and freedom desired by the peoples of the Associated States; and if those peoples and the other peoples of Asia remain aloof from the conflict, as they have in the past, then it is my hope that Secretary Dulles, before pledging our assistance at Geneva, will recognize the futility of channeling American men and machines into that hopeless internecine struggle.

The facts and alternatives before us are unpleasant, Mr. President. But in a nation such as ours, it is only through the fullest and frankest appreciation of such facts and alternatives that any foreign policy can be effectively maintained. In an era of supersonic attack and atomic retaliation, extended public debate and education are of no avail, once such a policy must be implemented. The time to study, to doubt, to review, and revise is now, for upon our decisions now may well rest the peace and security of the world, and, indeed, the very continued existence of mankind. And if we cannot entrust this decision to the people, then, as Thomas Jefferson once said: "If we think them not enlightened enough to exercise their control with a wholesome discretion, the remedy is not to take it from them but to inform their discretion by education."

CHAPTER 2

America Commits to South Vietnam

Chapter Preface

On May 8, 1954, one day after France's surrender at Dien Bien Phu in Vietnam, diplomatic delegations from the United States, the Soviet Union, Great Britain, France, the People's Republic of China, Ho Chi Minh's Democratic Republic of Vietnam (DRV), the State of Vietnam (headed by Emperor Bao Dai), Cambodia, and Laos opened negotiations in Geneva, Switzerland, to discuss the political future of Indochina. The United States was a minor and reluctant participant in the conference, as indicated by the fact that Secretary of State John Foster Dulles stayed in Geneva for only one week. American officials would have preferred that France continue to fight in Indochina, and the U.S. government did not want any direct diplomatic contact with the Chinese delegation, whose Communist government it refused to recognize.

In July the Geneva Conference produced a cease-fire agreement, signed by the military commanders of the DRV and of France, and a "Final Declaration," which on July 21 received recorded oral endorsement from (but was not signed by) China, the DRV, the Soviet Union, Great Britain, and France. The cease-fire agreement called for the temporary division of Vietnam near the seventeenth parallel, with French forces to be relocated south of the line and Vietminh forces to be regrouped north of it, "pending the general elections which will bring about the unification of Viet Nam." The Final Declaration noted that the division of the country into North Vietnam and South Vietnam "was provisional and should not be interpreted as constituting a political or territorial boundary," and it specified that nationwide elections were to be held in July 1956 under the auspices of an international commission.

The settlement in Geneva meant different things to different countries. For France, it allowed a peaceful and orderly extrication from war in Indochina. For the leaders of the Democratic Republic of Vietnam, it was a military compromise; they had to give up territory that they controlled in order to gain the chance to reunify the country through elections. Officials of Bao Dai's government in South Vietnam denounced the Final Declaration and dubbed July 21 a "day of shame."

The United States did not sign or endorse the Geneva Accords, but it did pledge to "refrain from the threat or use of force to disturb them." Some Americans decried the agreements as a defeat in the Cold War, while others argued that they provided the

United States with a new opportunity to take a stand against Communism. Dulles stated in the fall of 1956, "We have a clean base there now, without a taint of colonialism. Dien Bien Phu was a blessing in disguise." Dulles had determined that, with France's withdrawal, the United States could step in to ensure that Communism would spread no further. In September 1954 Dulles helped forge the Southeast Asia Treaty Organization (SEATO), in which Great Britain, France, Australia, New Zealand, Thailand, Pakistan, and the Philippines agreed to "meet and confer" if one of the signatories was attacked. A separate protocol extended SEATO protection to Laos, Cambodia, and Bao Dai's State of Vietnam (South Vietnam), providing a legal basis for American intervention there. Dulles's efforts to form SEATO reflected America's decision to intervene directly in Vietnam and to work to establish a separate non-Communist state in the southern region established by the Geneva Accords. Historian George McT. Kahin, in his book *Intervention*, argues that the commitment to establish and nurture such a state was America's "most fundamental decision of its thirty-year involvement [in Vietnam]—the critical prerequisite to the subsequent incremental steps that culminated in President Johnson's famous escalation a decade later."

Ngo Dinh Diem was the person the United States looked to to govern South Vietnam and to be a nationalist leader to rival Ho Chi Minh. Appointed prime minister of the State of Vietnam by Bao Dai in 1954, Diem defeated Bao Dai in a 1955 plebiscite and proclaimed the existence of the Republic of Vietnam with himself as president—a position he would hold until 1963. Diem was a strong opponent both of Communism *and* of French colonial rule—a combination that made him attractive to American policy makers. Over the next several years the United States displaced France as the leading foreign power in South Vietnam and assisted the Diem regime in several ways, including economic aid and secret CIA operations aimed at North Vietnam and Diem's opponents in South Vietnam. The United States also backed Diem when he refused to cooperate with North Vietnam in planning and holding the 1956 elections called for by the Geneva Accords.

In the United States, Diem was strongly praised as an exemplary leader who was saving Vietnam from Communist rule. However, American efforts to promote Diem in Vietnam as a popular nationalist alternative to Ho Chi Minh foundered for several reasons, including Diem's aloof and autocratic political style, his inability to gain the support of Vietnamese Buddhists (Diem was Catholic, a minority group in Vietnam), and his failure to promote significant land and social reforms within South Vietnam.

In 1957 Communist-backed rebels in South Vietnam began to carry out terrorist attacks. The National Liberation Front of South

Vietnam (NLF) was created in 1960 with the assistance of North Vietnam's Communist government. The United States responded by increasing its military assistance and its number of advisers to Diem's government, a policy continued by President John F. Kennedy when he entered office in 1961. Under Kennedy, the number of U.S. military personnel in South Vietnam rose from several hundred to sixteen thousand, but despite such aid South Vietnam remained a country in turmoil.

VIEWPOINT 1

"A wholly unexpected political miracle has occurred in South Viet Nam."

American Aid Has Helped Create a Stable Government in South Vietnam

William Henderson (b. 1903)

The 1954 Geneva agreements divided Vietnam along the seventeenth parallel, to be united following internationally supervised elections in July 1956. In the northern half of the country, the Communists, led by Ho Chi Minh, consolidated their power and embarked on programs of land reform and industrialization. In the southern half, the Republic of Vietnam was created. Its first president, Ngo Dinh Diem, had the strong support of the United States, which soon displaced France as the dominant foreign influence in the region. Diem, with U.S. backing, refused to participate in the scheduled 1956 elections (which most observers, including U.S. president Dwight D. Eisenhower, believed Ho Chi Minh would have won). Vietnam thus remained divided between a Communist North Vietnam and an anti-Communist and American-backed South Vietnam. Some Americans considered this development a significant victory in America's quest to prevent the spread of communism in the world, and praised Diem as a hero.

The following viewpoint is taken from a January 1957 article in *Foreign Affairs* by William Henderson, a former associate executive

Excerpted from William Henderson, "South Viet Nam Finds Itself," *Foreign Affairs*, January 1957. Copyright 1957 by the Council on Foreign Relations, Inc. Reprinted by permission of *Foreign Affairs*.

director of the Council on Foreign Relations. In the article, written after a 1956 visit to South Vietnam, Henderson describes Diem's struggles to create a viable government in South Vietnam. Henderson argues that Diem has been mostly successful in this endeavor, due in large part to American aid and diplomatic backing.

When the Geneva Agreement of 1954 terminated the fighting in Indochina on the basis of the partition of Viet Nam along the seventeenth parallel, most observers felt that the Communists had won a striking victory. Their conquest of the North, with somewhat more than half of Viet Nam's 26 million people, most of its mineral deposits and the bulk of its modest industrial establishment, represented the most important Communist territorial advance since the collapse of Nationalist China and posed an ominous challenge to all of Southeast Asia. South Viet Nam, war-weary and desolated, was conceded little chance of survival. Laos and Cambodia would then be outflanked and the whole region placed in imminent danger. This at least was the implication of the famous "domino theory" propounded by President Eisenhower in the spring of 1954, when the United States was still considering active military intervention in Indochina.

To the extent that the theory had validity after Geneva, the key to the salvation of Southeast Asia—with its vast population, incalculable wealth in natural resources and critical strategic position—was South Viet Nam. There the situation could scarcely have been worse. The authority of the local government hardly extended beyond the environs of its capital. Its leadership appeared incapable of constructive action, incapacitated as much by inexperience as by the incubus of the continued presence of the French. Everywhere the population was sullen and resentful, bitterly disillusioned by military defeat after a long, costly and unpopular war. The army could not be counted on. The police were controlled by an organized band of gangsters known as the Binh Xuyen, which ruled Saigon and ran its lucrative vice rackets. Great stretches of the countryside were in the hands of two politico-religious sects, the Cao Dai and Hoa Hao, which disposed of formidable armed strength and governed their territories as autonomous states within the state.

There were also the Communists. While the Geneva Agreement called for the withdrawal of all Viet Minh forces from the South, in fact several thousand trained political and military cadres were left behind. Besides ubiquitous efforts at infiltration, the Communists dominated many rural districts and also maintained some organized military units in the South. The economy was in chaos. Long years of warfare had disrupted most productive activity, and inflation was rampant. Meanwhile hundreds of thousands of refugees poured into South Viet Nam from the North, hopelessly overtaxing the inadequate facilities of the Saigon government to cope with them.

It is against this somber background that the record of the two years since Geneva should be judged. The general expectation was that South Viet Nam would quickly succumb to Communist pressures. If the tactics of subversion failed, nation-wide elections scheduled for July 1956 by the Final Declaration at Geneva would surely produce the same result. The efficacy of totalitarian control techniques in the North, where a majority of the population lived, guaranteed a Communist victory at the polls. In any case South Viet Nam, deeply divided within itself, seemed certain to sink into the abyss of bloody internecine strife ending in complete collapse.

Remarkable Progress

Yet none of this came to pass. Far from collapsing, the government of Ngo Dinh Diem, which took office early in July 1954 in the darkest days of Geneva, has made remarkable progress in putting its house in order and establishing the bases of stability and future progress. Today South Viet Nam is very much in business, and barring the catastrophe of a third world war in the foreseeable future, is likely to remain in business. The achievements of Diem's government won international recognition of an impressive sort when the July 1956 elections, which it had adamantly opposed, were indefinitely postponed by the United Kingdom and the Soviet Union, co-chairmen of the Geneva Conference. The Viet Minh, although it had based its propaganda on the certainty of the elections and its triumph in them, had no alternative but to accept this decision. In short, a wholly unexpected political miracle has occurred in South Viet Nam.

How are we to account for this? Certainly the principal credit should be given to President Ngo Dinh Diem himself. Diem has shown himself a man of courage and determination, capable of ruthless decision and forceful action when the occasion called for it. His reputation as an implacable Vietnamese nationalist enabled him to rally enough support to consolidate his position in the face of bitter opposition from the sects, the Communists and even the French. In the early days after Geneva, Diem was often characterized as a bumbling political innocent lost in the labyrinthine mazes of Vietnamese politics. No doubt he often appeared hesitant and indecisive, but in those days there was nothing and no one on whom he could rely, neither the army nor the

America's Stake in Vietnam

In the following excerpts from a June 1956 address before the American Friends of Vietnam, a private lobbying group that supported South Vietnam and its leader, Ngo Dinh Diem, Senator John F. Kennedy of Massachusetts argues that the fate of a free and non-Communist South Vietnam is important for the United States.

Let us briefly consider exactly what is "America's Stake in Vietnam":

(1) *First,* Vietnam represents the cornerstone of the Free World in Southeast Asia, the keystone to the arch, the finger in the dike. Burma, Thailand, India, Japan, the Philippines and obviously Laos and Cambodia are among those whose security would be threatened if the red tide of Communism overflowed into Vietnam. . . .

(2) *Secondly,* Vietnam represents a proving ground of democracy in Asia. However we may choose to ignore it or deprecate it, the rising prestige and influence of Communist China in Asia are unchallengeable facts. Vietnam represents the alternative to Communist dictatorship. If this democratic experiment fails, if some one million refugees have fled the totalitarianism of the North only to find neither freedom nor security in the South, then weakness, not strength, will characterize the meaning of democracy in the minds of still more Asians. . . .

(3) *Third* and in somewhat similar fashion, Vietnam represents a test of American responsibility and determination in Asia. If we are not the parents of little Vietnam, then surely we are the godparents. We presided at its birth, we gave assistance to its life, we have helped to shape its future. As French influence in the political, economic and military spheres has declined in Vietnam, American influence has steadily grown. This is our offspring—we cannot abandon it, we cannot ignore its needs. And if it falls victim to any of the perils that threaten its existence—Communism, political anarchy, poverty and the rest—then the United States, with some justification, will be held responsible; and our prestige in Asia will sink to a new low.

(4) *Fourth* and finally, America's stake in Vietnam, in her strength and in her security, is a very selfish one—for it can be measured, in the last analysis, in terms of American lives and American dollars. It is now well known that we were at one time on the brink of war in Indo-China—a war which could well have been more costly, more exhausting and less conclusive than any war we have ever known. The threat of such war is not now altogether removed from the horizon. Military weakness, political instability or economic failure in the new state of Vietnam could change almost overnight the apparent security which has increasingly characterized that area under the leadership of President Diem. And the key position of Vietnam in Southeast Asia, as already discussed, makes inevitable the involvement of this nation's security in any new outbreak of trouble.

police, neither the government nor any significant segment of popular opinion. As the record shows, he learned quickly. . . .

American Backing

Despite his undoubted personal qualities, however, and the large element of luck that enters into every successful political enterprise, Diem could never have survived without American support. We cannot claim credit for selecting Diem or having pushed him into office, but we have since been his most ardent and effective champion. American funds have sustained Diem's government from the beginning. Allocations of United States aid totalled $320,300,000 in the fiscal year 1954–55 and $196,500,000 in 1955–56. Estimates for the current fiscal year are of the same general magnitude. American aid equals about 65 percent of South Viet Nam's total budget. We finance most of the military budget and three quarters of the country's imports. Almost the entire program of refugee relief and rehabilitation is being paid for with American funds.

Scarcely less important has been our diplomatic backing. United States support was a decisive factor in keeping Diem afloat during his first year in office. It is true that we played a less distinguished role at the time of the [April 1955] showdown with the Binh Xuyen. General J. Lawton Collins, President Eisenhower's special ambassador in Saigon at the time, is known to have wavered in his evaluation of Diem's prospects during that moment of supreme danger. But fortunately the State Department, ignoring French pressure, decided not to alter its course. Since May 1955 our support has been unshakeable. The United States fully endorsed Diem's position in refusing to go through with the nationwide elections on unification scheduled at Geneva; and their indefinite postponement sharply reduced popular fears of an imminent Communist takeover in the South. This whole episode was an important factor in rallying public opinion behind the Diem regime. The mantle of protection afforded by the Manila Pact [that formed the Southeast Asia Treaty Organization (SEATO)] was also thrown over South Viet Nam (as well as Laos and Cambodia); and American officers, putting to use the experience gained in Korea, are training the South Vietnamese army.

We must also concede the part played by shifts in Communist world strategy. South Viet Nam does not yet have the military capability of defending itself successfully against a determined attack from the North; and despite our commitments under the Manila Pact, it will always be uncertain whether the United States would intervene militarily in Indochina if the Communists renewed open aggression. But they have not done so. Nor have they made a serious attempt to subvert South Viet Nam from within, although in the early months of the Diem government such an effort might well have succeeded.

Early Struggles

Diem's first task after assuming office was to gain control over the Vietnamese army. A prolonged crisis in the fall of 1954, in which the United States gave Diem decisive support, resulted in the withdrawal of the pro-French Chief of Staff, General Nguyen Van Hinh, and his replacement by Le Van Ty, Diem's own choice for the job. Thereafter the army gave its loyalties increasingly to the Diem government rather than to Bao Dai, the ex-Emperor of Annam who was still titular Chief of State, or to the French, and thus provided Diem with the power essential for the struggle that was already shaping up with the sects.

A showdown was not long in coming. Recognizing the extreme danger of a pitched battle, Diem maneuvered skillfully to divide and destroy the sects one by one. A major break occurred in March 1955 when the Chief of Staff of the Cao Dai army, General Nguyen Thanh Phuong, was induced by bribery and other means to "rally" to the national cause with most of his units. But the Binh Xuyen had to be crushed by force. An initial flurry of skirmishing in Saigon late in March was ended by French intervention. When fighting broke out again at the end of April, Diem this time defied the French and ordered the national army, now almost completely loyal to him, to destroy the bandit sect. In a brief but bloody struggle, which devastated part of central Saigon, the Binh Xuyen were defeated and fled in disorder to the dense swamps south of the city. Subsequent operations eliminated them as a significant factor in Vietnamese politics. At the height of the crisis an attempted coup by General Nguyen Van Vy, acting under orders from Bao Dai, who correctly assessed the trend of events as fatal to his own position in Viet Nam, failed when the national army remained steadfast in its support of Diem.

There remained only the Hoa Hao to be dealt with. While some elements came over to the government side, protracted operations were necessary against their two strongest generals, Tran Van Soai and Le Quang Vinh (alias Ba Cut). The military forces at Diem's disposal were now so overwhelming, however, that the results were a foregone conclusion. Shrewdly accepting the inevitable, General Soai eventually made the best deal he could with the government and "rallied" in March 1956. A month later Ba Cut was captured while fleeing with the remnant of his forces in the extreme southwestern corner of the country. He was quickly brought to trial as a rebel, found guilty and guillotined in July. His death marked the end of the sects as important political forces in South Viet Nam. Their authority over large parts of

South Viet Nam has been eliminated and their military power destroyed. Some scattered sect units are still holding out in the maquis, but they no longer constitute a serious threat.

Containing Communism

Diem has also contained the menace of Communism. The exact strength of the Communists in South Viet Nam is a matter of speculation. After May 18, 1955, the date on which all Viet Minh forces were supposedly withdrawn from the South, the Communists continued to exercise effective political authority in many rural areas. They had extensively infiltrated the government apparatus, the police and armed forces; and they enjoyed considerable support, or at least acquiescence, among large segments of the rural population. Apparently in keeping with the overriding dictates of Communist world strategy, however, the Communists in South Viet Nam played a fairly passive role after Geneva. Although they gave sporadic assistance to the sects, they did not themselves engage in widespread guerrilla operations. Where possible they maintained their positions in the countryside. They carried on persistent clandestine propaganda and made half-hearted efforts to sabotage the two elections held by the Diem government. But otherwise they bided their time.

As the Diem regime waxed in strength and confidence, it gave increasing attention to rooting out the Communist danger. All the techniques of political and psychological warfare, as well as pacification campaigns involving extensive military operations, have been brought to bear against the underground. Some of the methods employed, such as anti-Communist denunciation rallies and self-criticism meetings, smack of practices which the Communists themselves perfected long ago; and it is clear that the usual democratic safeguards have not always been upheld. The consensus is that this all-out effort has been reasonably effective. Infiltration within the various organs of government and armed forces is apparently under control, and real progress has been made in extending the effective authority of the regime in rural districts formerly subject to the Communists. Perhaps the best evidence of this is that the ordinary peasant is beginning to turn against the cadres and give information to the government even in areas long under Communist influence. Today the Communists could still cause a lot of trouble in South Viet Nam. They could isolate extensive if fairly remote areas in the event of a renewed outbreak of civil war. But barring outside aid in the form of an invasion from the North, it is doubtful if they could any longer seriously challenge the authority of the Diem regime over most of its territory.

Diem also got rid of the French. In a sense this was the most critical problem of all, for without the achievement of complete independence his long-run prospects were hopeless. If Diem was ever to rival Ho Chi Minh as an authentic champion of the Vietnamese people he had to end any semblance of French control in the South, as Ho had successfully done in the North. Even after Geneva the French sought to salvage something of their political and military position in South Viet Nam. Their support of Diem was always lukewarm at best. For many months they continued to intrigue with the sects, to which they had given extensive economic and military support in the past; and their covert propaganda against Diem at times reached savage proportions. Doubtless they would have been glad to see his government collapse and replaced by a more tractable regime. At the height of the Binh Xuyen crisis in April 1955 Premier [Edgar] Faure openly tried to

The Achievements of Diem

In his June 1956 speech to the American Friends of Vietnam, John F. Kennedy praised the accomplishments of South Vietnam's president Ngo Dinh Diem.

Let us stop to review what the Diem government has already accomplished. . . . Most striking of all, perhaps, has been the rehabilitation of more than ¾ of a million refugees from the North. For these courageous people dedicated to the free way of life, approximately 45,000 houses have been constructed, 2,500 wells dug, 100 schools established and dozens of medical centers and maternity homes provided.

Equally impressive has been the increased solidarity and stability of the Government, the elimination of rebellious sects and the taking of the first vital steps toward true democracy. Where once colonialism and Communism struggled for supremacy, a free and independent republic has been proclaimed, recognized by over 40 countries of the Free World. Where once a playboy emperor [Bao Dai] ruled from a distant shore, a constituent assembly has been elected.

Social and economic reforms have likewise been remarkable. The living conditions of the peasants have been vastly improved, the wastelands have been cultivated, and a wider ownership of the land is gradually being encouraged. Farm cooperatives and farmer loans have modernized an outmoded agricultural economy; and a tremendous dam in the center of the country has made possible the irrigation of a vast area previously uncultivated. Legislation for better labor relations, health protection, working conditions and wages has been completed under the leadership of President Diem.

Finally, the Vietnamese army—now fighting for its own homeland and not its colonial masters—has increased tremendously in both quality and effectiveness.

torpedo Diem. He gave up only when events in Saigon outran his policy and after the United States, overcoming grave apprehensions of its own, decided to continue its support of Diem.

Thereafter the French were finished. When Diem demanded that France withdraw its armed forces from South Viet Nam in accordance with the terms of the Geneva Agreement, Paris quickly complied. The release of French advisers and other personnel by the Saigon administration was hastened and today only a handful remain. Even the training of the Vietnamese army has been turned over entirely to the Americans. . . .

Diem's first year in office was necessarily devoted almost entirely to his tenacious struggle for survival. Correspondingly less attention could be given to economic and social matters, but some important steps were taken none the less. South Viet Nam established its own national bank on January 1, 1955. Direct contacts were inaugurated with the international trading community, and normal political relationships with the outside world were also broadened. A land reform program was promulgated, calling for sweeping rent reductions rather than land redistribution. Tentative steps were also taken toward rehabilitating the war devastated economy, and inflation was brought under control.

Perhaps the most difficult economic and social problem confronting the harassed Diem government during its first year was the wholly unexpected flood of refugees that streamed into the South after Geneva. A movement of refugees was foreseen and provided for at Geneva, but was not expected to reach very great proportions. As it developed, more than 850,000 individuals, including Vietnamese military personnel, fled the North in the year after Geneva. The reception of this enormous number of destitute persons would have taxed the facilities of any government. Yet after a brief period of confusion, the challenge was met and somehow surmounted. France and the United States provided air and sea transport for the initial movement southward. Makeshift facilities were improvised for preliminary reception of the refugees, who were then redistributed as quickly as possible to hastily built temporary villages. There was no outbreak of epidemic diseases, no starvation and little if any unrest.

The satisfactory emergency handling of the refugee crisis reflected great credit on the struggling Vietnamese government, where failure might have brought about its collapse. Of course, the main problem of permanent resettlement and rehabilitation has still to be met. But even here significant progress has been made during the past year. Despite inevitable mistakes, lassitude and some corruption in the implementation of long-range programs, it is not unreasonable to expect that the whole problem will be substantially liquidated by the end of 1958. The vast influx of refugees may eventually turn out, in fact, to have been a blessing in disguise. Their numbers have added significantly to the total population, and thus helped to redress the unfavorable balance with the Communist North; and their skills and industry, mostly agricultural, could add much to a land that is not suffering from overpopulation.

Reorganizing the Government

In the last year several important steps have been taken toward reorganizing the constitutional structure of the government and broadening its political base. A popular referendum in October 1955 resulted in the deposition of Bao Dai as Chief of State and the establishment of a republic with Ngo Dinh Diem as first President. Bao Dai had never attracted much support as a nationalist leader. . . . The referendum, which registered a majority of 98 percent against the ex-Emperor, simply formalized a foregone conclusion. But Diem's ability to stage the referendum, and win such a thumping majority without the exercise of undue official coercion, enormously enhanced his prestige both at home and abroad.

Less than six months later, with the sect problem now well in hand, Diem felt strong enough to conduct elections for a Constituent Assembly. The elections of March 4, 1956, have been widely criticized, and certainly many of the practices employed by the government were highly questionable. The whole weight of government support, including its efficient propaganda machine, was thrown behind officially sponsored candidates. Many individual candidacies repugnant to the government were terminated under official pressure. The press remained closely muzzled during the brief campaign period, and opportunities for public rallies and speech-making, especially on the part of non-government candidates, were severely restricted. Most of the principal opposition parties refused to campaign under these circumstances and boycotted the elections.

Criticism of these practices should, however, be placed in the proper political setting. South Viet Nam is not Great Britain or the United States. Its people have no experience of normal democratic processes. After more than a decade of turmoil, which brought to an end a long period of colonial domination, there was a crying need to establish in an orderly fashion a political structure resting on a reasonably convincing popular base. The elections did serve this essential purpose. Where they fell short of customary democratic practice, Diem argued that circumstances did not permit him to risk real electoral freedom. Moreover, while the government won a heavy majority in the new Assembly, a number of candidates lacking the imprimatur of the regime were also successful. . . .

Much effort was also devoted to improving the administrative machinery of the state. South Viet Nam inherited a grossly outmoded colonial government and lacked the trained administrators and technicians necessary to make it work. The result was heart-breaking inefficiency in the face of almost overwhelming problems. Fortunately there has been some awareness of the dangers inherent in this situation. Large-scale technical assistance has been accepted from the United States to reorganize the administrative structure from top to bottom. A National Institute of Administration has been established, advantage is being taken of foreign educational opportunities, and as rapidly as possible expert administrators are being trained. Special attention has been given to reorganizing and training the municipal and national police forces. Corruption has also kept within bounds. The technical capacity and perhaps even more important the esprit de corps of the civil service have been gradually improving in consequence of these and other measures. One evidence is that the area of effectiveness of the South Vietnamese government has been steadily expanding both geographically and functionally. It is increasingly turning its attention to the elaboration and implementation of programs of economic and social reconstruction, with greater prospects for success than ever before.

A Continuing Challenge

The Diem regime has still to prove itself in these fields. South Viet Nam faces problems of economic backwardness and social upheaval which are common to most of Southeast Asia. They are perhaps no more acute here than elsewhere. But popular expectations of change are already high, and they are rising rapidly. Today only a small minority in the South favors the Communists. But as time goes on comparisons are bound to be made with progress in the North, where the Viet Minh are putting forth tremendous efforts to hasten economic development and social reorganization. Unless the Diem government can successfully meet the fundamental demands of Viet Nam's economic and social revolution, its achievement of political stability and constitutional consolidation in the South may in the long run prove ephemeral.

South Viet Nam thus represents a continuing challenge for American policy in the Far East. Whether we like it or not, this exposed salient of the free world has become a showcase for what American friendship, support and material aid can do in Asia. So far a respite has been gained and a solid basis laid for the future. It is a profound and legitimate interest of the United States that the structure of a stable, prosperous and democratic society be erected on the foundations that have already been prepared.

VIEWPOINT 2

"The Americans must open their eyes. South Vietnam is a police state in which the Americans are training and equipping the police."

American Aid Has Not Created a Stable Government in South Vietnam

David Hotham (b. 1917)

David Hotham, a British journalist for the *London Times* and the *Economist*, worked from 1954 to 1957 as a correspondent in Saigon, South Vietnam. The following viewpoint is taken from a 1957 article published in the *New Republic*, a liberal American magazine, in which Hotham critically analyzes the South Vietnamese government and U.S. actions in Southeast Asia. Hotham asserts that the millions of dollars the United States has spent to aid South Vietnam has accomplished little in achieving America's objective, which he defines to be the establishment of an independent and prosperous South Vietnam that is able to resist a Communist takeover. He especially criticizes South Vietnam president Ngo Dinh Diem, arguing that he has failed to inspire popular support and has relied too heavily on force to maintain his power. Hotham concludes that the United States is in danger of finding itself in France's position as an unwanted foreign power in Vietnam.

Abridged from David Hotham, "South Vietnam—Shaky Bastion," *New Republic*, November 25, 1957. Reprinted by permission of the *New Republic*; ©1957, The New Republic, Inc.

South Vietnam has been represented by Western propaganda as the success story of Asia: While other parts of the continent are over-run by Communism or wavering in a dangerous neutralism, South Vietnam, under its stout President Ngo Dinh Diem, is the most stable country in the area and the "bastion of the free world in Southeast Asia." This is the story which has gone out to the world, almost without contradiction, and that is what most people in the West think about Indo-China when they think about it at all. There is only one flaw in this story—it is totally untrue! South Vietnam today is one of the least stable countries in Asia. It has been possible for Western propaganda to portray it as stable by drawing over the confused whirlpool of its internal ferment a massive but discreet curtain of dollars and misleading publicity.

The present writer spent nearly three years in Saigon as the correspondent of an English newspaper. He has no axe to grind other than to make what contribution he can to the over-riding objective of saving the people of this corner of Asia from the desperate system of Communism. It is his view that Western policy in South Vietnam has gone completely off the rails, and unless it is radically changed *now*, will utterly fail in its main objectives. If South Vietnam goes Communist, or is again plunged in chaos, it will be a dangerous shock for the Western world and a menace for the rest of Asia. Such, however, is the danger today, and the Western nation mainly concerned is the United States.

Into this little country of 11 million inhabitants the US has pumped about $770 million of aid since the end of the Indo-China War in 1954. It has given the government of President Ngo Dinh Diem every kind of support that a great power can give to a small—diplomatic, military, economic, moral. Yet, it has to be admitted, and the Americans themselves do admit it, that those who bring this unstinting aid are not liked in the country to which they bring it, and that the economic situation there, instead of improving as the result of it, is rapidly deteriorating. What is wrong?

Three Objectives

When the Indo-China War was lost the best hope of saving the South from Communism depended on three main objectives of Western policy being achieved—and achieved with the least possible delay. These were: *first*, to unite South Vietnam under a political leadership which had a popular basis among its own people; *second*, to give the South genuine political and economic independence so that it could stand up against, and indeed outbid, Communist North Vietnam in this respect; *third*, a more long-term, but perhaps even more important objective than the other two, to lift the standard of living of the Asian masses south of the 17th parallel at a speed greater than those masses might suppose that Communism could do it for them. The fulfillment of these three objectives within a measurable period was the pre-condition of a victory for the West in what was left to them of Indo-China. Despite the massive aid program none of these objectives have been achieved. They have hardly even been tried.

Let us take them one by one. First, the political leadership. Western policy-makers justify themselves often by pointing out that President Ngo Dinh Diem, despite prophecies of his imminent fall, is still in place. Diem has held the fort, true. But how has he managed to hold it? In two ways: he has been provided by American aid with an immense army and police force which, during the period of exhaustion which followed the long wars, enabled him to defeat the sects and his other political enemies, who had small armies and little money. Second, he has held, let it be frankly admitted, because of Communist abstention. During the three years since he came to power there has been neither aggression from the North, nor any determined attempt by the Communists to subvert the Southern regime from within. We should not deceive ourselves by putting the cart before the horse. We should not suppose that the Communists have done nothing because Diem has been in power; it is rather that Diem has remained in power because the Communists have done nothing. Moreover, to assume that because Diem has remained in place his regime has therefore a popular basis is a flagrant error, as any dispassionate person in Saigon will tell you.

I have no wish to depreciate Diem personally. He is a courageous man, with numerous good qualities. But he is not a popular leader, and it is only by dint of intense and continuous propaganda that his name has even become widely known among the people of the South. (Diem is a native of Hue, in Central Annam.)

What is more serious is that Diem has failed completely to unite the South. To do this was a *sine qua non* of any successful resistance to the Communists. It is often forgotten that the national hero of Vietnam was not Diem, but the Communist Ho Chi Minh, and the national party which outbid all the others for independence from French rule was the Communist Viet-Minh. There was no hope of fighting against this strong natural current unless all the anti-Communist elements in the South could be strongly led against it. The opportunity to do this was lost from the very beginning. Diem crushed the sects, the natural enemies of the Viet-Minh, instead of leading them. He suppressed the revolutionary committees, which at least represented something of a popular movement. He used his police to squelch the anti-Communist intellectual opposition. All these imbecilities were ignored or openly supported by the Western powers.

More recently Diem has taken an even more foolish step. He has humiliated the powerful Chinese community in the South by compelling all Chinese born in Vietnam to take Vietnamese nationality without the option. (This is roughly equivalent to Guatemala forcing all Americans born in that country to become Guatemalans.) By this means he has turned the Chinese, about 800,000 strong, who were hitherto politically neutral, if not immediately toward Peking at least away from Formosa [Taiwan]. As they control the more important commerce in the country, a blow has been struck at the economy of the South which all the massive foreign aid program may not suffice to put right. What is extraordinary is that these incredible mistakes of policy have been represented by Western publicity services as successes of the regime. In fact they have annihilated the forces of anti-Communist nationalism in the South, on which alone the West could hope to rely in the long run to lead the population against the powerful natural influence of the Communists among a materially backward people.

So much for the political leadership. Let us now turn to the other two Western aims, independence for the South, and the raising of the standard of living. These two hang together, as they both depend on the American aid program. South Vietnam has been much vaunted as having true independence, because the French army withdrew last year and political institutions and a constitution etc. have been framed. In fact it has no independence at all. How can a country be independent when its entire army is financed by a foreign power? The very idea is an absurdity! How can a country be independent when more than 80 percent of its imports are paid for, not by its own exports, but by the Treasury in Washington? These facts alone suffice to make the point. In this context political institutions mean nothing. Far from being independent, South Vietnam today is one of the most dependent countries in the world! The Vietnamese in the South know this, and it riles them to the danger point.

American Aid

US aid has been generous. But how has it been spent? 64 percent of the $770 million poured into the little country since 1954 has been used simply to pay the wages of the 150,000-strong army. There is much talk of "the blessing of security" which the army bequeaths to the people. But in South Vietnam today it does nothing of the sort. Since the defeat of the sects in 1955, Diem's army and police have been notorious for their activities in the villages—widespread arrests and imprisonment without evidence and without trial of persons suspected of being Communists or "enemies of the State." According to reliable sources, about 14,000 persons were arrested in Central Annam alone at the time of the March, 1956, elections. Since then the process has, according to all reports, increased rather than diminished. Far from giving security, there is every reason to suppose that the army, buttressed by the Civil Guard (a sort of rural police of 50,000 men), is regarded by the Southern peasant as a symbol of insecurity and repression.

Questioning Diem

Although South Vietnamese president Ngo Dinh Diem had the strong backing of the United States, within government circles many U.S. officials expressed doubts about his effectiveness. Elbridge Durbrow, the U.S. ambassador to South Vietnam from 1957 to 1961, wrote the following critique of Diem in a January 1957 report to Washington.

Certain problems now discernible have given us a warning which, if disregarded, might lead to a deteriorating situation in Viet Nam within a few years.

Diem achieved notable successes in the first two years of his regime and remains the only man of stature so far in evidence to guide this country. He has unified free Viet Nam, brought it relative security and stability, and firmly maintains a pro-West, anti-communist position.

In the last year, however, Diem has avoided making decisions required to build the economic and social foundations necessary to secure Viet Nam's future independence and strength. He has made it clear that he would give first priority to the build-up of his armed forces regardless of the country's requirements for economic and social development. Events abroad which increase the danger of communist infiltration and subversion, and which threaten Viet Nam with possible isolation in this area have contributed to his concern and to his determination to strengthen his armed forces.

Certain characteristics of Diem—his suspiciousness and authoritarianism—have also reduced the Government's limited administrative capabilities. He assumes responsibility for the smallest details of Government and grants his Ministers little real authority.

At the same time, discontent is felt in different segments of the population for varied reasons. The base of the regime's popular support remains narrow. The regime might overcome such discontent and finally win over the loyalty of a majority of Vietnamese both in the North and South if it could show its ability to give the country stronger protection and create sound economic and social bases for progress. Progress, which is demanded in Viet Nam as throughout Asia, is perhaps the touchstone of the regime's enduring viability. Yet precisely because Diem is now procrastinating in making decisions affecting fundamental problems of his country's development, the lag between the people's expectations and the Government's ability to show results will grow.

From there we go to the other argument: that so large an army is required by the exigencies of the international situation to ward off an attack by the Communists across the 17th parallel. This argument is founded on a false premise. An aggression across the parallel, should it occur, would be decided in Moscow and Peking. The deterrent to such an aggression is not the South Vietnamese army, the fighting value of which is very doubtful: it is the Manila Treaty [that created the Southeast Asia Treaty Organization (SEATO)], the possibility of Western intervention with tactical atomic weapons or even the hydrogen bomb, and behind that world opinion, the guardian of which on the spot is the International Control Commission in Indo-China.

If Diem's army contributes little or nothing to the advancement of the Southern people, neither does the resettlement of the Northern refugees. This was a great, successful human operation (though it was also of course a maneuver in the Cold War). But to settle nearly 900,000 Tonkinese refugees, two-thirds of them Catholics, among the primarily Buddhist population of Cochin China, was not calculated to endear a Catholic president and his Western supporters to the people of the South. The latter have besides every reason to be envious of the money spent on these undesirable visitants from the North, and of the houses, work and land—all of which are short in the South—with which they were provided.

The Foreign Aid Program

The upshot is that more than four-fifths of the whole gigantic aid program has failed to contribute in any direct way to the well-being of the Southern population, which should of course have been the primary objective since the beginning. None of it has been used to cure the growing unemployment. Almost none has been used to build houses for the people. Not a single industry has been created in the South since the end of the Indo-China War. The Southern population, which knows well enough what large sums have been spent in its country, knows equally well that almost none of this money has come its way. This not only breeds hatred of the West, it contradicts the whole principle of Western aid to "backward" countries—the principle of preventing Communism by improving the lot of most of the people.

In passing, one wonders whether the best method has been chosen to give this aid—a cumbrous bureaucracy in Saigon, many offices and much paper work, large houses and cars for the officials, the PX stores, pay far above local wages for the US staff, and facilities for that staff to change their dollars at advantageous rates not available to others. The result is that the American residents form an extra-rich class. Can this be a help in averting Communism in a poor country? This class, moreover, has very few links with the people. Very few of the officials can speak the language. Is this method likely to endear these men, whose devotion to their duties is not in question, to the Asian masses? The Vietnamese have recently thrown out one Western power, France, and patently have no desire to install another.

Why is it necessary, for example, for the American military advisory headquarters in Saigon, which until recently was housed in a suitably discreet suburb, to move into a vast building in the most central square of the city, immediately opposite, and several stories higher than, the South Vietnamese National Assembly? A greater psychological error is hardly conceivable. But, to revert to the general question of the method of giving aid to these countries, would it not be better to send out men who are trained in the language, who can live in the villages among the people, who can teach the people how to breed chickens, to improve their cattle, to dig wells, increase their crop yields, drive tractors, and all the innumerable techniques which we in the West have learnt, and could pass on to those who have not done so?

It is untrue to say that South Vietnam is a colony of the United States, but American policy is falling into the same error in Asia as that of the colonial nations—failure to realize what the dependent people are thinking. "South Vietnam is the bastion of the free world against Communism in Southeast Asia," says the State Department over and over again. This phrase alone betrays what is wrong. It shows that Washington thinks of Vietnam simply in strategic terms—a mere piece of territory, a salient in the Cold War. It does not seem to occur to the strategists that 11 million human beings live in the "bastion," 11 million people whose wishes and interests may be, and almost certainly are, quite different to theirs. These people have no reason to love the West. They have no reason whatever to hate Communism. The Communists, under Ho Chi Minh, fought for and won their national independence against the regular French army, supported by the US at a time when Ngo Dinh Diem was living piously in a seminary in New Jersey. For the people of Vietnam, North and South, Diem is not an outstanding national leader at all. He is *"l'homme de l'Amerique"* [America's man].

A Repressive Regime

The most serious side of the whole affair, in the long run, is perhaps that the West, and the US in particular, will be identified in the minds of this particular lot of Asians with an inefficient and yet at the same time repressive regime. There is in South Vietnam no freedom of the press; there are ordered verdicts in the courts, and the clauses of the liberal constitution are a dead letter. The whole regime is a façade, propped up by money from across the seas. . . . Behind the façade, the economic situation rots hourly. The

Franco-Chinese commercial system is collapsing; and there is nothing yet to replace it. The unemployed number hundreds of thousands. Beggars, disguised as photographers or the sellers of impossible objects, accumulate in the Rue Catinat. A deep lethargy hangs over the economy. With all the huge influx of aid—American . . . United Nations, and a multitude of charitable organizations—nothing is done to build houses for the people, nothing is done to create new industries. How is it imagined that the standard of living of a whole Asian people can be raised appreciably in a short time without the creation of a single new industry?

A Police State

If the Americans do not act, their identification in the Vietnamese mind with a repressive and incompetent regime may prejudice the whole Western position in Asia, for Vietnam is only typical of what is happening in the other "containment" countries. The Americans must open their eyes. South Vietnam is a police state in which the Americans are training and equipping the police. It is no use saying: "It is better than in the Communist North!" No doubt it is, but how can you convince the people of the South, who have never lived under Communism, that it is?

It is easy to be critical; it is less easy to be constructive. But in this case what ought to be done sticks out a mile. It is to take the original principles of policy out of the pigeon-holes, dust them off, and them simply *apply* them. To unite the South, all the anti-Communist elements available in the country should be brought in to help the running of the country, instead of being kept out. It is painful to see so many able men kicking their heels in idleness and frustration in South Vietnam. Secondly, the aid program should be recast (whether or not the volume of aid is cut) so that it aims at making South Vietnam economically independent of the US within the shortest time possible. At the same time, the total amount of the aid should be spent on improving the living standards of the people who live in the country to whom it is given, and not on anything else.

If these objectives are clear, the means to achieve them will become clear. Some industrialization will certainly be involved—probably a good deal. The execution of the long-paralyzed land reform will be imperative. Some policy for the reunification of the country—instead of, as at present, no policy at all—will be essential. The idea of the "bastion of Southeast Asia" should be discarded. To persevere with it is to make absolutely sure that the "bastion" crumbles within the next few years.

A final point may be added. If President Ngo Dinh Diem objects to such a change in policy, the West should remember that South Vietnam is *not* in fact economically independent today. Pressure can and should be used. Gross mistakes have been made in South Vietnam. The Western policy-makers should realize that the whole aim and object of their policy is not merely to keep one particular man or group of men in power. It is to live up to their declared principles. If they do not act now, it will be too late. They will have done permanent harm to their future in Asia.

"We should be prepared to introduce United States combat forces if that should become necessary for success."

The United States Should Increase Its Military Commitment to South Vietnam

Dean Rusk (1909–1994) and Robert S. McNamara (b. 1916)

By the time John F. Kennedy was inaugurated as president of the United States in January 1961, South Vietnam was locked in war between the government of Ngo Dinh Diem and the rebels of the National Liberation Front (NLF), whom Diem labeled the Vietcong (Vietnamese Communists). The rebels, with arms and support from North Vietnam, were successful in gaining control of many rural areas of South Vietnam.

During his first year of office, Kennedy responded to the deteriorating situation in South Vietnam by approving significant increases in military aid, including providing the Army of the Republic of (South) Vietnam (ARVN) with helicopters and additional military advisers. In doing so, Kennedy acted in agreement with most of his key advisers, including Secretary of Defense Robert S. McNamara and Secretary of State Dean Rusk. The following viewpoint is taken from a November 11, 1961, report prepared for Kennedy by the two cabinet members. They argue that the United States, utilizing U.S. troops if necessary, must commit itself to preventing the fall of South Vietnam to Communism.

Excerpted from Dean Rusk and Robert S. McNamara's report to President Kennedy, November 11, 1961.

1. United States National Interests in South Viet-Nam.

The deteriorating situation in South Viet-Nam requires attention to the nature and scope of United States national interests in that country. The loss of South Viet-Nam to Communism would involve the transfer of a nation of 20 million people from the free world to the Communism bloc. The loss of South Viet-Nam would make pointless any further discussion about the importance of Southeast Asia to the free world; we would have to face the near certainty that the remainder of Southeast Asia and Indonesia would move to a complete accommodation with Communism, if not formal incorporation with the Communist bloc. The United States, as a member of SEATO [Southeast Asia Treaty Organization], has commitments with respect to South Viet-Nam under the Protocol to the SEATO Treaty. Additionally, in a formal statement at the conclusion session of the 1954 Geneva Conference, the United States representative stated that the United States "would view any renewal of the aggression . . . with grave concern and seriously threatening international peace and security."

American Credibility at Stake

The loss of South Viet-Nam to Communism would not only destroy SEATO but would undermine the credibility of American commitments elsewhere. Further, loss of South Viet-Nam would stimulate bitter domestic controversies in the United States and would be seized upon by extreme elements to divide the country and harass the Administration. . . .

3. The United States' Objective in South Viet-Nam.

The United States should commit itself to the clear objective of preventing the fall of South Viet-Nam to Communism. The basic means for accomplishing this objective must be to put the Government of South Viet-Nam [GVN] into a position to win its own war against the Guerrillas. We must insist that that Government itself take the measures necessary for that purpose in exchange for large-scale United States assistance in the military, economic and political fields. At the same time we must recognize that it will probably not be possible for the GVN to win this war as long as the flow of men and supplies from North Viet-Nam continues unchecked and the guerrillas enjoy a safe sanctuary in neighboring territory.

We should be prepared to introduce United States combat forces if that should become necessary for success. Dependent upon the circumstances, it may also be necessary for United States forces to strike at the source of the aggression in North Viet-Nam.

4. The Use of United States Forces in South Viet-Nam.

The commitment of United States forces to South Viet-Nam involves two different categories: (A) Units of modest size required for the direct support of South Vietnamese military effort, such as communications, helicopter and other forms of airlift, reconnaissance aircraft, naval patrols, intelligence units, etc., and (B) larger organized units with actual or potential direct military mission.

Communist Aggression and the Strategic Importance of Vietnam

Secretary of State Dean Rusk, in an address before the Economic Club of New York on April 22, 1963, argues that the war in South Vietnam is not a local conflict but an attack by North Vietnam. He emphasizes the strategic importance to the United States of preventing South Vietnam's fall to communism.

According to Communist propaganda, the war in South Viet-Nam is a civil war, a local uprising. The truth is that it is an aggression organized, directed, and partly supplied from North Viet-Nam. It is conducted by hardened Communist political organizers and guerrilla leaders trained in North Viet-Nam, who, upon their arrival in the South, recruit local assistance. This has been done in a variety of ways, including terror and assassination. Schoolteachers, health workers, malaria eradication teams, local officials loyal to the Republic—these were the first targets of the assassins. But many ordinary villagers who refused to cooperate with the Communist guerrillas likewise have been ruthlessly killed.

This assault on South Viet-Nam was a major Communist enterprise, carefully and elaborately prepared, heavily staffed, and relentlessly pursued. It made headway. In 1961 President Diem appealed for further assistance and President Kennedy responded promptly and affirmatively.

The strategic importance of South Viet-Nam is plain. It controls the mouth of the Mekong River, the main artery of Southeast Asia. The loss of South Viet-Nam would put the remaining states of Southeast Asia in mortal danger.

But there are larger reasons why the defense of South Viet-Nam is vital to us and to the whole free world. We cannot be indifferent to the fate of 14 million people who have fought hard against communism—including nearly 1 million who fled their former homes to avoid living under Communist tyranny. Since we went to the aid of Greece and Turkey 16 years ago, it has been the attitude of the United States to assist peoples who resist Communist aggression. We have seen this form of attack fail in Burma, Malaya, and the Philippines. The South Vietnamese are determined to win their battle, and they deserve our help.

Category (A) should be introduced as speedily as possible. Category (B) units pose a more serious problem in that they are much more significant from the point of view of domestic and international political factors and greatly increase the probabilities of Communist bloc escalation. Further, the employment of United States combat forces (in the absence of Communist bloc escalation) involves a certain dilemma: if there is a strong South Vietnamese effort, they may not be needed; if there is not such an effort, United States forces could not accomplish their mission in the midst of an apathetic or hostile population. Under present circumstances, therefore, the question of injecting United States and SEATO combat forces should in large part be considered as a contribution to the morale of the South Vietnamese in their own effort to do the principal job themselves. . . .

Recommendations

In the light of the foregoing, the Secretary of State and the Secretary of Defense recommend that:

1. We now take the decision to commit ourselves to the objective of preventing the fall of South Viet-Nam to Communism and that, in doing so, we recognize that the introduction of United States and other SEATO forces may be necessary to achieve this objective. (However, if it is necessary to commit outside forces to achieve the foregoing objective our decision to introduce United States forces should not be contingent upon unanimous SEATO agreement thereto.)

2. The Department of Defense be prepared with plans for the use of United States forces in South Viet-Nam under one or more of the following purposes:

(a) Use of a significant number of United States forces to signify United States determination to defend Viet-Nam and to boost South Viet-Nam morale.

(b) Use of substantial United States forces to assist in suppressing Viet Cong insurgency short of engaging in detailed counter-guerrilla operations but including relevant operations in North Viet-Nam.

(c) Use of United States forces to deal with the situation if there is organized Communist military intervention.

3. We immediately undertake the following actions in support of the GVN: . . .

(c) Provide the GVN with small craft, including such United States uniformed advisers and operating personnel as may be necessary for quick and effective operations in effecting surveillance and control over coastal waters and inland waterways. . . .

(e) Provide such personnel and equipment as may be necessary to improve the military-political intelligence system beginning at the provincial level and extending upward through the Government and the armed forces to the Central Intelligence Organization.

(f) Provide such new terms of reference, reorganization and additional personnel for United States military forces as are required for increased United States participation in the direction and control of GVN military operations and to carry out the other increased responsibilities which accrue to MAAG [Military Assistance Advisory Group] under these recommendations.

VIEWPOINT 4

"A truly massive commitment of American military personnel and other resources . . . is an alternative which I most emphatically do not recommend."

The United States Should Try to Minimize Its Military Commitment to South Vietnam

Mike Mansfield (b. 1903)

Mike Mansfield, a Democrat, was a U.S. senator from Montana from 1953 to 1977 and majority leader of the Senate from 1961 to 1977. A former professor of political science and Far Eastern history at Montana State University (later named the University of Montana), Mansfield was an early and influential supporter of Ngo Dinh Diem, who with America's backing became leader of South Vietnam following the 1954 Geneva Agreement.

In 1962 Mansfield was sent by President John F. Kennedy on a fact-finding trip to South Vietnam. The following viewpoint is excerpted from his December 1962 report to the president. Mansfield gives a pessimistic assessment of Ngo Dinh Diem's leadership and concludes that the United States is in serious danger of being drawn into an unwinnable war. He argues against the deployment of large numbers of U.S. troops to the area, asserting that the primary responsibility for defending South Vietnam "rests with the Vietnamese."

As American involvement in Vietnam escalated, Mansfield con-

Excerpted from Mike Mansfield, "Two Reports on Viet Nam and Southeast Asia to the President of the United States," U.S. Congress, Senate, Committee on Foreign Relations, 93rd Cong., 1st sess. (April 1973).

tinued to voice his concerns about Vietnam in private conversations and memorandums to Kennedy and his successor, Lyndon B. Johnson. In the early 1970s he sponsored legislation designed to end the war and withdraw U.S. forces. After his retirement as senator in 1977, Mansfield served for twelve years as U.S. ambassador to Japan.

Even assuming that aid over a prolonged period would be available, the question still remains as to the capacity of the present Saigon government to carry out the task of social engineering. Ngo Dinh Diem remains a dedicated, sincere, hardworking, incorruptible and patriotic leader. But he is older and the problems which confront him are more complex than those which he faced when he pitted his genuine nationalism against, first, the French and Bao Dai and then against the sects with such effectiveness. The energizing role, which he played in the past, appears to be passing to other members of his family, particularly Ngo Dinh Nhu. The latter is a person of great energy and intellect who is fascinated by the operations of political power and has consummate eagerness and ability in organizing and manipulating it. But it is Ngo Dinh Diem, not Ngo Dinh Nhu, who has such popular mandate to exercise power as there is in South Vietnam. In a situation of this kind there is a great danger of the corruption of unbridled power. This has implications far beyond the persistent reports and rumors of fiscal and similar irregularities which are, in any event, undocumented. More important is its effect on the organization of the machinery for carrying out the new concepts. The difficulties in Vietnam are not likely to be overcome by a handful of paid retainers and sycophants. The success of the new approach in Vietnam presupposes a great contribution of initiative and self-sacrifice from a substantial body of Vietnamese with capacities for leadership at all levels. Whether that contribution can be obtained remains to be seen. For in the last analysis it depends upon a diffusion of political power, essentially in a democratic pattern. The trends in the political life of Vietnam have not been until now in that direction despite lip service to the theory of developing democratic and popular institutions "from the bottom up" through the strategic hamlet program.

To summarize, our policies and activities are designed to meet an existing set of internal problems in South Vietnam. North Vietnam infiltrates some supplies and cadres into the south; together with the Vietnamese we are trying to shut off this flow. The Vietcong has had the offensive in guerrilla warfare in the countryside; we are attempting to aid the Vietnamese military in putting them on the defensive with the hope of eventually reducing them at least to ineffectiveness. Finally, the Vietnamese peasants have sustained the Vietcong guerrillas out of fear, indifference or blandishment and we are helping the Vietnamese in an effort to win the peasants away by offering them the security and other benefits which may be provided in the strategic hamlets.

Unfounded Optimism on Vietnam

State department official Chester Bowles recommended to President John F. Kennedy on several occasions that the United States seek a negotiated settlement on Vietnam and reappraise its military commitment to South Vietnam. The following passage is taken from a memorandum to the president written on March 7, 1963, shortly before Bowles left the State Department to become ambassador to India.

I hesitate to play the role of Cassandra again in regard to Vietnam and Southeast Asia. However, I remain deeply concerned about the outlook there, and having talked to Mike Mansfield about his report and the fragile nature of our present position, I feel that I should frankly express my misgivings to you.

I see nothing in the present course of events to dispel my conviction, expressed to you and the Secretary on several occasions, that if this course is pursued, the Southeast Asia situation will ultimately have a serious impact on the Administration's position at home and abroad.

Although the general outlook here in Washington and in Saigon now seems to be cautiously optimistic, it may be worthwhile to remind ourselves of the confident assumptions of the Eisenhower Administration in a somewhat similar situation during the winter of 1954 [when France was at war with the Vietminh]. . . .

Nine years have passed and now it is we who appear to be striving, in defiance of powerful indigenous political and military forces, to insure the survival of an unpopular Vietnamese regime with inadequate roots among the people. And now, as in 1954, many able U.S. military authorities are convinced that the situation is moving in our favor and that victory can be foreseen within two to three years.

I wonder if these assurances are not based on a dangerously false premise, i.e., that the Communists will not embarrass us by upping the military ante . . . ?

That, in brief, is the present situation. As noted, there is optimism that success will be achieved quickly. My own view is that the problems can be made to yield to present remedies, *provided* the problems and their magnitude do not change significantly and *provided* that the remedies are pursued by both Vietnamese and Americans (and particularly the former) with great vigor and self-dedication.

Our Role Must Be Secondary

Certainly, if these remedies do not work, it is difficult to conceive of alternatives, with the possible exception of a truly massive commitment of American military personnel and other resources—in short going to war fully ourselves against the guerrillas—and the establishment of some form of neocolonial rule in South Vietnam. That is an alternative which I most emphatically do not recommend. On the contrary, it seems to me most essential that we make crystal clear to the Vietnamese government and to our own people that while we will go to great lengths to help, the primary responsibility rests with the Vietnamese. Our role is and must remain secondary in present circumstances. It is their country, their future which is most at stake, not ours.

To ignore that reality will not only be immensely costly in terms of American lives and resources but it may also draw us inexorably into some variation of the unenviable position in Vietnam which was formerly occupied by the French. We are not, of course, at that point at this time. But the great increase in American military commitment this year has tended to point us in that general direction and we may well begin to slide rapidly toward it if any of the present remedies begin to falter in practice.

As indicated, our planning appears to be predicated on the assumption that existing internal problems in South Vietnam will remain about the same and can be overcome by greater effort and better techniques. But what if the problems do not remain the same? To all outward appearances, little if any thought has been given in Saigon at least, to the possibilities of a change in the nature of the problems themselves. Nevertheless, they are very real possibilities and the initiative for instituting change rests in enemy hands largely because of the weakness of the Saigon government. The range of possible change includes a step-up in the infiltration of cadres and supplies by land or sea. It includes the use of part or all of the regular armed forces of North Vietnam, reported to be about 300,000 strong, under Vo Nguyen Giap. It includes, in the last analysis, the possibility of a major increase in any of many possible forms of Chinese Communist support for the Vietcong.

None of these possibilities may materialize. It would be folly, however, not to recognize their existence and to have as much clarification in advance of what our response to them will be if they do.

Determining Our Interests

This sort of anticipatory thinking cannot be undertaken with respect to the situation in Vietnam alone. The problem there can be grasped, it seems to me, only as we have clearly in mind our interests with respect to all of Southeast Asia. If it is essential in our own interests to maintain a quasi-permanent position of power on the Asian mainland as against the Chinese then we must be prepared to continue to pay the present cost in Vietnam indefinitely and to meet any escalation on the other side with at least a commensurate escalation of commitment of our own. This can go very far, indeed, in terms of lives and resources. Yet if it is essential to our interests then we would have no choice.

But if on the other hand it is, at best, only desirable rather than essential that a position of power be maintained on the mainland, then other courses are indicated. We would, then, properly view such improvement as may be obtained by the new approach in Vietnam primarily in terms of what it might contribute to strengthening our diplomatic hand in the Southeast Asian region. And we would use that hand as vigorously as possible and in every way possible not to deepen our costly involvement on the Asian mainland but to lighten it.

VIEWPOINT 5

"South Viet Nam still faces a long, hard fight. But the national effort is gathering momentum."

South Vietnamese Forces Are Making Significant Progress

Time

Vietnam remained relatively obscure to most Americans even as the U.S. commitment to South Vietnam deepened in the early 1960s. Much of what little media coverage there was of Vietnam reflected the optimism of American officials, who in their public statements remained upbeat about the progress of the American-backed government of Ngo Dinh Diem in defeating the Vietcong rebels.

The following viewpoint is taken from a September 21, 1962, article in *Time*, an influential newsweekly. The article reports on the trip of Paul Harkins and Maxwell D. Taylor to Vietnam and their assessments of improving military and political conditions in South Vietnam. Harkins was the military commander of U.S. forces in Vietnam. Taylor, who later became the U.S. ambassador to South Vietnam, was then the personal military representative of President John F. Kennedy. One of the positive developments in South Vietnam reported by *Time* was the "strategic hamlet" counterinsurgency program, in which Vietnamese peasants were relocated to armed stockades in order to protect them from the Vietcong (and to deprive the Vietcong of a source of support).

"Their Own Battle," *Time*, September 21, 1962. Copyright ©1962, Time Inc. Reprinted by permission.

Over rutted jungle roads and through remote mountain villages, General Maxwell D. Taylor Jeeped and walked last week on a first-hand inspection tour of South Viet Nam's hard, ugly war against the Communist Viet Cong. Taylor, who takes over as chairman of the Joint Chiefs of Staff next month, last visited Viet Nam a year ago; from that trip came the stepped-up program of U.S. military and economic aid to the embattled nation. Last week, in talks with President Ngo Dinh Diem and General Paul Harkins, boss of U.S. forces in Viet Nam, hard-bitten Maxwell Taylor sought to assess the results. His conclusion: "We are making progress."

Since last October, the U.S. has boosted its force of military advisers to more than 10,000, and is now spending $1,000,000 daily to beat the Viet Cong. This year the U.S. will help arm some 130,000 members of the Civil Guard and the Self-Defense Corps, and train them both to defend their villages and to make short-range thrusts against the Viet Cong. The regular army will be boosted from seven to nine divisions, with a total force of 200,000 men; U.S.-backed training programs will also double the size of the army's officer and NCO corps.

Clear & Hold

With the growth of the militiamen, the army is being released from static holding operations to make major offensive sweeps against the Viet Cong, sometimes clearing them from areas where no government forces have been in 15 years. In Kien Phong and Vinh Long provinces, where the Reds once dominated up to 65% of the population, swiftly mounted government raids against guerrilla training centers and supply depots have reduced the Communist-controlled populace to less than 30%. In the past year, the army's striking power has been massively enhanced by U.S. helicopters that can airlift Vietnamese troops in hours to isolated areas that once took days to reach—if they were not ambushed en route. In the next month, the four helicopter units now ferrying troops will be reinforced with three new companies, including a number of new models armed with machine guns and rockets.

Taylor and Harkins were particularly encouraged by the government's ambitious strategic hamlet program [*see map*]. Its aim is to concentrate the rural population in fortified villages that are guarded by Self-Defense Corpsmen, and thus deprive the Viet Cong guerrillas of the supplies and shelter they have long exacted from the terrified peasants. To date, nearly 3,000 of the 11,500 strategic hamlets that the government expects to build have been completed, and 2,700 more are under construction. In

Phu Yen province alone, 200 miles northeast of Saigon, 170,000 Vietnamese out of a population of 345,000 have been relocated in strategic hamlets. Though the Viet Cong have repeatedly attacked the strategic hamlets, they have been unable to subdue any of them. In 60 attacks last month, the government claimed that the Reds lost 109 men while only twelve Self-Defense Corpsmen were killed.

But the country is under considerable and mounting strain.

Politically, despite the pleadings of U.S. officials—and rumbles of discontent from his opponents—Diem is in no mood to relax his authoritarian rule. Economically, the war has taken a heavy toll. The Viet Cong have cut off rice shipments from the interior and rubber production is down sharply. Gold and foreign exchange reserves have dipped from $222 million in 1960 to $158

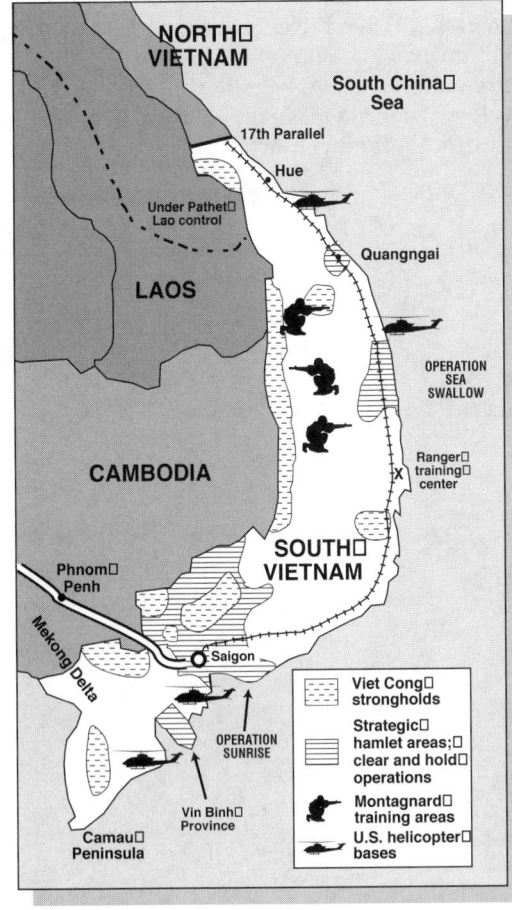

South Vietnam in 1962.

million, and export earnings will drop this year from $70 million to $55 million. Nearly $2.5 billion in U.S. aid has only made South Viet Nam more dependent on—and more critical of—its friends.

A National Character

Yet U.S. aid is essential not only to South Viet Nam's survival as a free nation; it is also helping subtly to foster what General Taylor called a "growing national character, a great national movement." The strategic hamlet program alone has given thousands of peasants their first experience of self-government: bolstered by U.S. economic aid, the experiment has also brought teachers, doctors and agricultural advisers to large areas that, in consequence, are undergoing what a top Vietnamese official calls "a social revolution, with a whole new scale of values."

As the Vietnamese clear and hold the countryside, Taylor said last week, "the emphasis will shift more to economic and social activities." In this realm alone, U.S. advisers admit, a vast amount remains to be done. Militarily, also, South Viet Nam still faces a long, hard fight. But the national effort is gathering momentum. Declared Maxwell Taylor: "South Viet Nam is moving toward victory because the South Vietnamese are fighting their own battle."

VIEWPOINT 6

"Most observers believe official American statements have been too optimistic, and that a greater U.S. effort is needed to win."

South Vietnamese Forces Are Not Making Significant Progress

Sol W. Sanders (b. 1926)

In August 1963 Henry Cabot Lodge replaced Frederick Nolting as U.S. ambassador to South Vietnam. *U.S. News & World Report*, a weekly newsmagazine, took the occasion to publish an assessment of the war in Vietnam by staff writer Sol W. Sanders. In his article, reprinted here, Sanders argues that, although U.S. military advisers in Vietnam have made some progress, past statements by U.S. public officials have often been too optimistic in their assessments of the war in Vietnam and the performance of the South Vietnamese. Two major problems he cites are the ability of Communist guerrillas to establish trails and retreats in the neighboring countries of Laos and Cambodia and the failure of South Vietnam's president Ngo Dinh Diem to inspire popular support. He argues that the United States may have to choose one of three stark alternatives: abandon South Vietnam, assume direct command of the war effort and send combat troops, or simply accept that the struggle "is going to be a long, tough haul."

Many people blamed the foundering war effort on the political shortcomings of Diem, who had been the U.S.-supported leader of South Vietnam since 1954. Clashes between government troops and Buddhist protesters in 1963 raised discontent with Diem both within South Vietnam and among officials of the U.S. government. On November 1, 1963, Diem was overthrown by a group of Vietnamese generals, with the tacit backing of Lodge and the United States. However, the coup led to a period of political instability in South Vietnam while doing little, from America's perspective, to improve the military situation.

"The U.S. acts like a blind, drunk elephant thrashing around out here."

That's the verdict of one of the most experienced American officials in South Vietnam, where U.S. troops are deeply involved in a war against Communists.

This man feels—as do many other veteran observers—that despite the 1.5 million dollars a day America is spending here [South Vietnam], Washington has, in his words "failed to focus on the problems."

Those problems are complicated ones.

The U.S. is trying to build a Vietnamese Army that can match the Communists who chased the French out of Indo-China—one of the best guerrilla forces in the history of warfare. It is trying to bring the villagers around to support the anti-Communist cause—though the vast majority of them are neutral in the 20-year-old civil war in this country. They want only to be left alone. And, perhaps the most difficult problem of all, the U.S. has thrown its weight behind the Government of President Ngo Dinh Diem in an effort to rally the educated elite against the Communist regime of North Vietnam.

Totting up the score. A year and a half after President Kennedy announced it was here that America intended to make a stand against Communist encroachment into Southeast Asia, this is the way observers here add up the score:

• The U.S. has made fair progress in building a Vietnamese Army.

• It has made some progress in winning the peasant population.

• It—along with the Diem Government—has failed to get the general support of the educated.

Now there are two new threats:

The Diem Government is up against strong internal opposition which has rallied around Buddhist agitation, ostensibly against religious discrimination.

At the same time, events in neighboring Laos have become more menacing. The Communists are now threatening to out-

86

flank the whole American effort here.

That's the situation that faces the new American Ambassador, Henry Cabot Lodge, when he arrives here soon. Most observers believe official American statements have been too optimistic, and that a greater U.S. effort is needed to win.

An old story. There is a recurrent rhythm to this war in South Vietnam.

I walked into a bar where, years ago, I watched Germans of the French Foreign Legion playing with a pet tiger. This time the bar was full of American soldiers.

In a Saigon office I was cornered by a typical Vietnamese intellectual. He berated me for U.S. support of the "dictator" regime. His arguments were the same I had heard a decade ago directed against the French and former Emperor Bao Dai. It finally turned out that the Government had refused to let this man go to France, where a large Vietnamese population is sitting out the war.

Why Are We Here?

A basic question was put to me by a young American airman in Saigon. He complained about the way his airplane was being used, and about relations with the Vietnamese Army. Then he said: "What are we doing here, anyway?"

It's a question many want answered considering that 92 Americans have been killed here since the first of last year.

The reasons why. People here tell you there are basic reasons why the U.S. chose South Vietnam to make its stand. Most important, of course, is that here is where the Communists have chosen to take on the Americans. The Communists want to overthrow South Vietnam's Government. If that happens, most Western observers see two results:

There would be a "domino effect," as former Secretary of State John Foster Dulles called it. Other countries in Southeast Asia—all weaker than Vietnam—would rush to make peace with the Chinese Communists. In the long run, as most Asians see it, this would mean the resources of Southeast Asia would fall to the Chinese Communist block.

But perhaps as important, a new Communist state that would arise in a unified Vietnam would be the most powerful country in this part of the world.

A different temperament. The Vietnamese are not the easygoing, chubby little people of other countries in Southeast Asia. They have drive, and their thin bodies are as hard as their harsh language that, to foreign ears, always sounds like argument. They seem high-strung almost to the point of hysteria.

Here there is a real war. I visited a battlefield less than 50 miles from Saigon a few days ago. Corpses littered the ground. Communist dead were lying in foxholes half filled with water.

A young American West Pointer—adviser to the Vietnamese forces—told how the native unit he is with had moved in on the well-armed Communists, and lost 14 men. There were 58 Communist dead and 18 prisoners. The rest of a Communist force of perhaps 400 men got away.

The Question of Time

One of the basic problems here is the question of time.

A senior military man reminds his listeners over and over that it took the British in Malaya eight years to defeat a Communist guerrilla movement which at its height never involved more than 3,000 men. The Communist guerrillas in South Vietnam probably total 30,000.

The British had many advantages. The guerrillas in Malaya had virtually no contact beyond the country's borders. The Communists here have moved in training units from North Vietnam, through Laos, and have sent recruits north for training. In many areas, when hard pressed, they move into Cambodia or Laos.

"Neither side wants to win this war quickly," said one young

On June 11, 1963, Buddhist monk Thich Quang Duc set himself ablaze with gasoline to protest the government of Ngo Dinh Diem. The photograph of the self-immolation brought home to many Americans the extent and depth of Vietnamese discontent with the Diem government.

American official in Saigon. He put in extreme form something you hear over and over—that neither the Communists nor their opponents are willing, at this point, to make the all-out effort that would be necessary for victory.

The Communists in North Vietnam are convinced—they have said so repeatedly—they will eventually wear down the Americans just as they wore down the French. Ho Chi Minh, Communist leader of North Vietnam, has said it took six years to drive out the French, and since the Americans are twice as strong it may take 12 years to get them out.

President Diem obviously believes that he cannot ask the immense sacrifices of the people in South Vietnam that any crash program for a quick victory would demand. And, after looking around Saigon, many observers believe he is right.

Nothing new in disaster. This is a city that has lived on the edge of disaster for a quarter of a century—and lived very well. Saigon students, for example, probably live better than any other students in Asia. There is always the unspoken fear among South Vietnam's leaders that to ask for any greater sacrifice would push these students into the arms of the Reds. Communist propaganda is constantly directed at the students—harping on the lack of good jobs and the "miserliness" of American scholarships.

Reshaping American Attitudes

Needed: new attitudes. Those on the ground here say that if this is going to be the long-drawn-out contest that it now appears, then American attitudes will have to be reshaped.

"We have set down a whole little Pentagon here with all its complications," said one American critic of the present policy. "We don't need so many people. What we do need are more men who know their job, better training."

To understand what he was getting at, you have to look at just what it is the Americans are trying to do.

For example, American officers are acting as "sector advisers." In effect they are military-government officers in each province.

In one province I visited last winter, there were clandestine Communist publications being distributed, but no Government newspaper. The sector adviser—an American infantry colonel—cranked up the U.S. Information Service in Saigon and got it to help the Vietnamese chief of the province to put one out.

Help, or "interference"? Anyone who has visited provincial areas of this country is impressed by the ability of American officers to take on jobs in which they have had neither experience nor training. Often, they need diplomatic skills to work with feudal Vietnamese local officials, many of whom resent what they call "American interference."

One obvious defect of the American program is rotation: Between February and May of this year there was an almost complete turnover of military advisers. They had been here one year.

War in peacetime. The Army's explanation is that it is not possible to keep up the morale of American soldiers—many of them senior officers with families—when they are assigned to a war theater in peacetime.

Not only do they run the risk of infection from tropical diseases, but they face the possibility of being killed in combat. So they are rotated. Yet—particularly in the case of the sector advisers—one year's experience only begins to make the man effective. Then he leaves.

The Pentagon says that this way practically the whole American military is being put through a training school in guerrilla warfare—something that may come in handy in the future. The answer you get here on the ground is: "We'd better win this one first."

Although there is much talk about this being an unconventional kind of war for which U.S. military techniques have been modified, that's not always the case. A young Special Forces sergeant complained to me about "sneak" inspections. "They came to see whether our trucks were being kept up and 'gigged' us for mud that was on them. Look, we're *living* in mud and thatch huts. We're hip deep in mud."

Yet there are signs of progress in the military effort. And, as one veteran guerrilla fighter points out, "signs are about all you ever get in this kind of war until it's nearly won."

The shape of war. Roughly, South Vietnam is divided into three main battle areas:

There is the high plateau which runs along the Laotian border up to the seventeenth parallel, dividing South Vietnam from the Communist North. There, American Special Forces have been extremely successful in bringing mountain tribesmen into the Vietnamese Government's fold.

The tribesmen are good fighters. Many of them served for years as guides and porters for Communist guerrillas. Winning them over has been possible partly because the Americans have succeeded in breaking down the traditional Vietnamese racial prejudices against the mountaineers.

On the strip that stretches up the coast, there has also been some progress. This area is a narrow band of rice fields lying between the mountains and the South China Sea. It has a long history of revolt against Vietnamese Governments. The Communist Party has a big following in its impoverished villages.

Still, in one of the provinces most heavily infiltrated by the Communists, the Government beat off a Red attack against 40 strategic hamlets not long ago. More important, Government forces had the help of local people who reported on Communist movements.

A Resistance to Fight

John Paul Vann, a lieutenant colonel in the U.S. Army who was sent as a military adviser to South Vietnam in 1962, emerged as one of the strongest critics of the South Vietnamese regime of Ngo Dinh Diem and of the progress of the war. Shortly after his resignation from the army, he granted an interview to U.S. News & World Report, *which was published in the magazine's September 16, 1963, issue. In the interview, Vann attributes the lack of battlefield success in Vietnam to the poor leadership of Diem and the unwillingness of South Vietnamese troops to fight.*

Question: Colonel Vann, is the war against the Communists being won in South Vietnam?

Answer: From what I saw firsthand, as a senior U.S. military adviser, the answer has to be "No." This is especially true about the Mekong Delta region, where 80 per cent of the fighting is going on. This is the area directly south of Saigon. . . .

The best you can say about the war in the Delta is that we are holding our own against a far fewer number of Communists. That would be an optimistic approach to it.

Question: What seems to be the trouble—is there a lack of arms and equipment and manpower in South Vietnam?

Answer: No, that's not it at all, although many top Vietnamese refuse to recognize that their own forces are better trained, better equipped and better supported than the enemy is.

The trouble is this: The Government in Saigon, and some top commanders of the Vietnamese Army, are unwilling to take or inflict casualties. Moreover, they deliberately refuse to come to grips with the enemy, for internal political reasons. There is a marked reluctance to go out and do what is necessary to defeat the Communists. You can't win a war that way. . . .

Question: What is it that accounts for the optimistic military reports from Vietnam often brought back by U.S. officials?

Answer: There has been a lack of firsthand information. High-ranking people are sent there from Washington and told to get results. It becomes a kind of consuming desire on their part to show some palpable results. I believe this causes a tendency to play down the real picture—that is, to give more weight to those areas where we are having success and less weight to those areas where we're having setbacks. So, overall, these reports reflect a favorable side of the picture. . . .

Question: Is your view that the Vietnamese aren't going all-out to win this war shared by other Americans in Vietnam?

Answer: I believe that view is almost universal among military people who are not afraid to speak out.

Where it's bad. In the Mekong River Delta—where 70 per cent of the population lives—it's a much grimmer story. Repeatedly, the Communists have eluded Government forces there. A look at the terrain shows why: This delta is one of the largest river systems in the world. Its swamps, canals, streams and rice fields provide an intricate system of hideouts for the Communists. The Mekong flows into South Vietnam from Cambodia and Laos, a kind of superhighway for infiltration.

A New Threat

Now a new threat has developed.

Until recently, Communist guerrillas have lived off the countryside—buying or stealing rice from the peasants, capturing arms from Government forces. But now the Vietnamese Communists have unrestricted access to Southern Laos and Northeastern Cambodia. What was the "Ho Chi Minh Trail" has become a good highway, and it is being extended into Laos. Within six months to a year, the North Vietnamese will have a jump-off point for pouring men and supplies into the Delta country.

The big failure. In the face of this threat to outflank what's been done in Central Vietnam and in the Delta, there is real concern here over the failure of the Diem Government to win the support of the educated elite. That concern is pointed up by the current controversy between the Government and organized Buddhists. Few veteran observers here believe this is a religious issue. Most of them see it rather as an effort by its opponents to topple the Diem Government.

Most observers tell you there has been no tradition of persecution of Buddhists in Vietnam. But American officials here say the Diem Government has handled the issue badly and that the recent repressive tactics are only creating long-term problems.

The way out. Americans on the ground here say there are three possible choices for the U.S. in South Vietnam:

It could decide there is no hope of building a local Government that could defeat the Communists, and withdraw. That could send shivers through the rest of non-Communist Asia.

It could try to assume direct command of the whole operation and send in American troops for direct combat. But to do so would arouse the cry of "imperialism" which the Communists use so effectively throughout Southeast Asia. Furthermore, there are few people here who think winning this war is just a question of manpower.

The third choice is to stick it out and, according to many here, face up to the prospect that it is going to be a long, tough haul. For that sort of policy, observers say the American organization needs to be streamlined, and has to take a tougher, more direct line in dealing with President Diem.

No alternative. Denouncing the Diem Government is about as popular a pastime among Americans here in Saigon as it is among Vietnamese intellectuals. But you find few people who have been in this country over a long period who believe there is any alternative to the present regime.

One British diplomat told me:

"We British felt we had to hold the Northwest Frontier in India during the nineteenth century. For almost 100 years we had to live with a bad situation, losing the lives of our young men, spending large sums of money to buy tribesmen and to fight wars. South Vietnam may be your Northwest Frontier."

An increasing number of people here feel that the decision lies in Washington—that what's needed is fewer optimistic statements from high military officers but a frank answer to the question: Is the United States willing to pay the price of winning in Vietnam?

That's the question Ambassador Henry Cabot Lodge will need the answer for when he arrives.

CHAPTER 3

The Johnson Years

Chapter Preface

Lyndon B. Johnson, president of the United States from November 1963 to January 1969, presided over the peak of America's involvement in Vietnam. His decisions essentially "Americanized" the war in Vietnam as he committed American ground troops and air power to fight against the Vietcong rebels and the North Vietnamese. During Johnson's presidency, the Vietnam War emerged from relative obscurity in America to become one of the country's central and controversial public issues—a controversy that eventually led to Johnson's decision not to run for reelection in 1968.

Johnson became president on November 22, 1963, following the assassination of John F. Kennedy. Kennedy's death came just a few weeks after South Vietnam's president Ngo Dinh Diem was killed during a military coup that had at least the tacit support of Henry Cabot Lodge, America's ambassador to South Vietnam, and the CIA. The United States had helped establish Diem as the leader of South Vietnam in 1954 but had grown increasingly unhappy with his dictatorial governing style and with what they viewed as his weak military leadership in fighting the Communist rebels. The coup did not resolve South Vietnam's political problems, however, as Diem was replaced by a series of unstable military governments that were unable to raise popular support or to win military victories in the conflict. Indeed, some American officials feared that South Vietnam was on the verge of collapse.

Senator Barry Goldwater of Arizona, the Republican challenger to Johnson in the 1964 presidential race, argued that the situation in South Vietnam called for an aggressive strategy that included bombing and/or invading North Vietnam. In a campaign speech on October 21, 1964, Johnson responded by pledging, "We are not going to send American boys nine or ten thousand miles away from home to do what Asian boys ought to be doing for themselves." But Johnson also stated in his campaign speeches that America would not abandon its commitments in Vietnam. In the months before and after his November 1964 electoral victory, Johnson made several key decisions that escalated American involvement in Vietnam.

In August 1964, two U.S. destroyers in the Gulf of Tonkin were reportedly attacked by North Vietnamese gunboats. Johnson responded by launching a retaliatory air strike and asking Congress to pass a special resolution giving him the authority to use "all necessary steps, including the use of armed force," in Southeast Asia. In February 1965, after a Vietcong shelling killed U.S. soldiers stationed in Pleiku, he ordered air attacks on military targets in North Vietnam. In March, he began a sustained bombing campaign against North Vietnam and ordered the first combat ground troops to South Vietnam; in July he committed still more forces. By the end of 1965 there were some 180,000 American troops in South Vietnam. Two years later the number had increased to 485,000. During these years, Johnson periodically announced bombing halts to indicate his willingness to begin peace talks with the North Vietnamese. However, both North Vietnam and the United States demanded concessions as a precondition to negotiations. The United States wanted North Vietnam to guarantee the existence of an independent non-Communist South Vietnam (one that excluded the Communist-led National Liberation Front), while North Vietnam called for the withdrawal of U.S. troops and the replacement of the South Vietnamese regime with a coalition government that included the NLF. These conflicting demands impeded various attempts to begin negotiations in 1966 and 1967.

Although Johnson sharply escalated U.S. involvement in Vietnam, several of his key decisions were made in order to minimize the conflict and its impact on the United States. Johnson chose not to seek an official declaration of war from Congress, to call up members of the armed reserves into active duty, to invade North Vietnam, or to invade Cambodia and Laos (neighboring countries that North Vietnam used as sanctuaries and as corridors for transporting troops and arms down the "Ho Chi Minh Trail"). In addition, he was reluctant to call for tax increases and economic controls on the home front.

Johnson's decision to keep the Vietnam conflict a limited war for the United States stemmed in part from his fear that a wider war might result in a direct military confrontation with the Soviet Union or China. U.S. officials did not want to risk a repetition of the events of 1950, when China had sent hundreds of thousands of troops into Korea to fight U.S.-led forces in the Korean War, nor did they wish to provoke a nuclear confrontation with China or the Soviet Union. Another important factor was Johnson's desire to focus on domestic concerns, especially his "Great Society" legislative agenda. In July 1965, while Johnson and his staff were considering various proposals to escalate American involvement in Vietnam, Congress was debating such landmark Great Society items as Medicare, the Voting Rights Act, and federal aid to education. Johnson was afraid that if the Vietnam War became too large, it would jeopardize his domestic agenda.

Initially, Johnson's political maneuvers succeeded. He won the

1964 presidential election over Goldwater by a wide margin, marshaled nearly unanimous votes in Congress in support of the Gulf of Tonkin Resolution and other war-related measures, and passed much of his domestic legislation. However, by 1966 the nation was becoming increasingly divided over the Vietnam War. "Hawks" in Congress and in the public advocated sending additional soldiers and implementing more aggressive strategies to win the conflict, while "doves" called for a stop to America's bombing of North Vietnam and for a negotiated settlement. Voices in Congress, the media, religious groups, and academia expressed their criticisms of the conflict. The Vietnam War also divided the Democratic Party; first Eugene McCarthy and then Robert Kennedy decided to challenge Johnson for the 1968 Democratic nomination for president.

Johnson steadily escalated America's involvement in Vietnam until the February 1968 Tet Offensive. This massive Vietcong and North Vietnamese assault throughout South Vietnam resulted in heavy losses for the attacking forces, but it also shattered the American public's confidence in the war effort and intensified opposition to the war. Shortly after the battle, American military officials requested an additional 206,000 troops to be sent to Vietnam—a step that would likely have forced Johnson to activate the armed reserves. Instead of granting the request, on March 31 Johnson announced on television that he would send only 13,500 more troops to Vietnam. Furthermore, he declared an unconditional partial halt of U.S. bombing missions in an effort to persuade North Vietnam to begin negotiations (somewhat unexpectedly, the North Vietnamese agreed, and peace negotiations began in Paris in May). Finally, Johnson surprised the nation by saying that he would not run for reelection—a decision both he and later historians attributed directly to the stalemated war in Vietnam.

VIEWPOINT 1

"If we are driven from . . . Viet Nam, then no nation can ever again have the same confidence . . . in American protection. In each land, the forces of independence would be considerably weakened."

America Is Fighting for a Just Cause in Vietnam

Lyndon B. Johnson (1908–1973)

Lyndon B. Johnson became president of the United States in November 1963, following the assassination of John F. Kennedy; he was elected to a full term in 1964. Over the course of his presidency Johnson greatly escalated American military involvement in Vietnam, although he never asked Congress to officially declare war. Johnson's decisions prompted protests on college campuses and elsewhere and ensured that Vietnam would become one of the dominant controversies of his presidency.

Johnson made several key decisions concerning Vietnam in 1965. In February, following attacks on U.S. Marines stationed at Pleiku, he began a sustained bombing campaign of North Vietnam. In March he began sending army combat troops to Vietnam, increasing their number at regular intervals. The following viewpoint is taken from a July 28, 1965, press conference in which Johnson announced that he was increasing the number of American troops in Vietnam from 75,000 to 125,000, with additional forces to be "sent as requested." Johnson argues that sending these soldiers is a necessary step to prevent the spread of Communism in Asia and to fulfill past pledges to protect South Vietnam. He describes his actions as "carefully measured" to "bring an end to aggression and a peaceful settlement" in the region.

Johnson closes his remarks by speaking of his personal anguish

Excerpted from Lyndon B. Johnson, statement at a White House news conference, July 28, 1965.

at sending young men off to war and of his goals for ending poverty and ensuring equality for all Americans (in July 1965 he was trying to pass an ambitious domestic agenda through Congress, including antipoverty and health care legislation). But he argues that, to preserve the nation and its freedoms, America must "stand in Viet Nam."

My fellow Americans. Not long ago, I received a letter from a woman in the Midwest. She wrote:

> Dear Mr. President,
>   In my humble way I am writing to you about the crisis in Vietnam. My husband served in World War II. Our country was at war. But now, this time, it's just something that I don't understand. Why?

Well, I've tried to answer that question dozens of times and more in practically every state in this Union. I have discussed it fully in Baltimore in April, in Washington in May, in San Francisco in June. And let me again now discuss it here in the East Room of the White House.

Why must young Americans, born into a land exultant and with hope and with golden promise, toil and suffer and sometimes die in such a remote and distant place?

No Easy Answers

The answer, like the war itself, is not an easy one. But it echoes clearly from the painful lessons of half a century.

Three times in my lifetime—in two world wars and in Korea—Americans have gone to far lands to fight for freedom. We have learned at a terrible and a brutal cost that retreat does not bring safety, and weakness does not bring peace.

And it is this lesson that has brought us to Viet Nam.

This is a different kind of war. There are no marching armies or solemn declarations. Some citizens of South Viet Nam, at times with understandable grievances, have joined in the attack on their own Government.

But we must not let this mask the central fact that this is really war. It is guided by North Viet Nam and it is spurred by Communist China. Its goal is to conquer the south, to defeat American power and to extend the Asiatic dominion of communism.

And there are great stakes in the balance.

Most of the non-Communist nations of Asia cannot, by themselves and alone, resist the growing might and the grasping ambition of Asian communism.

Our power therefore is a very vital shield. If we are driven from the field in Viet Nam, then no nation can ever again have the same confidence in American promise or in American protection.

In each land, the forces of independence would be considerably weakened, and an Asia so threatened by Communist domination would certainly imperil the security of the United States itself.

We did not choose to be the guardians at the gate, but there is no one else. Nor would surrender in Viet Nam bring peace, because we learned from Hitler at Munich that success only feeds the appetite of aggression. The battle would be renewed in one country, and then another country bringing with it perhaps even larger and crueler conflict, as we have learned from the lessons of history.

American Promises

Moreover, we are in Viet Nam to fulfill one of the most solemn pledges of the American nation. Three Presidents—President Eisenhower, President Kennedy and your present President— over eleven years have committed themselves and have promised to help defend this small and valiant nation.

Strengthened by that promise, the people of South Viet Nam have fought for many long years. Thousands of them have died. Thousands more have been crippled and scarred by war. And we just cannot now dishonor our word, or abandon our commitment, or leave those who believed us and who trusted us to the terror and repression and murder that would follow.

This, then, my fellow Americans, is why we are in Viet Nam.

What are our goals in that war-stained land?

First, we intend to convince the Communists that we cannot be defeated by force of arms or by superior power. They are not easily convinced. In recent months they have greatly increased their fighting forces and their attacks and the numbers of incidents.

I have asked the commanding general, General [William C.] Westmoreland, what more he needs to meet this mounting aggression. He has told me. And we will meet his needs.

I have today ordered to Viet Nam the Airmobile Division and certain other forces which will raise our fighting strength from 75,000 to 125,000 men almost immediately. Additional forces will be needed later and they will be sent as requested.

This will make it necessary to increase our active fighting forces by raising the monthly draft call from 17,000 over a period of time to 35,000 per month and for us to step up our campaign for voluntary enlistments.

After this past week of deliberations, I have concluded that it is not essential to order Reserve units into service now. If that necessity should later be indicated, I will give the matter most careful consideration and I will give the country due and adequate notice before taking such action, but only after full preparations.

We have also discussed with the Government of South Viet Nam lately the steps that will—we will take to substantially increase their own effort, both on the battlefield and toward reform and progress in the villages. Ambassador [Henry Cabot] Lodge is now formulating a new program to be tested upon his return to that area.

Why America Fights in Vietnam

President Johnson made a major speech at Johns Hopkins University on April 7, 1965, in which he defended American actions in Vietnam.

Tonight Americans and Asians are dying for a world where each people may choose its own path to change.

This is the principle for which our ancestors fought in the valleys of Pennsylvania. It is the principle for which our sons fight tonight in the jungles of Viet-Nam.

Viet-Nam is far away from this quiet campus. We have no territory there, nor do we seek any. The war is dirty and brutal and difficult. And some 400 young men, born into an America that is bursting with opportunity and promise, have ended their lives on Viet-Nam's steaming soil.

Why must we take this painful road?

Why must this Nation hazard its ease, and its interest, and its power for the sake of a people so far away?

We fight because we must fight if we are to live in a world where every country can shape its own destiny. And only in such a world will our own freedom be finally secure.

This kind of world will never be built by bombs or bullets. Yet the infirmities of man are such that force must often precede reason, and the waste of war, the works of peace.

We wish that this were not so. But we must deal with the world as it is, if it is ever to be as we wish.

I have directed Secretary [of State Dean] Rusk and Secretary [of Defense Robert S.] McNamara to be available immediately to the Congress to review with these committees—the appropriate Congressional committees—what we plan to do in these areas. I have asked them to be able to answer the questions of any member of Congress.

And Secretary McNamara, in addition, will ask the Senate Appropriations Committee to add a limited amount to present legislation to help meet part of this new cost until a supplemental measure is ready and hearings can be held when the Congress assembles in January. In the meantime, we will use the authority contained in the present defense appropriation bill under consideration to transfer funds in addition to the additional money that we will ask.

These steps, like our actions in the past, are carefully measured to do what must be done to bring an end to aggression and a peaceful settlement.

We do not want an expanding struggle with consequences that no one can foresee, nor will we bluster or bully or flaunt our power. But we will not surrender, and we will not retreat.

For behind our American pledge lies the determination and resources, I believe, of all of the American nation.

We Are Ready to Negotiate

Second, once the Communists know, as we know, that a violent solution is impossible, then a peaceful solution is inevitable. We are ready now, as we have always been, to move from the battlefield to the conference table.

I have stated publicly and many times, again and again, America's willingness to begin unconditional discussions with any Government at any place at any time.

Fifteen efforts have been made to start these discussions, with the help of forty nations throughout the world. But there has been no answer. But we are going to continue to persist, if persist we must, until death and desolation have led to the same conference table where others could now join us at a much smaller cost.

I have spoken many times of our objectives in Viet Nam. So has the Government of South Viet Nam. Hanoi has set forth its own proposals. We are ready to discuss their proposals and our proposals and any proposals of any Government whose people may be affected, for we fear the meeting room no more than we fear the battlefield. And in this pursuit we welcome and we ask for the concern and the assistance of any nation and all nations.

And if the United Nations and its officials or any one of its 114 members can by deed or word, private initiative or public action, bring us nearer an honorable peace, then they will have the support and gratitude of the United States of America. . . .

We do not seek the destruction of any Government nor do we covet a foot of any territory. But we insist and we will always insist that the people of South Viet Nam shall have the right of choice, the right to shape their own destiny in free elections in the south or throughout all Viet Nam under international supervision, and they shall not have any Government imposed upon them by force and terror so long as we can prevent it.

This was the purpose of the 1954 [Geneva] agreements which the Communists have now cruelly shattered. And if the machinery of those agreements was tragically weak, its purposes still guide our action. And as battle rages we will continue as best we can to help the good people of South Viet Nam enrich the condition of their life, to feed the hungry, and to tend the sick, and teach the young, and shelter the homeless and help the farmer to increase his crops and the worker to find a job. . . .

Sending Men to Battle

And let me also add now a personal note. I do not find it easy to send the flower of our youth, our finest young men, into battle. I have spoken to you today of the divisions and the forces and the battalions and the units but I know them all, everyone. I have seen them in a thousand streets of a hundred towns in every state in this Union—working and laughing and building and filled with hope and life. And I think I know, too, how their mothers weep and how their families sorrow.

And this is the most agonizing and the most painful duty of your President.

And there is something else, too. When I was young, poverty was so common that we didn't know it had a name. An education was something that you had to fight for, and water was really life itself. I have now been in public life for thirty-five years, more than three decades, and in each of those thirty-five years I have seen good men and wise leaders struggle to bring the blessings of this land to all of our people.

And now I am the President. It is now my opportunity to help every child get an education, to help every Negro and every American citizen have an equal opportunity, to help every family get a decent home, and to help bring healing to the sick and dignity to the old.

As I have said before, that is what I've lived for, that's what I've wanted all my life since I was a little boy, and I do not want to see all those hopes and all those dreams of so many people for so many years now drowned in the wasteful ravages of cruel wars. And I'm going to do all I can do to see that that never happens.

But I also know, as a realistic public servant, that as long as there are men who hate and destroy we must have the courage to resist or we'll see it all—all that we have built, all that we hope to build, all of our dreams for freedom—all will be swept away on the flood of conquest.

So, too, this shall not happen. We will stand in Viet Nam.

VIEWPOINT 2

"We believe that the entire war in Vietnam is criminal and immoral."

America Is Not Fighting for a Just Cause in Vietnam

Vietnam Day Committee

As American military involvement in Vietnam sharply escalated in 1965, increasing numbers of Americans were questioning this mobilization, forming the basis for an organized protest movement. Among the earliest manifestations of the antiwar movement were the "teach-ins" held at many colleges and universities (beginning with the University of Michigan on March 24, 1965), at which participants debated and criticized American policy on the Vietnam War in forums and demonstrations. One of the largest of the "teach-ins" was the Vietnam Day held on May 21 and 22 at the University of California at Berkeley, in which thirty thousand people participated. The Vietnam Day Committee, the group that organized the event, continued to function afterward as the leading antiwar organization in northern California. Among their efforts was the publication of a pamphlet, reprinted here, that was distributed to new army personnel at military bases in California. The writers of the pamphlet take issue with several basic assumptions behind the U.S. military effort in Vietnam, argue that the United States is not fighting for freedom or justice in Vietnam, and urge soldiers to oppose the war.

From the Vietnam Day Committee's pamphlet *Attention All Military Personnel*, May 1965.

You may soon be sent to Vietnam. You have heard about the war in the news; your officers will give you pep talks about it. But you probably feel as confused and uncertain as most Americans do. Many people will tell you to just follow orders and leave the thinking to others. But you have the right to know as much about this war as anyone. After all, it's you—not your Congressman—who might get killed.

Why Are We Fighting in Vietnam? We are supposed to be fighting to protect democracy in Vietnam, and yet your own government admits that South Vietnam is run by a dictatorship. General [Nguyen Cao] Ky, the latest military dictator, is as bad as they come. In a recent interview he said: "People ask me who my heroes are. I have only one—Hitler. I admire Hitler because he pulled his country together when it was in a terrible state" *(London Sunday Mirror,* July 4, 1965).

General Ky doesn't mean much to us; we're not even sure how to pronounce his name, but the South Vietnamese have lived under men like him for years. As far as the Vietnamese are concerned, we are fighting on the side of Hitlerism: and they hope we lose.

Who Is the Enemy? U.S. military spokesmen have often said that their greatest problem is finding the enemy. The enemy, they say, is everywhere. The old woman feeding her chickens may have a stock of hand grenades in her hut. The little boy who trails after the American soldiers during the day slips out to give information to the guerrillas at night. The washerwoman at the American air base brings a bomb to work one day. It is impossible, say the military, to tell which are the Viet Cong and which are the civilians.

A Dirty War

And so, because the whole Vietnamese people seem to be the enemy, the military is taking no chances. They use tear gas—a weapon designed for use against civilians. They order American troops to fire at women and children—because women and children, after all, are firing at American troops. American fighter planes destroy civilian villages with napalm; American B-52s are flattening whole regions. That is why the war in Vietnam is so often called a "dirty war."

When the South Vietnamese people see you in your foreign uniform, they will think of you as *their* enemy. You are the ones bombing their towns. They don't know whether you're a draftee or a volunteer, whether you're for the war or against it; but they're not taking any chances either.

Free Elections. The Vietnamese would like to *vote* the foreigners out of their country, but they have been denied the chance. According to the Geneva Agreement of 1954, there were supposed to be elections throughout Vietnam in 1956. But the U.S. government was certain that our man in Vietnam, Premier [Ngo Dinh] Diem, would lose. So we decided not to allow any election until we were sure we could win. Diem set up a political police force and put all political opposition—Communist and anti-Communist—in jail. By 1959, it was clear there weren't going to be any elections, and the guerrillas known as the Viet Cong began to fight back. By 1963 our government was fed up with Diem, but still wasn't willing to risk elections. Our CIA helped a group of Vietnamese generals to overthrow Diem and kill him. Since then there have been a series of "better" military dictators. General Ky—the man who admires Hitler—is the latest one.

Fighting for Democracy. Your job as a soldier is supposed to be "to win the people of South Vietnam." Win them to democracy? No, we keep military dictators in power. What then? The American way of life? But why should they care any more about our way of life than we care about theirs? We can't speak their language or even pronounce their names. We don't know anything about their religion or even what it is. We never even heard of Vietnam until Washington decided to run it.

You are supposed to be fighting "to save the Vietnamese people from Communism." Certainly Communist influence is very strong in the National Liberation Front [NLF], the rebel government. Yet most of the people support the NLF. Why? Many of the same people who now lead the NLF led the Vietnamese independence movement against the Japanese during World War II, and then went on to fight against French colonial rule. Most Vietnamese think of the NLF leaders as their country's outstanding patriots. In fact, many anti-Communists have joined the guerrilla forces in the belief that the most important thing is to get rid of foreign domination and military dictators. On the other hand, very few Vietnamese support the official government of General Ky. His army has low morale and a high desertion rate.

The Guerrillas. The newspapers and television have told us again and again what a tough fighter the Vietnamese guerrilla is. Short of ammunition and without any air cover, he can beat forces that outnumber him five or ten to one. Why do they have such high morale? They are not draftees; no draftees ever fight like that. They are not high-paid, professional soldiers. Most of them are peasants who work their fields; they can't even spare the ammunition for target practice.

Their secret is that they know why they are fighting. They didn't hear about Vietnam in the newspapers; they've lived there all their lives. While we were in high school, they were living under the Diem regime and hating it. Now American planes are bombing their towns and strafing their fields; American troops have occupied their country; and if they complain out loud, an American-supported dictator sentences them to jail or the firing squad. Is it any wonder that they fight so fiercely?

Crushing the Resistance. The war in Vietnam is not being fought according to the rules. Prisoners are tortured. Our planes drop incendiary bombs on civilian villages. Our soldiers shoot at women and children. Your officers will tell you that it is all necessary, that we couldn't win the war any other way. *And they are right.* Americans are no more cruel than any other people; American soldiers don't enjoy this kind of war. But if you are going to wage war against an entire people, you have to become cruel.

The ordinary German soldier in occupied Europe wasn't especially cruel, either. But as the resistance movements grew, he *became* cruel. He shot at women and children because they were shooting at him; he never asked himself *why* they were shooting at him. When a certain town became a center of resistance activity, he followed his orders and destroyed the whole town. He knew that SS men were torturing captured resistance fighters, but it wasn't his business to interfere.

A Soldier's Responsibility

Following Orders. As a soldier you have been trained to obey orders, but as a human being you must take responsibility for your own acts. International and American law recognize that an individual soldier, even if acting under orders, must bear final legal and moral responsibility for what he does. This principle became a part of law after World War II, when the Allied nations, meeting in London, decided that German war criminals must be punished even if they committed war crimes under orders. This principle was the basis of the Nuremberg trials. We believe that the entire war in Vietnam is criminal and immoral. We believe that the atrocities which are necessary to wage this war against the people of Vietnam are inexcusable.

We Are Not Defending Freedom in Vietnam

Students for a Democratic Society (SDS) held an antiwar rally in Washington, D.C., on April 17, 1965. At the end of the protest, Paul Potter, the president of SDS, made a speech in which he argued that America was not defending freedom in Vietnam.

The President says that we are defending freedom in Vietnam. Whose freedom? Not the freedom of the Vietnamese. The first act of the first dictator, Diem, the United States installed in Vietnam, was to systematically begin the persecution of all political opposition, non-Communist as well as Communist. The first American military supplies were not used to fight Communist insurgents; they were used to control, imprison or kill any who sought something better for Vietnam than the personal aggrandizement, political corruption and the profiteering of the Diem regime. The elite of the forces that we have trained and equipped are still used to control political unrest in Saigon and defend the latest dictator from the people. . . .

The pattern of repression and destruction that we have developed and justified in the war is so thorough that it can only be called cultural genocide. I am not simply talking about napalm or gas or crop destruction or torture, hurled indiscriminately on women and children, insurgent and neutral, upon the first suspicion of rebel activity. That in itself is horrendous and incredible beyond belief. But it is only part of a larger pattern of destruction to the very fabric of the country. We have uprooted the people from the land and imprisoned them in concentration camps called "sunrise villages." Through conscription and direct political intervention and control, we have destroyed local customs and traditions, trampled upon those things of value which give dignity and purpose to life. . . .

The President mocks freedom if he insists that the war in Vietnam is a defense of American freedom. Perhaps the only freedom that this war protects is the freedom of the warhawks in the Pentagon and the State Department to experiment with counter-insurgency and guerrilla warfare in Vietnam.

Oppose the War. We hope that you too find yourself, as a human being, unable to tolerate this nightmare war, and we hope that you will oppose it. We don't know what kind of risks we are taking in giving you this leaflet; you won't know what risk you will be taking in opposing the war. A growing number of GIs have already refused to fight in Vietnam and have been court-martialed. They have shown great courage. We believe that they, together with other courageous men who will join them, will have influence far out of proportion to their numbers.

There may be many other things you can do; since you are in the service, you know better than civilians what sorts of opposition are possible. But whatever you do, keep your eyes open. Draw your own conclusions from the things you see, read, and hear. At orientation sessions, don't be afraid to ask questions, and if you're not satisfied with the answers, keep asking. Take every chance you get to talk to your fellow soldiers about the war.

You may feel the war is wrong, and still decide not to face a court-martial. You may then find yourself in Vietnam under orders. You might be forced to do some fighting—but don't do any more than you have to. Good luck.

VIEWPOINT 3

"I recommend that the deployment of US ground troops in Vietnam be increased."

America Must Send More Troops to Vietnam

Robert S. McNamara (b. 1916)

Robert S. McNamara was secretary of defense from 1961 to 1968, serving under Presidents John F. Kennedy and Lyndon B. Johnson. A former Ford Motor Company executive noted for his management skills, McNamara made numerous trips to Vietnam and was one of the key planners of American escalation there.

The following viewpoint is excerpted from a memo from Mc-Namara to Johnson, written on July 1, 1965, and revised on July 20. McNamara lays out three possible choices for the president: maintaining current U.S. policy, negotiating a settlement and withdrawing from Vietnam, or increasing America's military effort there. McNamara recommends the third choice and urges the president to increase American troop levels in Vietnam to 175,000 by October (and possibly higher in future years), warning that the failure to do so would mean the fall of South Vietnam and the loss of U.S. credibility around the world. Johnson accepted most of McNamara's proposals, and by the end of 1965 the number of U.S. military personnel in Vietnam had reached 184,000.

Toward the end of his tenure as secretary of defense McNamara harbored growing doubts about the Vietnam War and U.S. policy. Following his resignation in 1968 he became president of the World Bank.

Excerpted from Robert S. McNamara, memo to Lyndon Johnson, July 20, 1965.

SUBJECT: Recommendations of additional deployments to Vietnam

1. *Introduction.* Our object in Vietnam is to create conditions for a favorable outcome by demonstrating to the VC/DRV [Vietcong Democratic Republic of Vietnam] that the odds are against their winning. We want to create these conditions, if possible, without causing the war to expand into one with China or the Soviet Union and in a way which preserves support of the American people and, hopefully, of our allies and friends. . . .

2. *Favorable outcome.* To my view, a "favorable outcome" for purposes of these assessments and recommendations has nine fundamental elements.

a. VC stop attacks and drastically reduce incidents of terror and sabotage.

b. DRV reduces infiltration to a trickle, with some reasonably reliable method of our obtaining confirmation of this fact.

c. US/GVN [Government of (South) Vietnam] stop bombing of North Vietnam.

d. GVN stays independent (hopefully pro-US, but possibly genuinely neutral).

e. GVN exercising governmental functions over substantially all of South Vietnam.

f. Communists remain quiescent in Laos and Thailand.

g. DRV withdraw PAVN [People's Army of Vietnam] forces and other North Vietnamese infiltration (not regroupees) from South Vietnam.

h. VC/NLF [National Liberation Front] transform from a military to a purely political organization.

i. US combat forces (not advisors or AID [Agency for International Development]) withdraw.

A favorable outcome could include also arrangements, regarding elections, relations between North and South Vietnam, participation in peace-keeping by international forces, membership for North and South Vietnam in the UN, and so on. The nine fundamental elements can evolve with or without an express agreement and, except for what might be negotiated incidental to a ceasefire, are more likely to evolve without an express agreement than with one. We do not need now to address the question whether ultimately we would settle for something less than the nine fundamentals; because deployment of the forces recommended in paragraph 5 is prerequisite to the achievement of *any* acceptable settlement, and a decision can be made later, when bargaining becomes a reality, whether to compromise in any particular.

3. *Estimate of the situation.* The situation in South Vietnam is

worse than a year ago (when it was worse than a year before that). After a few months of stalemate, the tempo of the war has quickened. A hard VC push is now on to dismember the nation and to maul the army. The VC main and local forces, reinforced by militia and guerrillas, have the initiative and, with large attacks (some in regimental strength), are hurting ARVN [Army of the Republic of (South) Vietnam] forces badly. . . .

The odds are less than even that the Ky government will last out the year. [Nguyen Cao] Ky is "executive agent" for a directorate of generals. His government is youthful and inexperienced, but dedicated to a "revolutionary" program. His tenure depends upon unity of the armed forces behind him. If the directorate holds together and the downward trend of the war is halted, the religious and regional factions will probably remain quiescent; otherwise there will be political turbulence and possibly uncoordinated efforts to negotiate settlement with the DRV. The Buddhists, Catholics, out-politicians and business community are "wait-and-seeing"; the VC, while unable alone to generate effective unrest in the cities, can "piggyback" on any anti-government demonstration or cause. . . .

There are no signs that we have throttled the inflow of supplies for the VC. . . . Nor have our air attacks in North Vietnam produced tangible evidence of willingness on the part of Hanoi to come to the conference table in a reasonable mood. The DRV/VC seem to believe that South Vietnam is on the run and near collapse; they show no signs of settling for less than a complete take-over.

Three Options

4. *Options open to us.* We must choose among three courses of action with respect to Vietnam all of which involve different probabilities, outcomes and costs:

a. Cut our losses and withdraw under the best conditions that can be arranged—almost certainly conditions humiliating the United States and very damaging to our future effectiveness on the world scene.

b. Continue at about the present level, with the US forces limited to say 75,000, holding on and playing for the breaks—a course of action which, because our position would grow weaker, almost certainly would confront us later with a choice between withdrawal and an emergency expansion of forces, perhaps too late to do any good.

c. Expand promptly and substantially the US military pressure against the Viet Cong in the South and maintain the military pressure against the North Vietnamese in the North while launching a vigorous effort on the political side to lay the groundwork for a favorable outcome by clarifying our objectives and establishing channels of communication. This alternative would stave off defeat in the short run and offer a good chance of producing a favorable settlement in the longer run; at the same time it would imply a commitment to see a fighting war clear through at considerable cost in casualties and material and would make any later decision to withdraw even more difficult and even more costly than would be the case today.

The Decision to Commit Troops

In his memoirs, published in 1971 under the title The Vantage Point, *Lyndon B. Johnson recollects discussing and dismissing the advice of George Ball to negotiate a withdrawal from Vietnam.*

We discussed Ball's approach for a long time and in great detail. I think all of us felt the same concerns and anxieties that Ball had expressed, but most of these men in the Cabinet Room were more worried about the results, in our country and throughout the world, of our pulling out and coming home. I felt the Under Secretary had not produced a sufficiently convincing case or a viable alternative.

Dean Rusk expressed one worry that was much on my mind. It lay at the heart of our Vietnam policy. "If the Communist world finds out that we will not pursue our commitments to the end," he said, "I don't know where they will stay their hand."

I felt sure they would *not* stay their hand. If we ran out on Southeast Asia, I could see trouble ahead in every part of the globe—not just in Asia but in the Middle East and in Europe, in Africa and in Latin America. I was convinced that our retreat from this challenge would open the path to World War III.

My recommendations in paragraph 5 below are based on the choice of the third alternative (Option c) as the course of action involving the best odds of the best outcome with the most acceptable cost to the United States.

5. *Military recommendations.* There are now 15 US (and 1 Australian) combat battalions in Vietnam; they, together with other combat personnel and non-combat personnel, bring the total US personnel in Vietnam to approximately 75,000.

a. I recommend that the deployment of US ground troops in Vietnam be increased by October to 34 maneuver battalions (or, if the Koreans fail to provide the expected 9 battalions promptly, to 43 battalions). The battalions—together with increases in helicopter lift, air squadrons, naval units, air defense, combat support and miscellaneous log support and advisory personnel which I also recommend—would bring the total US personnel in Vietnam to approximately 175,000 (200,000 if we must make up for the Korean failure). It should be understood that the deployment of more men (perhaps 100,000) may be necessary in early 1966, and that the deployment of additional forces thereafter is possible but will depend on developments.

b. I recommend that Congress be requested to authorize the call-up of approximately 235,000 men in the Reserve and National Guard. (Deleted)

The call-up would be for a two-year period; but the intention would be to release them after one year, by which time they could be relieved by regular forces if conditions permitted.

c. I recommend that the regular armed forces be increased by approximately 375,000 men (approximately 250,000 Army, 75,000 Marines, 25,000 Air Force and 25,000 Navy). (Deleted)

The increase would be accomplished by increasing recruitment, increasing the draft and extending tours of duty of men already in the service.

d. I recommend that a supplemental appropriation of approximately $X for FY 1966 be sought from the Congress to cover the first part of the added costs attributable to the build-up in and for the war in Vietnam. A further supplemental appropriation might be required later in the fiscal year.

It should be noted that in mid-1966 the United States would, as a consequence of the above method of handling the build-up, have approximately 600,000 additional men (deleted) as protection against contingencies. . . .

10. *South Vietnamese reaction to expansion of US forces.* Three factors dominate the psychological situation in South Vietnam: (a) the military situation (i.e., the security problem), (b) the effectiveness of the government as a vehicle for dynamic leadership, and (c) the implications of the growing American presence. The deployments recommended in paragraph 5 run some risk of causing the Vietnamese to "turn the war over to us" and of generating an "anti-colonial" type resentment toward us. The GVN has requested the additional US forces urgently (indeed, they want 9 battalions more than the 44 recommended here). When Ky was asked about the popular reaction, he said, "We will explain it to our people." [Nguyen Van] Thieu agreed saying, "They know that you are not here to make us a colony." Former Prime Minister [Plan Huy] Quat told me, "The only way to save Vietnam is to send a large number of troops." He added, "The people of South Vietnam will not object." The spectres of widespread adverse public reaction have been raised each time we deployed personnel in the past, and, while no deployment has been so massive as this one, no such reaction appeared. Furthermore, the key requirement for continued viability of the Vietnamese spirit in the short

run is evidence that RVNAF [Republic of (South) Vietnam Armed Forces]/US/third-country forces can contain the VC/DRV. . . .

12. *Evaluation.* ARVN overall is not capable of successfully resisting the VC initiatives without more active assistance from more US/third-country ground forces than those thus far committed. Without further outside help, the ARVN is faced with successive tactical reverses, loss of key communication and population centers particularly in the highlands, piecemeal destruction of ARVN units, attrition of RVNAF will to fight, and loss of civilian confidence. Early commitment of additional US/third-country forces in sufficient quantity, in general reserve and offensive roles, should stave off GVN defeat.

The success of the program from the military point of view turns on whether the Vietnamese hold their own in terms of numbers and fighting spirit, and on whether the US forces can be effective in a quick-reaction reserve role, a role in which they are only now being tested. The number of US troops is too small to make a significant difference in the traditional 10-1 government-guerrilla formula, but it is not too small to make a significant difference in the kind of war which seems to be evolving in Vietnam—a "Third Stage" or conventional war in which it is easier to identify, locate and attack the enemy.

The plan is such that the risk of escalation into war with China or the Soviet Union can be kept small. US and South Vietnamese casualties will increase—just how much cannot be predicted with confidence, but the US killed-in-action might be in the vicinity of 500 a month by the end of the year. The South Vietnamese under one government or another will probably see the thing through* and the United States public will support the course of action because it is a sensible and courageous military-political program designed and likely to bring about a success in Vietnam.

It should be recognized, however, that success against the larger, more conventional, VC/PAVN forces could merely drive the VC back into the trees and back to their 1960–64 pattern—a pattern against which US troops and aircraft would be of limited value but with which the GVN, with our help, could cope. The questions here would be whether the VC could maintain morale after such a setback, and whether the South Vietnamese would have the will to hang on through another cycle. It should be recognized also that, even in "success," it is not obvious how we will be able to disengage our forces from Vietnam. It is unlikely that a formal agreement good enough for the purpose could possibly be

---

*Ambassador [Henry Cabot] Lodge points out that we may face a neutralist government at some time in the future and that in those circumstances the US should be prepared to carry on alone.

negotiated—because the arrangement can reflect little more than the power situation. A fairly large number of US (or perhaps "international") forces may be required to stay in Vietnam.

The overall evaluation is that the course of action recommended in this memorandum—if the military and political moves are properly integrated and executed with continuing vigor and visible determination—stands a good chance of achieving an acceptable outcome within a reasonable time in Vietnam.

"No one can assure you that we can beat the Viet Cong or even force them to the conference table on our terms, no matter how many hundred thousand white, foreign (U.S.) troops we deploy."

America Must Not Send More Troops to Vietnam

George Ball (1909–1994)

In late 1964 and early 1965, South Vietnam appeared to be on the verge of collapse; it suffered military defeats against the Vietcong and North Vietnamese forces as well as chronic political instability in its government. In response, President Lyndon B. Johnson made several crucial decisions that sharply escalated American involvement in Vietnam and that, in essence, "Americanized" the Vietnam War. In February 1965, following an attack on U.S. Marines stationed at Pleiku, he authorized a sustained bombing campaign in North Vietnam. In March he ordered two Marine Corps battalions to Vietnam to guard a U.S. Air Force base in Da Nang. These were the first American combat troops sent to Vietnam (soldiers already in Vietnam had been designated as military "advisers" and were kept from official combat roles). In April, Johnson authorized an additional 20,000 combat troops. The war continued to go badly for South Vietnam, and in June 1965 General William C. Westmoreland, the U.S. commander in Vietnam, requested an additional 150,000 troops and the freedom to engage in a broad offensive strategy in order to stave off defeat.

The following viewpoint is taken from a July 1, 1965, memorandum to the president by George Ball, then undersecretary of state. Ball was one of only a few of Johnson's high-placed civilian advisers to counsel against sending large numbers of American

Excerpted from George Ball, memo to Lyndon Johnson, "A Compromise Solution in South Vietnam," July 1, 1965.

troops to Vietnam. In the July memorandum, he argues for an alternative to increasing military escalation, which he asserts is approaching the point of no return. He proposes that America seek a compromise solution in Vietnam in which U.S. objectives—including an independent non-Communist South Vietnam—may not be fully realized. Ball contends that such a development would be better for America than a protracted war in Vietnam.

---

(1) *A Losing War:* The South Vietnamese are losing the war to the Viet Cong. No one can assure you that we can beat the Viet Cong or even force them to the conference table on our terms, no matter how many hundred thousand *white, foreign* (U.S.) troops we deploy.

No one has demonstrated that a white ground force of whatever size can win a guerrilla war—which is at the same time a civil war between Asians—in jungle terrain in the midst of a population that refuses cooperation to the white forces (and the South Vietnamese) and thus provides a great intelligence advantage to the other side. Three recent incidents vividly illustrate this point: (a) the sneak attack on the Da Nang Air Base which involved penetration of a defense perimeter guarded by 9,000 Marines. This raid was possible only because of the cooperation of the local inhabitants; (b) the B-52 raid that failed to hit the Viet Cong who had obviously been tipped off; (c) the search and destroy mission of the 173rd Air Borne Brigade which spent three days looking for the Viet Cong, suffered 23 casualties, and never made contact with the enemy who had obviously gotten advance word of their assignment.

(2) The Question to Decide: Should we limit our liabilities in South Vietnam and try to find a way out with minimal long-term costs?

The alternative—no matter what we may wish it to be—is almost certainly a protracted war involving an open-ended commitment of U.S. forces, mounting U.S. casualties, no assurance of a satisfactory solution, and a serious danger of escalation at the end of the road.

(3) Need for a Decision Now: So long as our forces are restricted to advising and assisting the South Vietnamese, the struggle will remain a civil war between Asian peoples. Once we deploy substantial numbers of troops in combat it will become a war between the U.S. and a large part of the population of South Vietnam, organized and directed from North Vietnam and backed by the resources of both Moscow and Peiping [Beijing].

118

The decision you face now, therefore, is crucial. Once large numbers of U.S. troops are committed to direct combat, they will begin to take heavy casualties in a war they are ill-equipped to fight in a non-cooperative if not downright hostile countryside.

Once we suffer large casualties, we will have started a well-nigh irreversible process. Our involvement will be so great that we cannot—without national humiliation—stop short of achieving our complete objectives. *Of the two possibilities I think humiliation would be more likely than the achievement of our objectives—even after we have paid terrible costs.*

A Compromise Solution

(4) Compromise Solution: Should we commit U.S. manpower and prestige to a terrain so unfavorable as to give a very large advantage to the enemy—or should we seek a compromise settlement which achieves less than our stated objectives and thus cut our losses while we still have the freedom of maneuver to do so?

(5) Costs of a Compromise Solution: The answer involves a judgment as to the cost to the U.S. of such a compromise settlement in terms of our relations with the countries in the area of South Vietnam, the credibility of our commitments, and our prestige around the world. In my judgment, if we act before we commit substantial U.S. troops to combat in South Vietnam we can, by accepting some short-term costs, avoid what may well be a long-term catastrophe. I believe we tended grossly to exaggerate the costs involved in a compromise settlement. . . .

(6) With these considerations in mind, I strongly urge the following program:

(a) Military Program

(1) Complete all deployments already announced—15 battalions—but decide not to go beyond a total of 72,000 men represented by this figure.

(2) Restrict the combat role of the American forces to the June 9 announcement, making it clear to General [William C.] Westmoreland that this announcement is to be strictly construed [A White House statement gave Westmoreland authority to use troops "in support of Vietnamese forces faced with aggressive attack."].

(3) Continue bombing in the North but avoid the Hanoi-Haiphong area and any targets nearer to the Chinese border than those already struck.

(b) Political Program

(1) In any political approaches so far, we have been the prisoners of whatever South Vietnamese government that was momentarily in power. If we are ever

Debate over Vietnam

George Ball and President Lyndon B. Johnson discussed American strategy in Vietnam at a secret White House meeting on July 21, 1965, that also included Dean Rusk, McGeorge Bundy, and other ranking officials. The following exchange was recorded by presidential assistant Jack Valenti.

BALL: We cannot win, Mr. President. This war will be long and protracted. The most we can hope for is a messy conclusion. There remains a great danger of intrusion by the Chinese. But the biggest problem is the problem of the long war. . . . As casualties increase, the pressure to strike at the very jugular of North Vietnam will become very great. I am concerned about world opinion. . . . If the war is long and protracted, as I believe it will be, then we will suffer because the world's greatest power cannot defeat guerrillas. Then there is the problem of national politics. Every great captain in history was not afraid to make a tactical withdrawal if conditions were unfavorable to him. The enemy cannot even be seen in Vietnam. He is indigenous to the country. I truly have serious doubt that an army of westerners can successfully fight orientals in an Asian jungle. . . . The least harmful way to cut losses in SVN [South Vietnam] is to let the government decide it doesn't want us to stay there. Therefore, we should put such proposals to the SVN that they can't accept. Then, it would move to a neutralist position. I have no illusions that after we were asked to leave South Vietnam, that country would soon come under Hanoi control. . . . If we wanted to make a stand in Thailand, we might be able to make it. . . . Between a long war and cutting our losses, the Japanese would go for the latter. . . .

JOHNSON: But George, wouldn't all these countries say that Uncle Sam was a paper tiger, wouldn't we lose credibility breaking the word of three presidents. . . .

BALL: The worse blow would be that the mightiest power on earth is unable to defeat a handful of guerrillas.

to move toward a settlement, it will probably be because the South Vietnamese government pulls the rug out from under us and makes its own deal *or* because we go forward quietly without advance prearrangement with Saigon.

(2) So far we have not given the other side a reason to believe there is *any* flexibility in our negotiating approach. And the other side has been unwilling to accept what *in their terms is* complete capitulation.

(3) Now is the time to start some serious diplomatic feelers looking towards a solution based on some application of a self-determination principle.

(4) I would recommend approaching Hanoi rather than any of the other probable parties, the NLF [National Liberation Front], ————— or Peiping. Hanoi is the only one that has given any signs of interest in discussion. Peiping has been rigidly opposed. Moscow has recommended that we negotiate with Hanoi. The NLF has been silent.

(5) There are several channels to the North Vietnamese, but I think the best one is through their representative in Paris, Mai van Bo. Initial feelers of Bo should be directed toward a discussion both of the four points we have put forward and the four points put forward by Hanoi as a basis for negotiation. We can accept all but one of Hanoi's four points, and hopefully we should be able to agree on some ground rules for serious negotiations—including no preconditions.

(6) If the initial feelers lead to further secret, exploratory talks, we can inject the concept of self-determination that would permit the Viet Cong some hope of achieving some of their political objectives through local elections or some other device.

(7) The contact on our side should be handled through a nongovernmental cutout (possibly a reliable newspaper man who can be repudiated).

(8) If progress can be made at this level a basis can be laid for a multinational conference. At some point, obviously, the government of South Vietnam will have to be brought on board, but I would postpone this step until after a substantial feeling out of Hanoi.

(7) Before moving to any formal conference we should be prepared to agree once the conference is started:

(a) The U.S. will stand down its bombing of the North,

(b) The South Vietnamese will initiate no offensive operations in the South, and

(c) The DRV [Democratic Republic of (North) Vietnam] will stop terrorism and other aggressive action against the South.

(8) The negotiations at the conference should aim at incorporating our understanding with Hanoi in the form of a multinational agreement guaranteed by the U.S., the Soviet Union and possibly other parties, and providing for an international mechanism to supervise its execution. . . .

World Reaction

On balance, I believe we would more seriously undermine the effectiveness of our world leadership by continuing the war and deepening our involvement than by pursuing a carefully plotted course toward a compromise solution. In spite of the number of powers that have—in response to our pleading—given verbal support from feelings of loyalty and dependence, we cannot ignore the fact that the war is vastly unpopular and that our role in it is perceptively eroding the respect and confidence with which other nations regard us. We have not persuaded either our friends or allies that our further involvement is essential to the defense of freedom in the cold war. Moreover, the more men we deploy in the jungles of South Vietnam, the more we contribute to a growing world anxiety and mistrust.

In the short run, of course, we could expect some catcalls from the sidelines and some vindictive pleasure on the part of Europeans jealous of American power. But that would, in my view, be a transient phenomenon with which we could live without sustained anguish. Elsewhere around the world I would see few unhappy implications for the credibility of our commitments.

*"I am absolutely certain that whereas in 1965 the
enemy was winning, today he is certainly losing."*

The United States
Is Winning the
War in Vietnam

William C. Westmoreland (b. 1914)

William C. Westmoreland was commander of the United States
Military Assistance Command, Vietnam (MACV) from 1964 to
1968. A veteran of both World War II and the Korean War, Westmoreland had achieved a long and notable career in the U.S.
Army before assuming command over U.S. forces in Vietnam.
Over the course of the Vietnam War he became a controversial
figure, both among antiwar doves and among war supporters
who questioned his military strategy and tactics. In Vietnam,
Westmoreland and his staff developed and implemented a military strategy of attrition: American and South Vietnamese forces
were sent on search and destroy missions in an effort to deplete
the numbers of enemy troops faster than they could be replaced.
To pursue this strategy, Westmoreland persistently requested
more U.S. troops to be sent to Vietnam. By the time he left Vietnam to become the chief of staff of the army in 1968, more than
half a million U.S. military personnel were stationed there.

While serving in Vietnam, Westmoreland returned to the
United States to speak about the war on several occasions. The
following viewpoint is taken from a speech given on November

Excerpted from William C. Westmoreland, address to the National Press Club (November 21,
1967), *Department of State Bulletin*, December 11, 1967.

21, 1967, to the National Press Club. Like most of Westmoreland's public pronouncements, it is an optimistic assessment of America's progress in the Vietnam War. Westmoreland lays out his strategic goals and argues that American and South Vietnamese forces are well on their way to victory.

I would like to give you today a short progress report on some aspects of the war in Viet-Nam, because we in Viet-Nam are keenly aware of the genuine concern being expressed at home about the complex situation in that country.

The war in Viet-Nam eludes any precise numerical system of measurement or any easy portrayal of progress on battle maps. The war is unique and complicated in origin, in diversity of form, and in its diffusion throughout Viet-Nam. It is a war which probably could not have occurred in this pattern in any other country in these times. But if we had not met it squarely, it well could have been the precedent for countless future wars of a similar nature.

But we have confronted this challenge. We have found it to be like no other war we have fought before. There are no moving front lines—just a changing picture of small actions scattered over the country. Only a few of these actions are reported in detail. Even the trained observer is drawn to the unusual and the spectacular, and finds his attention shifting to another action before the significance or impact of the first can be analyzed.

I have been observing the war in South Viet-Nam at close hand for almost 4 years. During the first 1½ years we were confined generally to an advisory role. In the past 2½ years I have seen the progressive commitment of U.S. troops in support of the Vietnamese. I am absolutely certain that whereas in 1965 the enemy was winning, today he is certainly losing. There are indications that the Viet Cong and even Hanoi know this.

However, the enemy may be operating from the delusion that political pressure here, combined with the tactical defeat of a major unit, might force the U.S. to "throw in the towel." If he does *not* believe this, there is very little logic to be found in his continuing the war in its present pattern.

The Enemy's Position

Let me review with you the enemy's situation and our own, and let me offer my estimate of our relative positions.

Since 1925, when Ho Chi Minh arrived in Canton, China, he has actively sought to gain control of the area known as Indochina. In

1930 the Indochina Communist Party was created, with Ho Chi Minh as its chief. However, since that time the cause and methods have been similar to those of other Asian Communist parties.

Ho Chi Minh's party came to power amid the chaotic conditions at the end of World War II. Although the present government of North Viet-Nam has taken a facade of democracy, it has remained under tight control of the same small, determined group of Communists who served Ho Chi Minh in the Communist Party of the 1930's.

Tet Was a U.S. Victory

The massive Tet offensive launched by North Vietnamese and Viet-cong forces on January 31, 1968, against cities and military bases in South Vietnam shook the confidence of many Americans. However, in a television interview on February 4, Secretary of Defense Robert S. McNamara maintained a public posture of optimism by arguing that the attackers had failed to achieve their objectives and had suffered heavy losses.

Question: Mr. Secretary, are you telling us the fact that the Viet Cong, after all these years, were able to, temporarily at least, grab control of some 20-odd Provincial capitals and the city of Saigon—are you telling us this has no military meaning at all?

Secretary McNamara: No; certainly not. I think South Viet-Nam is such a complex situation—one must always look at the pluses and the minuses, and I don't mean to say there haven't been any minuses for the South Vietnamese in the last several days. I think there have been, but there have been many, many pluses. The North Vietnamese and the Viet Cong have not accomplished either one of their major objectives: either to ignite a general uprising or to force a diversion of the troops which the South Vietnamese and the United States have moved into the northern areas of South Viet-Nam, anticipating a major Viet Cong and North Vietnamese offensive in that area.

And beyond that, the North Vietnamese and the Viet Cong have suffered very heavy penalties in terms of losses of weapons and losses of men in the past several days. They have, of course, dealt a very heavy blow to many of the cities of South Viet-Nam.

By 1954 it appeared to them that they had overcome the last major obstacle to the original goal. A million people had been displaced from the North, and although they were fleeing communism, they created a burden on the new government of South Viet-Nam. For the next few years the Communists believed that South Viet-Nam would succumb politically. These hopes were dashed by the vigor of the non-Communist government and by U.S. assistance.

In 1957 they reverted to terror, both indiscriminate and selective, with the assassination of teachers and local leaders. This terror rate went up every year. Despite that, it did not succeed. So, to guerrilla terror was added the military buildup of Viet Cong main-force units from 1959. Even this was not enough.

In 1963 and 1964 there started the military invasion from the North, when the first North Vietnamese regiments entered the South. This almost succeeded. By early 1965, the Vietnamese Government found its resolution exhausted by a decade of struggle and its last resources committed. It was at that point that the intervention of our Armed Forces restored a future to the long-suffering people of South Viet-Nam, who grasped the opportunity.

As you know, in the midst of war the South Vietnamese have in the past year held free elections and have turned out a larger percentage of the vote than we normally do in this country. The Viet Cong have tried desperately to stop these elections by terror and intimidation. But the Vietnamese voted despite the Viet Cong efforts. This mass disregard of Viet Cong initiatives killed the myth that the Viet Cong or the National Liberation Front speak for the people.

It is significant that the enemy has not won a major battle in more than a year. In general, he can fight his large forces only at the edges of his sanctuaries, as we have seen recently at Con Thien and along the DMZ [Demilitarized Zone], at Dak To opposite the Laotian border, at Song Be and Loc Ninh near the Cambodian border. His Viet Cong military units can no longer fill their ranks from the South but must depend increasingly on replacements from North Viet-Nam. His guerrilla force is declining at a steady rate. Morale problems are developing within his ranks.

Despite this, our enemy seeks to prolong the war, occasionally sallying forth from his sanctuaries and attempting by his counter-sweep operations to regain control of the population and to rebuild his guerrilla forces. Of essential importance is his desire to force us politically to stop, unconditionally, the bombing of his support base and his lines of communication. He appears to believe that he can defeat the Vietnamese forces, over 600,000 strong and getting stronger, reinforced by over 50,000 troops from free-world allies, and our commitment now approaching 500,000 men.

Buildup and Deployment of U.S. Forces

Our common plan with the Vietnamese has involved four distinct phases. In phase I we came to the aid of South Viet-Nam, prevented its collapse under the massive Communist thrust, built up our bases and began to deploy our forces.

In phase I we planned and did the following:

Built ports, airfields, and supply and maintenance areas.

Set up a 10,000-mile-long supply pipeline.

Constructed an extensive communication system.

Brought in 400,000 men and several thousand aircraft.

Deployed troops throughout South Viet-Nam.

Learned to work alongside the Vietnamese Army, while encouraging development of a representative government.

Equipped and revitalized the Vietnamese Armed Forces, whose morale was low.

Expanded the Armed Forces of South Viet-Nam in quantitative terms.

Defended South Viet-Nam against defeat and against being cut in half.

Learned to cope with guerrilla tactics.

Set up an intelligence system for this new type of war.

Limited inflation.

Developed our own confidence that we could operate successfully in the environment of Southeast Asia.

We did all this by the middle of 1966. It was a tribute to U.S. organization, technology, and concerted diplomatic and military professionalism by many people.

Military and Economic Aid

At that point, during the summer of 1966, we moved into the second phase of our plan. In phase II we continued the pattern and did the following:

Drove the enemy divisions back to sanctuary or into hiding.

Trained, expanded, and improved the quality of the Vietnamese Armed Forces.

Assisted free-world forces of the Pacific area to join the battle against Communist aggression.

Entered enemy base areas and destroyed his supplies.

Raised enemy losses beyond his input capability.

Helped train the Vietnamese Army as a territorial security force.

Encouraged combined U.S.-Vietnamese operations.

Continued to help the Vietnamese Armed Forces in professional development.

Completed free elections within South Viet-Nam.

Saw an elected civilian government installed.

Stabilized prices—opening roads and canals.

Encouraged enemy defection and resettlement.

Discovered and thwarted the enemy's battle plans before they could be executed.

Unified the U.S. pacification assistance effort for better management of widespread resources.

We will complete this second phase by the end of this year. . . .

Improving Vietnamese Effectiveness

With 1968, a new phase is now starting. We have reached an important point when the end begins to come into view. What is this third phase we are about to enter?

In phase III, in 1968, we intend to do the following:

Help the Vietnamese Armed Forces to continue improving their effectiveness.

Decrease our advisers in training centers and other places where the professional competence of Vietnamese officers makes this possible.

Increase our advisory effort with the younger brothers of the Vietnamese Army: the Regional Forces and Popular Forces.

Use U.S. and free-world forces to destroy North Vietnamese forays while we assist the Vietnamese to reorganize for territorial security.

Provide the new military equipment to revitalize the Vietnamese Army and prepare it to take on an ever-increasing share of the war.

Continue pressure on the North to prevent rebuilding and to make infiltration more costly.

Turn a major share of frontline DMZ defense over to the Vietnamese Army.

Increase U.S. support in the rich and populated delta.

Help the Government of Viet-Nam single out and destroy the Communist shadow government.

Continue to isolate the guerrilla from the people.

Help the new Vietnamese government to respond to popular aspirations and to reduce and eliminate corruption.

Help the Vietnamese strengthen their police forces to enhance law and order.

Open more roads and canals.

Continue to improve the Vietnamese economy and standard of living.

The Final Phase

Now for phase IV—the final phase. That period will see the conclusion of our plan to weaken the enemy and strengthen our friends until we become progressively superfluous. The object will be to show the world that guerrilla warfare and invasion do not pay as a new means of Communist aggression.

I see phase IV happening as follows:

Infiltration will slow.

The Communist infrastructure will be cut up and near collapse.

The Vietnamese Government will prove its stability, and the Vietnamese Army will show that it can handle Viet Cong.

The Regional Forces and Popular Forces will reach a higher level of professional performance.

U.S. units can begin to phase down as the Vietnamese Army is modernized and develops its capacity to the fullest.

The military physical assets, bases and ports, will be progressively turned over to the Vietnamese.

The Vietnamese will take charge of the final mopping up of the Viet Cong (which will probably last several years). The U.S., at the same time, will continue the developmental help envisaged by the President for the community of Southeast Asia.

You may ask how long phase III will take, before we reach the final phase. We have already entered parts of phase III. Looking back on phases I and II, we can conclude that we have come a long way.

I see progress as I travel all over Viet-Nam.

I see it in the attitudes of the Vietnamese.

I see it in the open roads and canals.

I see it in the new crops and the new purchasing power of the farmer.

I see it in the increased willingness of the Vietnamese Army to fight North Vietnamese units and in the victories they are winning.

Parenthetically, I might say that the U.S. press tends to report U.S. actions; so you may not be as aware as I am of the victories won by South Vietnamese forces.

The enemy has many problems:

He is losing control of the scattered population under his influence.

He is losing credibility with the population he still controls.

He is alienating the people by his increased demands and taxes, where he can impose them.

He sees the strength of his forces steadily declining.

He can no longer recruit in the South to any meaningful extent; he must plug the gap with North Vietnamese.

His monsoon offensives have been failures.

He was dealt a mortal blow by the installation of a freely elected representative government.

And he failed in his desperate effort to take the world's headlines from the inauguration by a military victory.

Lastly, the Vietnamese Army is on the road to becoming a competent force. Korean troops in Viet-Nam provide a good example for the Vietnamese. Fifteen years ago the Koreans themselves had problems now ascribed to the Vietnamese. The Koreans surmounted these problems, and so can and will the Vietnamese.

The Vietnamese Armed Forces have accomplished much in a short time. Here are a few examples:

Career management for officers, particularly infantry officers, has been instituted.

Sound promotion procedures have been put into effect.

Discipline and conduct is being stressed.

Increased emphasis is being devoted to small-unit tactics and leadership.

The promotion of enlisted men to the commissioned ranks is now commonplace (2,200 in 1966).

Officer candidates must now take basic training and prove that they have the leadership potential to be officers.

An Inspector General for the Vietnamese Armed Forces has been appointed and is now active in detailed inspections.

Corrupt and inefficient officials are being gradually eliminated.

The military school system has been revitalized.

The Military Academy has gone to a 4-year curriculum.

A school for battalion commanders has been established.

A 10-month National Defense College has been organized for selected senior officers.

The same personnel management programs which have been installed successfully in the Vietnamese Army are being expanded to the Regional Forces and Popular Forces.

We are making progress. We know you want an honorable and early transition to the fourth and last phase. So do your sons and so do I.

It lies within our grasp—the enemy's hopes are bankrupt. With your support we will give you a success that will impact not only on South Viet-Nam but on every emerging nation in the world.

VIEWPOINT 6

"A total military victory is not within sight or around the corner; . . . in fact, it is probably beyond our grasp."

The United States Cannot Win the War in Vietnam

Robert F. Kennedy (1925–1968)

Despite the official optimistic appraisals of U.S. progress in Vietnam by President Lyndon B. Johnson, General William C. Westmoreland, and other leading officials, by the end of 1967 a growing number of Americans were questioning whether America could achieve victory in Vietnam. These doubts became widespread following the Tet Offensive of 1968, the largest military campaign of the war.

Tet is the lunar new year, the most celebrated holiday in Vietnam. On January 31, 1968, the beginning of the Tet period, North Vietnamese and Vietcong forces staged large and synchronized surprise attacks on nearly every major city, town, and U.S. base in South Vietnam. They successfully attacked army installations, police headquarters, radio stations, and other targets (a small group broke into the compound of the U.S. embassy in Saigon). After being caught off guard, South Vietnamese and American forces were eventually able to retake most positions, killing an estimated thirty to forty thousand enemy soldiers. Westmoreland and others argued that Tet represented a major tactical victory for the United States. But many Americans were shocked that the North Vietnamese and Vietcong, supposedly on the verge of defeat, were capable of such a large offensive.

The following viewpoint is excerpted from a February 8, 1968, speech by Robert F. Kennedy, made shortly after the Tet offensive began. Kennedy had participated in the decisions leading to increasing U.S. involvement in Vietnam while serving as attorney

From Robert F. Kennedy, speech delivered before the U.S. Senate, February 8, 1968.

general (and close personal adviser) to his brother, President John F. Kennedy. During a 1962 trip to Saigon, he declared that "we are going to win." After John F. Kennedy was assassinated in November 1963, Robert F. Kennedy continued as attorney general for a short time under President Lyndon B. Johnson before leaving to become a U.S. senator from New York in 1964. While in the Senate, he began to voice increasingly critical opinions about the war in Vietnam. In his February 8 statement, Kennedy argues that the war in Vietnam cannot be won at an acceptable cost to the United States, despite the massive increase of U.S. troops there. The United States, he asserts, must give up its "illusions" about victory and seek a peaceful settlement in Vietnam.

Kennedy announced his candidacy for the presidency on March 16, 1968, running on a platform of opposition to the war. After several primary victories, he was assassinated on June 5, 1968.

Our enemy, savagely striking at will across all of South Vietnam, has finally shattered the mask of official illusion with which we have concealed our true circumstances, even from ourselves. But a short time ago we were serene in our reports and predictions of progress.

The Vietcong will probably withdraw from the cities, as they were forced to withdraw from the American Embassy. Thousands of them will be dead.

But they will, nevertheless, have demonstrated that no part or person of South Vietnam is secure from their attacks: neither district capitals nor American bases, neither the peasant in his rice paddy nor the commanding general of our own great forces.

No one can predict the exact shape or outcome of the battles now in progress, in Saigon or at Khesanh. Let us pray that we will succeed at the lowest possible cost to our young men.

But whatever their outcome, the events of the last two weeks have taught us something. For the sake of those young Americans who are fighting today, if for no other reason, the time has come to take a new look at the war in Vietnam; not by cursing the past but by using it to illuminate the future.

Facts and Illusions

And the first and necessary step is to face the facts. It is to seek out the austere and painful reality of Vietnam, freed from wishful thinking, false hopes and sentimental dreams. It is to rid ourselves of the "good company," of those illusions which have lured us into the deepening swamp of Vietnam.

We must, first of all, rid ourselves of the illusion that the events of the past two weeks represent some sort of victory. That is not so.

It is said the Vietcong will not be able to hold the cities. This is probably true. But they have demonstrated despite all our reports of progress, of government strength and enemy weakness, that half a million American soldiers with 700,000 Vietnamese allies, with total command of the air, total command of the sea, backed by huge resources and the most modern weapons, are unable to secure even a single city from the attacks of an enemy whose total strength is about 250,000. . . .

For years we have been told that the measure of our success and progress in Vietnam was increasing security and control for the population. Now we have seen that none of the population is secure and no area is under sure control.

Four years ago when we only had about 30,000 troops in Vietnam, the Vietcong were unable to mount the assaults on cities they have now conducted against our enormous forces. At one time a suggestion that we protect enclaves was derided. Now there are no protected enclaves.

The Will of the People

This has not happened because our men are not brave or effective, because they are. It is because we have misconceived the nature of the war: It is because we have sought to resolve by military might a conflict whose issue depends upon the will and conviction of the South Vietnamese people. It is like sending a lion to halt an epidemic of jungle rot.

This misconception rests on a second illusion—the illusion that we can win a war which the South Vietnamese cannot win for themselves.

You cannot expect people to risk their lives and endure hardship unless they have a stake in their own society. They must have a clear sense of identification with their own government, a belief they are participating in a cause worth fighting for.

People will not fight to line the pockets of generals or swell the bank accounts of the wealthy. They are far more likely to close their eyes and shut their doors in the face of their government—even as they did last week.

More than any election, more than any proud boast, that single fact reveals the truth. We have an ally in name only. We support a government without supporters. Without the efforts of American arms that government would not last a day.

The third illusion is that the unswerving pursuit of military victory, whatever its cost, is in the interest of either ourselves or the people of Vietnam.

For the people of Vietnam, the last three years have meant little but horror. Their tiny land has been devastated by a weight of bombs and shells greater than Nazi Germany knew in the Second World War.

We have dropped 12 tons of bombs for every square mile in North and South Vietnam. Whole provinces have been substantially destroyed. More than two million South Vietnamese are now homeless refugees.

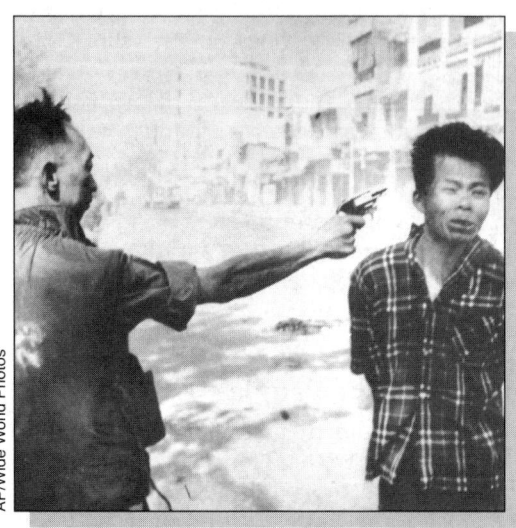

AP/Wide World Photos

The photograph mentioned by Robert F. Kennedy, reprinted here, was prominently featured in many newspapers, adding to the public's shock over events in Vietnam during the Tet Offensive. The photograph, taken on January 31, 1968, shows the chief of South Vietnam's national police summarily executing a Vietcong suspect.

Imagine the impact in our own country if an equivalent number—over 25 million Americans—were wandering homeless or interned in refugee camps, and millions more refugees were being created as New York and Chicago, Washington and Boston, were being destroyed by a war raging in their streets.

Whatever the outcome of these battles, it is the people we seek to defend who are the greatest losers.

Nor does it serve the interests of America to fight this war as if moral standards could be subordinated to immediate necessities. Last week, a Vietcong suspect was turned over to the chief of the Vietnamese Security Services, who executed him on the spot—a flat violation of the Geneva Convention on the Rules of War.

The photograph of the execution was on front pages all around the world—leading our best and oldest friends to ask, more in sorrow than in anger, what has happened to America?

The National Interest

The fourth illusion is that the American national interest is identical with—or should be subordinated to—the selfish interest of an incompetent military regime.

We are told, of course, that the battle for South Vietnam is in reality a struggle for 250 million Asians—the beginning of a Great Society for all of Asia. But this is pretension.

We can and should offer reasonable assistance to Asia; but we cannot build a Great Society there if we cannot build one in our own country. We cannot speak extravagantly of a struggle for 250 million Asians, when a struggle for 15 million in one Asian country so strains our forces, that another Asian country, a fourth-rate power which we have already once defeated in battle, dares to seize an American ship and hold and humiliate her crew. [On January 23, 1968, the USS *Pueblo*, an American naval intelligence ship, and its crew were seized by North Korea while patrolling Korea's coastal waters.]

The fifth illusion is that this war can be settled in our own way and in our own time on our own terms. Such a settlement is the privilege of the triumphant: of those who crush their enemies in battle or wear away their will to fight.

We have not done this, nor is there any prospect we will achieve such a victory.

Unable to defeat our enemy or break his will—at least without a huge, long and ever more costly effort—we must actively seek a peaceful settlement. We can no longer harden our terms every time Hanoi indicates it may be prepared to negotiate; and we must be willing to foresee a settlement which will give the Vietcong a chance to participate in the political life of the country.

Basic Truths

These are some of the illusions which may be discarded if the events of last week are to prove not simply a tragedy, but a lesson: a lesson which carries with it some basic truths.

First, that a total military victory is not within sight or around the corner; that, in fact, it is probably beyond our grasp; and that the effort to win such a victory will only result in the further slaughter of thousands of innocent and helpless people—a slaughter which will forever rest on our national conscience.

Second, that the pursuit of such a victory is not necessary to our national interest, and is even damaging that interest.

Third, that the progress we have claimed toward increasing our control over the country and the security of the population is largely illusory.

Fourth, that the central battle in this war cannot be measured by body counts or bomb damage, but by the extent to which the people of South Vietnam act on a sense of common purpose and hope with those that govern them.

Fifth, that the current regime in Saigon is unwilling or incapable of being an effective ally in the war against the Communists.

Sixth, that a political compromise is not just the best path to peace, but the only path, and we must show as much willingness to risk some of our prestige for peace as to risk the lives of young men in war.

Seventh, that the escalation policy in Vietnam, far from strengthening and consolidating international resistance to aggression, is injuring our country through the world, reducing the faith of other peoples in our wisdom and purpose and weakening the world's resolve to stand together for freedom and peace.

Eighth, that the best way to save our most precious stake in Vietnam—the lives of our soldiers—is to stop the enlargement of the war, and that the best way to end casualties is to end the war.

Ninth, that our nation must be told the truth about this war, in all its terrible reality, both because it is right—and because only in this way can any Administration rally the public confidence and unity for the shadowed days which lie ahead.

No war has ever demanded more bravery from our people and our Government—not just bravery under fire or the bravery to make sacrifices—but the bravery to discard the comfort of illusion—to do away with false hopes and alluring promises.

Reality is grim and painful. But it is only a remote echo of the anguish toward which a policy founded on illusion is surely taking us.

This is a great nation and a strong people. Any who seek to comfort rather than speak plainly, reassure rather than instruct, promise satisfaction rather than reveal frustration—they deny that greatness and drain that strength. For today as it was in the beginning, it is the truth that makes us free.

CHAPTER 4

Vietnamization and Withdrawal

Chapter Preface

Promising "peace with honor" in Vietnam, Republican nominee Richard M. Nixon won the presidential election of 1968. He defeated Vice President Hubert H. Humphrey, whom many voters closely associated with President Lyndon B. Johnson and the Vietnam War, which had become a divisive issue during Johnson's presidency. President Nixon continued the peace negotiations that had begun in Paris in 1968 and eventually did preside over a peace agreement and U.S. withdrawal from Vietnam. However, this end result was not reached until January 1973.

When Nixon took office, some observers believed that he had the opportunity to do what his predecessor could not—withdraw from South Vietnam at the risk of seeing it fall to North Vietnam. David Halberstam, a journalist who covered Vietnam in the early 1960s, wrote in 1969 that Vietnam was essentially "Johnson's war" and that Nixon was therefore free to withdraw with relatively few political repercussions. "He will be able to handle, should he seek peace, the one faction of Congress which partially supports the war, the Republicans," Halberstam maintained. "Most important, he is freed from past decisions and past mistakes; indeed, he can do what no one in official Washington has been able to do in the past—he can actually say that the war was a mistake and a miscalculation. The country will believe him."

Nixon did not take this course. He had built his political career on a strong anti-Communist record and, like Johnson before him, was determined not to preside over an American defeat in Vietnam. He argued that such "defeat and humiliation" would undermine the credibility and reliability of America's foreign policy commitments, would lead to international instability, and would "promote recklessness in the councils of those great powers who have not yet abandoned their goals of world conquest." Thus, in the ongoing Paris negotiations, Nixon and his principal foreign policy adviser and negotiator, Henry Kissinger, insisted that the North Vietnamese guarantee the future existence of a non-Communist South Vietnam. Nixon warned in a July 15, 1969, letter to Ho Chi Minh that the United States would have no choice but to resort to "measures of great consequence and force" if no progress in negotiations was made by November 1. However, North Vietnam and the South Vietnamese rebels of the National Liberation Front (renamed the Provisional Revolutionary Government, or PRG, in 1969) steadfastly refused to agree to America's demands. The death of Ho Chi Minh in 1969 did little to ease the negotiating impasse.

Nixon and Kissinger had hoped that by threatening greater military action, they would cause the North Vietnamese to be more flexible in peace negotiations. In September 1969, when it became apparent that such flexibility was not forthcoming, Nixon and Kissinger instructed a select group from the president's National Security Council to draw up plans for a "savage, punishing" blow against North Vietnam. The group's proposals, code-named Duck Hook, included mining Haiphong Harbor, launching a full-scale invasion of North Vietnam, implementing a naval blockade on North Vietnam's coast, bombing dikes to flood major portions of North Vietnam, and the possible use of tactical nuclear weapons. However, the staff who drew up these plans also concluded that such actions would probably not force any diplomatic concessions from North Vietnam or significantly diminish its war-making capability. In addition, Nixon's advisers, including Secretary of State William Rogers and Secretary of Defense Melvin Laird, warned that such military action would rouse great dissent within Congress and among the American public.

Rejecting both immediate withdrawal and the Duck Hook proposals, Nixon settled on a policy that became known as "Vietnamization," under which American soldiers would be gradually withdrawn from South Vietnam while the Army of the Republic of Vietnam (ARVN) would be trained and equipped to take their place. On June 8, 1969, Nixon announced that he was immediately pulling out 25,000 American troops. By the end of 1970 the number of U.S. soldiers in Vietnam had dropped from an April 1969 peak of 543,000 to 334,000; two years later it would stand at less than 25,000. Nixon coupled the reduction in American ground forces with increases in U.S. bombing, and he also expanded the war by attacking Communist sanctuaries and supply routes in Cambodia and Laos. Despite this escalation of fighting, the gradual troop withdrawals, along with reforms in America's military draft, did result in a lessening of public support for the antiwar protest movement.

Nixon's strategy in Vietnam included a series of diplomatic initiatives aimed at improving relations with the Soviet Union and China in the hopes that these two Communist giants (which were at odds with each other) would curtail their support for North Vietnam and encourage it to be more flexible in negotiations. Historian Walter LaFeber writes that "a strange reversal had taken place: Eisenhower, Kennedy, and Johnson had argued that the defeat of North Vietnam was necessary to contain China and Russia. Now Nixon and Kissinger argued that the friendship of China and

Russia was necessary to contain North Vietnam." Nixon made historic visits to China and the Soviet Union in 1972 that, while important and successful in many respects, were disappointing in terms of settling the Vietnam War to America's satisfaction.

A test of Vietnamization came in March 1972, when North Vietnam launched a full-scale conventional assault with 120,000 soldiers armed with Soviet tanks and weapons. Nixon responded by implementing some elements of the 1969 Duck Hook plans, including a massive bombing campaign in North Vietnam, a naval blockade, and the mining of Haiphong Harbor. With this support and the continued presence of American military advisers, the ARVN was able to inflict heavy casualties and beat back the invasion. At the same time, however, the Nixon administration was coming under growing pressure to further decrease American involvement as members of Congress debated bills that would cut off all funding of American military operations in Indochina. Such legislation was finally passed in 1973.

By late 1972 both North Vietnam and the United States had modified their negotiating demands. The Paris negotiations (which included secret talks between Kissinger and the North Vietnamese) finally resulted in the Paris Peace Accords, which were signed on January 27, 1973, by the PRG and the governments of North Vietnam, South Vietnam, and the United States. Under what was essentially a cease-fire agreement, the United States promised to withdraw all of its forces from South Vietnam within sixty days; North Vietnam agreed to return all American prisoners of war and was allowed to keep its 150,000 troops in South Vietnam. The political future of South Vietnam was to be determined by internationally supervised elections, in which the PRG would have a recognized role.

The agreement marked an end to American participation in the Vietnam War, but not to the war itself; both North and South Vietnam violated provisions of the accords. In 1975 North Vietnam launched another invasion. This time, without American advisers or bombing support, South Vietnam quickly fell. By then Nixon was no longer president. Although he had won reelection in 1972 by a wide margin, he resigned less than two years later after his involvement in and covering up of illegal activities—including the wiretapping and surveillance of suspected political opponents— became public in the Watergate scandal. Many historians and observers argue that Nixon authorized the criminal actions in large part because of his frustrations over his failure to end the Vietnam War and his concerns about news leaks regarding secret military operations in Vietnam. The Vietnam War thus became an indirect cause of Nixon's downfall.

"In the previous Administration, we Americanized the war in Vietnam. In this Administration, we are Vietnamizing the search for peace."

Vietnamization Provides America a Way Out of Vietnam

Richard M. Nixon (1913–1994)

Richard M. Nixon won a narrow election victory in 1968, due in large part to public dissatisfaction with the Johnson administration and the stalemated and costly Vietnam War. In his campaign for president, Nixon spoke of achieving "peace with honor" in Vietnam, but did not spell out how he would attain such a goal. Some observers argued that the change of administrations, coupled with Nixon's longtime record as an anti-Communist, gave the new president a political opportunity that Johnson lacked to admit America's past mistakes in Vietnam and negotiate an American military withdrawal there. Like his predecessors in the White House, however, Nixon was determined to preserve a noncommunist South Vietnam, and he opposed all proposals for unilateral American withdrawal.

The plan he settled on instead became known as "Vietnamization." America would redouble its efforts to train and supply the South Vietnamese army so that it could take over more of the fighting, enabling the United States to gradually pull its soldiers out of Vietnam. At the same time, the United States and North Vietnam would continue the peace talks that had begun in Paris in 1968. Nixon, who first announced a withdrawal of twenty-five thousand American troops from Vietnam in June 1969, presented

Excerpted from Richard M. Nixon, television speech, November 3, 1969.

his strategy as a fresh approach. However, George C. Herring and other historians have argued that Vietnamization was basically similar to the policies Nixon inherited from the final months of the Johnson administration.

The following viewpoint is taken from a televised address to the nation given by Nixon on November 3, 1969, in which he spells out his policy of Vietnamization and appeals for public support. Nixon argues that his approach would enable America to withdraw from Vietnam without conceding defeat.

Nixon made this speech at a time of increasing antiwar activity. On October 15, between half a million and a million people nationwide participated in a "moratorium" on business-as-usual to protest Vietnam; the work stoppages and mass demonstrations brought "new respectability and popularity" to the antiwar movement, according to *Time* magazine. Another national "moratorium" was scheduled to be held on November 15. In his speech of November 3, Nixon decries the antiwar protesters and asks the "silent majority" of Americans to support their government concerning Vietnam. His address was generally credited with putting the antiwar movement on the defensive and for gaining Nixon renewed public support for his policies.

Good evening, my fellow Americans:

Tonight I want to talk to you on a subject of deep concern to all Americans and to many people in all parts of the world—the war in Vietnam.

I believe that one of the reasons for the deep division about Vietnam is that many Americans have lost confidence in what their Government has told them about our policy. The American people cannot and should not be asked to support a policy which involves the overriding issues of war and peace unless they know the truth about that policy.

Tonight, therefore, I would like to answer some of the questions that I know are on the minds of many of you listening to me.

How and why did America get involved in Vietnam in the first place?

How has this administration changed the policy of the previous administration?

What has really happened in the negotiations in Paris and on the battlefront in Vietnam?

What choices do we have if we are to end the war?

What are the prospects for peace?

Now, let me begin by describing the situation I found when I was inaugurated on January 20.

The war had been going on for 4 years.

31,000 Americans had been killed in action.

The training program for the South Vietnamese was behind schedule.

540,000 Americans were in Vietnam with no plans to reduce the number.

No progress had been made at the negotiations in Paris and the United States had not put forth a comprehensive peace proposal.

The war was causing deep division at home and criticism from many of our friends as well as our enemies abroad.

Some Urge Withdrawal

In view of these circumstances there were some who urged that I end the war at once by ordering the immediate withdrawal of all American forces.

From a political standpoint this would have been a popular and easy course to follow. After all, we became involved in the war while my predecessor was in office. I could blame the defeat which would be the result of my action on him and come out as the peacemaker. Some put it to me quite bluntly: This was the only way to avoid allowing Johnson's war to become Nixon's war.

But I had a greater obligation than to think only of the years of my administration and of the next election. I had to think of the effect of my decision on the next generation and on the future of peace and freedom in America and in the world.

Let us all understand that the question before us is not whether some Americans are for peace and some Americans are against peace. The question at issue is not whether Johnson's war becomes Nixon's war.

The great question is: How can we win America's peace?

Well, let us turn now to the fundamental issue. Why and how did the United States become involved in Vietnam in the first place?

Fifteen years ago North Vietnam, with the logistical support of Communist China and the Soviet Union, launched a campaign to impose a Communist government on South Vietnam by instigating and supporting a revolution.

In response to the request of the Government of South Vietnam, President Eisenhower sent economic aid and military equipment to assist the people of South Vietnam in their efforts to prevent a Communist takeover. Seven years ago, President Kennedy sent 16,000 military personnel to Vietnam as combat advisers. Four years ago, President Johnson sent American combat forces to South Vietnam.

Now, many believe that President Johnson's decision to send American combat forces to South Vietnam was wrong. Any many others—I among them—have been strongly critical of the way the war has been conducted.

But the question facing us today is: Now that we are in the war, what is the best way to end it?

Vietnamization Has Been a Success

A 1971 Department of State publication praised President Nixon's program of Vietnamization, noting that the number of American troops in Vietnam was steadily decreasing.

While we continue to press for a reasonable settlement through negotiations, the U.S. Government is pursuing the alternative policy of Vietnamization, designed to reduce and eventually eliminate American participation in the war in a way which leaves the South Vietnamese a reasonable chance to survive as a free people. The rate of withdrawal of U.S. troops is determined on the basis of three criteria announced by the President at the beginning of the program: 1) the level of enemy military activity, 2) progress in the Paris talks, and 3) the ability of the South Vietnamese to assume an increasing share of the burden of their own defense. Two years ago:

The authorized American troop strength in Viet-Nam in 1969 was 549,500. More than 316,200 have now been withdrawn. By December 1, 1971, the authorized troop strength will be 184,000. The current pace of U.S. withdrawal is ahead of schedule.

Approximately three hundred Americans were being lost every week. This year that figure runs less than 50.

The ratio of South Vietnamese forces to U.S. forces in Viet-Nam changed from 2 to 1 in 1969 to 4 to 1 in early 1971.

Thus the President could announce on April 7, 1971, "The American involvement in Viet-Nam is coming to an end. The day the South Vietnamese can take over their own defense is in sight. Our goal is a total American withdrawal from Viet-Nam. We can and we will reach that goal . . .".

The Vietnamization program, which the Communists have consistently denounced, is in general succeeding. In some areas it is, inevitably, a mixed picture; in others, the picture is one of uniform progress.

In January I could only conclude that the precipitate withdrawal of American forces from Vietnam would be a disaster not only for South Vietnam but for the United States and for the cause of peace.

For the South Vietnamese, our precipitate withdrawal would inevitably allow the Communists to repeat the massacres which followed their takeover in the North 15 years before. . . .

For the United States, this first defeat in our Nation's history would result in a collapse of confidence in American leadership, not only in Asia but throughout the world. . . .

For the future of peace, precipitate withdrawal would thus be a disaster of immense magnitude.

A nation cannot remain great if it betrays its allies and lets down its friends.

Our defeat and humiliation in South Vietnam without question would promote recklessness in the councils of those great powers who have not yet abandoned their goals of world conquest.

This would spark violence wherever our commitments help maintain the peace—in the Middle East, in Berlin, eventually even in the Western Hemisphere.

Ultimately, this would cost more lives.

It would not bring peace; it would bring more war.

For these reasons, I rejected the recommendation that I should end the war by immediately withdrawing all of our forces. I chose instead to change American policy on both the negotiating front and battlefront. . . .

The Obstacle to Peace

It has become clear that the obstacle in negotiating an end to the war is not the President of the United States. And it is not the South Vietnamese.

The obstacle is the other side's absolute refusal to show the least willingness to join us in seeking a just peace. It will not do so while it is convinced that all it has to do is to wait for our next concession, and the next until it gets everything it wants.

There can now be no longer any question that progress in negotiation depends only on Hanoi's deciding to negotiate, to negotiate seriously.

I realize that this report on our efforts on the diplomatic fronts is discouraging to the American people, but the American people are entitled to know the truth—the bad news as well as the good news, where the lives of our young men are involved.

Now let me turn, however, to a more encouraging report on another front.

At the time we launched our search for peace I recognized we might not succeed in bringing an end to the war through negotiation. I, therefore, put into effect another plan to bring peace—a plan which will bring the war to an end regardless of what happens on the negotiating front.

The Nixon Doctrine

It is in line with a major shift in U.S. foreign policy which I described in my press conference at Guam on July 25. Let me briefly explain what has been described as the Nixon Doctrine—a policy which not only will help end the war in Vietnam, but which is an essential element of our program to prevent future Vietnams.

We Americans are a do-it-yourself-people. We are an impatient people. Instead of teaching someone else to do a job, we like to do it ourselves. And this trait has been carried over into our foreign policy.

In Korea and again in Vietnam, the United States furnished most of the money, most of the arms, and most of the men to help the people of those countries defend their freedom against the Communist aggression.

Before any American troops were committed to Vietnam, a leader of another Asian country expressed this opinion to me when I was traveling in Asia as a private citizen. He said, "When you are trying to assist another nation defend its freedom, U.S. policy should be to help them fight the war but not to fight the war for them."

Well, in accordance with this wise counsel, I laid down in Guam three principles as guidelines for future American policy toward Asia:

First, the United States will keep all of its treaty commitments.

Second, we shall provide a shield if a nuclear power threatens the freedom of a nation allied with us or of a nation whose survival we consider vital to our security.

Third, in cases involving other types of aggression, we shall furnish military and economic assistance when requested in accordance with our treaty commitments. But we shall look to the nation directly threatened to assume the primary responsibility of providing the manpower for its defense.

After I announced this policy, I found that the leaders of the Philippines, Thailand, Vietnam, South Korea, and other nations which might be threatened by Communist aggression, welcomed this new direction in American foreign policy.

Vietnamization

The defense of freedom is everybody's business—not just America's business. And it is particularly the responsibility of the people whose freedom is threatened. In the previous Administration, we Americanized the war in Vietnam. In this Administration, we are Vietnamizing the search for peace.

The policy of the previous Administration not only resulted in our assuming the primary responsibility for fighting the war but even more significantly did not adequately stress the goal of strengthening the South Vietnamese so that they could defend themselves when we left.

The Vietnamization Plan was launched following Secretary [of

Defense Melvin] Laird's visit to Vietnam in March. Under the plan, I ordered first a substantial increase in the training and equipment of South Vietnamese forces.

In July, on my visit to Vietnam, I changed General [Creighton] Abrams' orders so that they were consistent with the objectives of our new policies. Under the new orders, the primary mission of our troops is to enable the South Vietnamese forces to assume the full responsibility for the security of South Vietnam.

Our air operations have been reduced by over 20 percent.

And now we have begun to see the results of this long overdue change in American policy in Vietnam.

Significant Results

After five years of Americans going into Vietnam, we are finally bringing American men home. By December 15, over 60,000 men will have been withdrawn from South Vietnam—including 20 percent of all of our combat forces.

The South Vietnamese have continued to gain in strength. As a result they have been able to take over combat responsibilities from our American troops.

Two other significant developments have occurred since this Administration took office.

Enemy infiltration, infiltration which is essential if they are to launch a major attack, over the last three months is less than 20 percent of what it was over the same period last year.

Most important—United States casualties have declined during the last two months to the lowest point in three years.

Let me now turn to our program for the future.

We have adopted a plan which we have worked out in cooperation with the South Vietnamese for the complete withdrawal of all U.S. combat ground forces, and their replacement by South Vietnamese forces on an orderly scheduled timetable. This withdrawal will be made from strength and not from weakness. As South Vietnamese forces become stronger, the rate of American withdrawal can become greater.

I have not and do not intend to announce the timetable for our program. There are obvious reasons for this decision which I am sure you will understand. As I have indicated on several occasions, the rate of withdrawal will depend on developments on three fronts.

One of these is the progress which can be or might be made in the Paris talks. An announcement of a fixed timetable for our withdrawal would completely remove any incentive for the enemy to negotiate an agreement.

They would simply wait until our forces had withdrawn and then move in.

The other two factors on which we will base our withdrawal decisions are the level of enemy activity and the progress of the training program of the South Vietnamese forces. I am glad to be able to report tonight progress on both of these fronts has been greater than we anticipated when we started the program in June for withdrawal. As a result, our timetable for withdrawal is more optimistic now than when we made our first estimates in June. This clearly demonstrates why it is not wise to be frozen in on a fixed timetable.

We must retain the flexibility to base each withdrawal decision on the situation as it is at that time rather than on estimates that are no longer valid.

Along with this optimistic estimate, I must—in all candor—leave one note of caution.

If the level of enemy activity significantly increases we might have to adjust our timetable accordingly.

However, I want the record to be completely clear on one point.

At the time of the bombing halt just a year ago, there was some confusion as to whether there was an understanding on the part of the enemy that if we stopped the bombing of North Vietnam they would stop the shelling of cities in South Vietnam. I want to be sure that there is no misunderstanding on the part of the enemy with regard to our withdrawal program.

We have noted the reduced level of infiltration, the reduction of our casualties, and are basing our withdrawal decisions partially on those factors.

If the level of infiltration or our casualties increase while we are trying to scale down the fighting, it will be the result of a conscious decision by the enemy.

Hanoi could make no greater mistake than to assume that an increase in violence will be to its advantage. If I conclude that increased enemy action jeopardizes our remaining forces in Vietnam, I shall not hesitate to take strong and effective measures to deal with that situation.

This is not a threat. This is a statement of policy which as Commander-in-Chief of our Armed Forces I am making in meeting my responsibility for the protection of American fighting men wherever they may be.

Two Choices

My fellow Americans, I am sure you recognize from what I have said that we really only have two choices open to us if we want to end this war.

I can order an immediate, precipitate withdrawal of all Americans from Vietnam without regard to the effects of that action.

Or we can persist in our search for a just peace through a nego-

148

tiated settlement if possible, or through continued implementation of our plan for Vietnamization if necessary—a plan in which we will withdraw all our forces from Vietnam on a schedule in accordance with our program, as the South Vietnamese become strong enough to defend their own freedom.

I have chosen this second course.

It is not the easy way.

It is the right way.

It is a plan which will end the war and serve the cause of peace—not just in Vietnam but in the Pacific and in the world.

In speaking of the consequences of a precipitate withdrawal, I mentioned that our allies would lose confidence in America.

Far more dangerous, we would lose confidence in ourselves. Oh, the immediate reaction would be a sense of relief that our men were coming home. But as we saw the consequences of what we had done, inevitable remorse and divisive recrimination would scar our spirit as a people.

We have faced other crises in our history and have become stronger by rejecting the easy way out and taking the right way in meeting our challenges. Our greatness as a nation has been our capacity to do what had to be done when we knew our course was right.

Those Who Disagree

I recognize that some of my fellow citizens disagree with the plan for peace I have chosen. Honest and patriotic Americans have reached different conclusions as to how peace should be achieved.

In San Francisco a few weeks ago, I saw demonstrators carrying signs reading "Lose in Vietnam, bring the boys home."

Well, one of the strengths of our free society is that any American has a right to reach that conclusion and to advocate that point of view. But as President of the United States, I would be untrue to my oath of office if I allowed the policy of this Nation to be dictated by the minority who hold that point of view and who try to impose it on the Nation by mounting demonstrations in the street.

For almost 200 years, the policy of this Nation has been made under our Constitution by those leaders in the Congress and the White House elected by all of the people. If a vocal minority, however fervent its cause, prevails over reason and the will of the majority, this Nation has no future as a free society. . . .

And so tonight—to you, the great silent majority of my fellow Americans—I ask for your support.

I pledged in my campaign for the Presidency to end the war in a way that we could win the peace. I have initiated a plan of action which will enable me to keep that pledge.

The more support I can have from the American people, the sooner that pledge can be redeemed; for the more divided we are at home, the less likely the enemy is to negotiate at Paris.

Let us be united for peace. Let us also be united against defeat. Because let us understand: North Vietnam cannot defeat or humiliate the United States. Only Americans can do that.

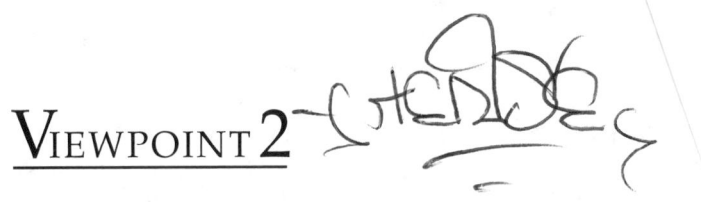

VIEWPOINT 2

"The policy of Vietnamization is a cruel hoax designed to screen from the American people the bankruptcy of a needless military involvement in the affairs of the Vietnamese people."

Vietnamization Is a Cruel Hoax

George S. McGovern (b. 1922)

George S. McGovern, the 1972 Democratic nominee for president, was one of the leading congressional critics of the Vietnam War. A bomber pilot during World War II, McGovern represented South Dakota in the U.S. Senate from 1962 to 1980.

The following viewpoint is excerpted from a statement made by McGovern before the Senate Committee on Foreign Relations on February 4, 1970, in support of a resolution calling for the withdrawal of all U.S. forces from Vietnam. In the statement, McGovern criticizes the "Vietnamization" policy of the administration of President Richard M. Nixon, in which U.S. troops were to be gradually replaced with South Vietnamese forces. McGovern argues that Vietnamization is an immoral and self-defeating policy that leaves the United States tied to what he calls the corrupt, "weak puppet regime" of South Vietnam. McGovern's advocacy of withdrawal from Vietnam was a central element of his campaign in the 1972 presidential election, which he lost to Nixon by a wide margin.

Excerpted from George S. McGovern, statement before the U.S. Senate Committee on Foreign Relations, February 4, 1970.

Mr. Chairman [of the Senate Committee on Foreign Relations], and members of the committee, the resolution that I have submitted with the cosponsorship of Senators [Frank] Church, [Alan] Cranston, [Charles] Goodell, [Harold] Hughes, [Eugene] McCarthy, [Frank] Moss, [Gaylord] Nelson, [Abraham] Ribicoff, and [Stephen] Young of Ohio calls for the withdrawal from Vietnam of all U.S. forces, the pace to be limited only by these three considerations: the safety of our troops during the withdrawal process, the mutual release of prisoners of war, and arrangements for asylum in friendly countries for any Vietnamese who might feel endangered by our disengagement. (I have recently been advised by the Department of Defense that the 484,000 men we now have in Vietnam could be transported to the United States at a total cost of $144,519,621.)

This process of orderly withdrawal could be completed, I believe, in less than a year's time.

Such a policy of purposeful disengagement is the only appropriate response to the blunt truth that there will be no resolution of the war so long as we cling to the [South Vietnam] Thieu-Ky regime. That government has no dependable political base other than the American military presence and it will never be accepted either by its challengers in South Vietnam or in Hanoi.

We can continue to pour our blood and substance into a never-ending effort to support the Saigon hierarchy or we can have peace, but we cannot have both General [Nguyen Van] Thieu and an end to the war.

Barrier to Peace and Healing

Our continued military embrace of the Saigon regime is the major barrier, both to peace in Southeast Asia and to the healing of our society. It assures that the South Vietnamese generals will take no action to build a truly representative government which can either compete with the NLF [National Liberation Front] or negotiate a settlement of the war. It deadlocks the Paris negotiations and prevents the scheduling of serious discussions on the release and exchange of prisoners of war. It diverts our energies from critical domestic needs. It sends young Americans to be maimed or killed in a war that we cannot win and that will not end so long as our forces are there in support of General Thieu.

I have long believed that there can be no settlement of the Vietnam struggle until some kind of provisional coalition government assumes control in Saigon. But this is precisely what General Thieu will never consider. After the Midway conference in June 1969 he said, "I solemnly declare that there will be no coalition government, no peace cabinet, no transitional government, not even a reconciliatory government."

Although President Nixon has placed General Thieu as one of the two or three greatest statesmen of our age, Thieu has brushed off the suggestion that he broaden his government and has denounced those who advocate or suggest a negotiated peace as pro-Communist racketeers and traitors. A coalition government means death, he has said.

Prescription for Endless War

Mr. Chairman, let us not delude ourselves. This is a clear prescription for an endless war, and changing its name to Vietnamization still leaves us tied to a regime that cannot successfully wage war or make peace.

Nixon and Vietnam

In the January 1969 issue of Harper's Magazine, *noted Vietnam journalist David Halberstam argues that newly elected president Richard M. Nixon has the opportunity to withdraw from "Johnson's war" in Vietnam.*

Mr. Nixon will enter the White House enjoying the benefit of the doubt both from those who voted for him and those who did not. He knows the nation is tired of the war, and if he has as keen a political sense as his friends think, he must know by now that the war is unwinnable. He will be able to handle, should he seek peace, the one faction of Congress which partially supports the war, the Republicans. Most important, he is freed from past decisions and past mistakes; indeed, he can do what no one in official Washington has been able to do in the past—he can actually say that the war was a mistake and a miscalculation. The country will believe him.

He will have that chance. Perhaps one chance, and it will come and go very quickly, for Vietnam is not just a quagmire, it is a tar-baby as well. It will not be easy for President Nixon. The North Vietnamese will not be particularly generous or flexible; they have come a long way and fought a long time for this, and one senses they are perfectly willing and content to go a longer way and wait a longer time for the settlement they demand. Even a dovish President would probably be surprised by the stiffness of their terms. Yet President Nixon, because *he* can be flexible, can settle at terms that Lyndon Johnson never could. We had committed 500,000 men and $30 billion a year and about two-thirds of Lyndon Johnson's ego to Vietnam—the last was the most difficult to extricate. Nixon's chance will come perhaps in the first four months, and if he fails, then his speeches will have to justify the war, and the failure to end the war, and soon it will no longer be Johnson's war, it will be Nixon's.

When administration officials expressed the view that American combat forces might be out of Vietnam by the end of 1970, General Thieu called a press conference and insisted that this was an "impossible and impractical goal" and that instead withdrawal "will take many years."

And yet there is wide currency to the view that America's course in Southeast Asia is no longer an issue, that the policy of Vietnamization promises an early end of hostilities. That is a false hope emphatically contradicted not only by our ally in Saigon but by the tragic lessons of the past decade.

As I understand the proposal, Vietnamization directs the withdrawal of American troops only as the Saigon armed forces demonstrate their ability to take over the war. Yet a preponderance of evidence indicates that the Vietnamese people do not feel the Saigon regime is worth fighting for. Without local support, "Vietnamization" becomes a plan for the permanent deployment of American combat troops, and not a strategy for disengagement. The President has created a fourth branch of the American Government by giving Saigon a veto over American foreign policy.

If we follow our present policy in Vietnam, there will still be an American army, in my opinion, of 250,000 or 300,000 men in Southeast Asia 15 or 20 years hence or perhaps indefinitely. Meanwhile American firepower and bombardment will have killed more tens of thousands of Vietnamese who want nothing other than an end of the war. All this to save a corrupt, unrepresentative regime in Saigon.

Any military escalation by Hanoi or the Vietcong would pose a challenge to American forces which would require heavier American military action and, therefore, heavier American casualties, or we would be faced with the possibility of a costly, forced withdrawal.

False Premises for Vietnamization

The Vietnamization policy is based on the same false premises which have doomed to failure our previous military efforts in Vietnam. It assumes that the Thieu-Ky regime in Saigon stands for freedom and a popularly backed regime. Actually, the Saigon regime is an oppressive dictatorship which jails its critics and blocks the development of a broadly based government. Last June 20, the Saigon minister for liaison for parliament, Von Huu Thu, confirmed that 34,540 political prisoners were being held and that many of those people were non-Communists who were guilty of nothing more than advocating a neutral peaceful future for their country. In proportion to population the political prisoners held by Saigon would be the equivalent of a half million political prisoners in the United States.

The Thieu-Ky regime is no closer to American ideals than its challenger, the National Liberation Front. Indeed self-determination and independence are probably far stronger among the Vietnamese guerrillas and their supporters than within the Saigon Government camp.

I have never felt that American interest and ideals were represented by the Saigon generals or their corrupt predecessors. We should cease our embrace of this regime now and cease telling the American people that it stands for freedom.

I should like to make clear that I am opposed to both the principle and the practice of the policy of Vietnamization. I am opposed to the policy, whether it works by the standard of its proponents or does not work. I oppose as immoral and self-defeating a policy which gives either American arms or American blood to perpetuate a corrupt and unrepresentative foreign regime. It is not in the interests of either the American or the Vietnamese people to maintain such a government.

I find it morally and politically repugnant for us to create a client group of Vietnamese generals in Saigon and then give them murderous military technology to turn against their own people.

Vietnamization is basically an effort to tranquilize the conscience of the American people while our Government wages a cruel and needless war by proxy.

An enlightened American foreign policy would cease trying to dictate the outcome of an essentially local struggle involving various groups of Vietnamese. If we are concerned about a future threat to Southeast Asia from China, let us have the common sense to recognize that a strong independent regime even though organized by the National Liberation Front and Hanoi would provide a more dependable barrier to Chinese imperialism than the weak puppet regime we have kept in power at the cost of 40,000 American lives and hundreds of thousands of Vietnamese lives.

A Cruel Hoax

Even if we could remove most of our forces from Vietnam, how could we justify before God and man the use of our massive firepower to continue a slaughter that neither serves our interests nor the interests of the Vietnamese.

The policy of Vietnamization is a cruel hoax designed to screen from the American people the bankruptcy of a needless military involvement in the affairs of the Vietnamese people. Instead of Vietnamizing the war let us encourage the Vietnamization of the government in South Vietnam. We can do that by removing the embrace that now prevents other political groups from assuming a leadership role in Saigon, groups that are capable of expressing the desire for peace of the Vietnamese people.

"We take this action not for the purpose of expanding the war into Cambodia but for the purpose of ending the war in Vietnam and winning the just peace we all desire."

Sending American Troops to Cambodia Is Necessary

Richard M. Nixon (1913–1994)

One of the most controversial acts undertaken by Richard M. Nixon during his presidency was his decision to send twenty thousand American and forty thousand South Vietnamese troops into Cambodia, a neighboring and officially neutral country, in April 1970. The military action had great repercussions for both the United States and Cambodia. The following viewpoint is excerpted from Nixon's televised address on April 30, 1970, explaining the reasons for his decision.

A major objective of the military action, Nixon argues, is to destroy communist bases in Cambodia. Although officially neutral, for some time Cambodia's leader, Prince Norodom Sihanouk, had allowed Vietcong and North Vietnamese forces to use regions of his country as staging areas and sanctuaries. In response, the United States had been secretly bombing Cambodian border areas since 1969; some U.S. military officers advocated direct military attacks on Cambodian areas. In March 1970 the political situation in Cambodia became further destabilized when Sihanouk was deposed by a pro-American regime led by Lon Nol. North Vietnam resisted the Lon Nol government's efforts to drive its forces out, and increased its assistance to Cambodia's own Communist revolutionaries, the Khmer Rouge.

Excerpted from Richard M. Nixon, television speech, April 3, 1970.

In his address, Nixon justifies the attack on Cambodia as being necessary to protect American soldiers in Vietnam and to strengthen the military position of South Vietnam. He also stresses the importance of avoiding the humiliation that would result from failure in Vietnam. American soldiers withdrew from Cambodia in June 1970.

Ten days ago, in my report to the Nation on Vietnam, I announced a decision to withdraw an additional one hundred and fifty thousand American troops over the next year. I said then I was making that decision despite our concern over increased enemy activity in Laos, in Cambodia, and in South Vietnam.

At that time, I warned that if I concluded that increased enemy activity in any of these areas endangered the lives of Americans remaining in Vietnam, I would not hesitate to take strong and effective measures to deal with that situation.

Despite that warning, North Vietnam has increased its military aggression in all three areas—particularly in Cambodia.

After full consultation with the National Security Council, Ambassador [Ellsworth] Bunker, General [Creighton] Abrams and my other advisers, I have concluded that the actions of the enemy in the last ten days clearly endanger the lives of Americans who are in Vietnam now and would constitute an unacceptable risk to those who will be there after our withdrawal of 150,000.

To protect our men who are in Vietnam and to guarantee the continued success of our withdrawal and Vietnamization programs, I have concluded the time has come for action.

Tonight, I shall describe the actions of the enemy, the actions I have ordered to deal with that situation, and the reasons for my decision.

Cambodia, a small country of seven million people has been a neutral nation since the Geneva Agreement of 1954—an agreement signed by the Government of North Vietnam.

American policy since then has been to scrupulously respect the neutrality of the Cambodian people. We have maintained a skeleton diplomatic mission of fewer than fifteen in Cambodia's capital since last August. For the previous four years—from 1965–1969, we did not have any diplomatic mission whatever. For the past five years, we have provided no military assistance and no economic assistance whatever to Cambodia.

North Vietnam, however, has not respected that neutrality.

For the past five years . . . North Vietnam has occupied military sanctuaries all along the Cambodian frontier with South Vietnam. Some of these extend up to 20 miles into Cambodia. They are used for hit-and-run attacks on American and South Vietnamese forces in South Vietnam.

These Communist occupied territories contain major base camps, training sites, logistics facilities, weapons and ammunition factories, air strips and prisoner of war compounds.

For five years, neither the United States nor South Vietnam moved against those enemy sanctuaries because we did not wish to violate the territory of a neutral nation. Even after the Vietnamese Communists began to expand these sanctuaries four weeks ago, we counselled patience to our South Vietnamese allies and imposed restraints on our commanders.

An Opportunity

On April 22, 1970, General William C. Westmoreland, then acting chairman of the Joint Chiefs of Staff, sent a memo to his Asian commanders discussing the possibility of direct U.S. attacks on border areas in Cambodia.

As you are certainly aware, there is highest level concern here with respect to the situation in Cambodia. . . .

Considerations are continuing as to how best to respond to this situation in a timely manner. As you know, limited US materiel support to the Cambodian Government has begun; however, we are of the view that this will have only minor impact on the current momentum of the VC/NVA [Vietcong/North Vietnamese Army]. Further, we believe that a more direct approach through attack of enemy support areas along the South Vietnam/Cambodian border would probably have much greater effect on the enemy in the near term. With the enemy over-extended, he presents us with opportunities that we should not let slip by. Further, the threat to Phnom Penh and the present concern of higher authority may be conducive to relaxation of some of the current constraints under which we are operating. If this happens we should be prepared to take advantage of the opportunity.

In contrast to our policy, the enemy in the past two weeks has stepped up his guerrilla actions and he is concentrating his main forces in the sanctuaries where they are building up to launch massive attacks on our forces and those of South Vietnam.

North Vietnam in the last two weeks has stripped away all pretense of respecting the sovereignty or neutrality of Cambodia. Thousands of their soldiers are invading the country from the sanctuaries; they are encircling the Capital of Phnom Penh. Cambodia has sent out a call to the United States and a number of other nations for assistance.

If this effort succeeds, Cambodia would become a vast enemy staging area and springboard for attacks on South Vietnam along 600 miles of frontier—and a refuge where enemy troops could return from combat without fear of retaliation.

North Vietnamese men and supplies could then be poured into that country jeopardizing not only the lives of our own men but the people of South Vietnam as well.

Confronted with this situation, we have three options.

First, we can do nothing. The ultimate result of that course of action is clear. Unless we indulge in wishful thinking, the Americans remaining in Vietnam after our next withdrawal would be gravely threatened.

Our second option is to provide massive military assistance to Cambodia. Unfortunately, while we deeply sympathize with the plight of seven million Cambodians whose country is being invaded, massive amounts of military assistance could not be rapidly and effectively utilized by the small Cambodian Army against the immediate threat. With other nations, we shall do our best to provide the small arms and other equipment which the Cambodian Army needs and can use now for its defense. The aid we will provide will be limited to the purpose of enabling Cambodia to defend its neutrality—not for the purpose of making it an active belligerent on one side or the other.

Our third choice is to go to the heart of the trouble. That means cleaning out major North Vietnamese and Viet Cong occupied sanctuaries which serve as bases for attacks on both Cambodia and American and South Vietnamese forces in South Vietnam. Some of these are as close to Saigon as Baltimore is to Washington.

This is my decision:

In cooperation with the armed forces of South Vietnam, attacks are being launched this week to clean out major enemy sanctuaries on the Cambodian-Vietnam border.

A major responsibility for the ground operations is being assumed by South Vietnamese forces. For example, the attacks in several areas including the Parrot's Beak are exclusively South Vietnamese ground operations under South Vietnamese command with the United States providing air and logistical support.

There is one area, however, where I have concluded that a combined American and South Vietnamese operation is necessary. Tonight, American and South Vietnamese units will attack the headquarters for the entire Communist military operation in South Vietnam. This key control center has been occupied by the North Vietnamese and Viet Cong for years in blatant violation of Cambodia's neutrality.

This is not an invasion of Cambodia. The areas in which these attacks will be launched are completely occupied and controlled by North Vietnamese forces. Our purpose is not to occupy the areas. Once enemy forces are driven out of these sanctuaries and their military supplies destroyed, we will withdraw.

These actions are in no way directed at the security interests of any nation. Any government that chooses to use these actions as a pretext for harming relations with the United States will be doing so on its own responsibility and at its own initiative and we will draw the appropriate conclusions.

A majority of the American people are for the withdrawal of our forces from Vietnam. The action I have taken tonight is indispensable for the continuing success of that withdrawal program.

A majority of the American people want to end this war rather than have it drag on interminably. The action I take tonight will serve that purpose.

A majority of the American people want to keep the casualties of our brave men in Vietnam at an absolute minimum. The action I take tonight is essential if we are to accomplish that goal.

We take this action not for the purpose of expanding the war into Cambodia but for the purpose of ending the war in Vietnam and winning the just peace we all desire. We have made and will continue to make every possible effort to end this war through negotiation at the conference table rather than through more fighting on the battlefield. . . .

This action puts the leaders of North Vietnam on notice that we will be patient in working for peace, we will be conciliatory at the conference table, but, we will not be humiliated. We will not be defeated. We will not allow American men by the thousands to be killed by an enemy from privileged sanctuaries.

The time came long ago to end this war through peaceful negotiations. We stand ready for those negotiations. We have made major efforts, many of which must remain secret. All the offers and approaches made previously remain on the conference table whenever Hanoi is ready to negotiate seriously.

But if the enemy response to our most conciliatory offers for peaceful negotiation continues to be to increase its attacks and humiliate and defeat us we shall react accordingly.

We live in an age of anarchy both abroad and at home. We see mindless attacks on all the great institutions which have been created by free civilizations in the last five hundred years. Here in the United States, great universities are being systematically destroyed. Small nations all over the world find themselves under attack from within and from without.

If when the chips are down the U.S. acts like a pitiful hapless giant, the forces of totalitarianism and anarchy will threaten free nations and free institutions throughout the world.

It is not our power but our will and character that is being tested tonight. The question all Americans must ask and answer tonight is this: Does the richest and strongest nation in the history of the world have the character to meet a direct challenge by a group which rejects every effort to win a just peace, ignores our warning, tramples on solemn agreements, violates the neutrality of an unarmed people, and uses our prisoners as hostages?

If we failed to meet this challenge all other nations will be on notice that despite its overwhelming power the United States, when a real crisis comes, will be found wanting.

VIEWPOINT 4

"The American invasion of Cambodia . . . was not a defensive response to a new threat. It was a ruthless, offensive act."

Sending American Troops to Cambodia Is Immoral

Commonweal

President Richard M. Nixon's decision in April 1970 to send U.S. troops into Cambodia created a storm of controversy in the United States. Critics accused the president of broadening the war, of exceeding the limits of his powers by acting without congressional authorization, and of disregarding the wishes of the American people to end, not expand, the war. An estimated four million students and faculty went on strike—the largest action of its kind in U.S. history. The National Guard was called out to maintain order in sixteen states because of the intensity and size of protests on college campuses; it was during one such protest that four students at Kent State University in Ohio were shot and killed by National Guard troops.

The following viewpoint is taken from an editorial in *Commonweal*, a biweekly Roman Catholic publication, in which the editors criticize the Cambodian invasion and America's subsequent bombing campaign against North Vietnam. They argue that the invasion reveals the flaws of Nixon's Vietnamization plan of withdrawing U.S. troops while still holding out for victory in Vietnam. Even a successful operation, they argue, will leave America embroiled in civil war in Cambodia in addition to Vietnam and will not place the United States any closer to a desirable outcome in Indochina.

From "Cold-Blooded Aggression," *Commonweal*, May 15, 1970. Reprinted by permission of *Commonweal*.

The American invasion of Cambodia, followed by resumption of bombing over North Vietnam, was not a defensive response to a new threat. It was a ruthless, offensive act, extending and intensifying the war. It cannot be considered a "blunder." It is the rationality and not the irrationality of this act which makes it ultimately so shocking. The land invasion of Cambodia and the air invasion of North Vietnam follow as logically from the twisted premises of our nation's leaders as did the [1968 Soviet] invasion of Czechoslovakia from the twisted premises of the Kremlin.

The North Vietnamese and Vietcong have occupied sanctuaries in Cambodia for some time. It is entirely hypocritical for a nation which crosses the ocean from its own sanctuary, hires mercenaries from other lands, and sends B-52s from Guam and Thailand to declare that the Cambodian sanctuaries are somehow "against the rules." That these sanctuaries created a problem for the Administration's scheme of Vietnamization cannot be denied. Critics have always said so; only the Administration pretended otherwise. The problem was not altered fundamentally by the overthrow of Prince Sihanouk. The right-wing, pro-American character of the new [Lon Nol] regime increased the danger of a Communist challenge to Phnom Penh; but Sihanouk, too, was faced with a long-run threat from "red Khmer" guerrillas. The new Cambodian regime threatened to cut off rebel Vietnamese supplies from the port of Sihanoukville; the Vietnamese struck back. Most observers agreed that the Communists were mainly concerned with maintaining rather than expanding their position.

The recent events in Cambodia did not force the President's hand. Instead, they presented him with an opportunity for an action long urged by the military and no doubt long planned. The Cambodian turmoil, like the Gulf of Tonkin affair before it, was only a fig-leaf. If the President's hand was forced by anything, it was the hollowness of a Vietnamization scheme, which has always been linked with military victory, in one form or another.

Without provocation, the United States has expanded the war. Several reasons have been suggested for this action; and in various combinations in the minds of various decision-makers, they all probably played a part. First, here was a chance to go for the jugular, the jugular being equated with the jungle "control center" of the enemy. Second, here was compensation for generals, in exchange for the very gradual withdrawal of U.S troops. Third, here was an opportunity to restore "credibility." Each reason strikes an ominous note. The first reflects the American belief in technology as the key to the Vietnamese conflict: knock out the enemy's switchboard and he'll fold. The second illustrates the

163

hold of the military on U.S. policy. The third fosters the kind of "credibility" which simply means that Moscow and Peking better believe Washington is apt to do anything, the kind of credibility a dangerous animal enjoys: you may give it a wide margin, but you don't strike bargains with it, and in the end you want to do away with the menace once and for all.

John Fischetti in the Chicago Daily News, 1970.

"I Never Did Say How, but I Told You I'd Get You Out of Vietnam."

Like the Soviet invasion of Czechoslovakia, the U.S. attack was a daring blow. The Administration has evidently surmised that the Soviet-Chinese dispute makes any solid response from those quarters unlikely. Certain signs, like Soviet Ambassador Malik's call for a new Geneva conference, although later withdrawn, may have been read as a green light from Moscow. China appears in no position to risk further involvement in its "rear." A daring blow, then—in the sense of getting away with it. Maybe even a successful operation militarily. We shall see. But to what end? We will kill more civilians, and perhaps some of the enemy. We will destroy villages. We may find a "central control" and destroy caches of weapons and ammunition. We will add more casualties onto the long, sad lists at home. And then will the U.S. troops turn around, head into Vietnam and start withdrawing? The *Times* quotes military planners as saying that a successful sweep would force the Vietcong and North Vietnamese to take "up to a year" to become a threat again in the southern half of South Vietnam. And after the year? When American forces will supposedly be 150,000 men weaker, will the remaining troops be less endangered than now? Will we then make another sweep? Will we bomb North Vietnam again? Or shall we bomb Cambodia con-

Questioning Nixon Administration Claims

During the debate over President Richard M. Nixon's controversial decision to move U.S. forces into Cambodia, five U.S. senators asked George McT. Kahin, a political science professor and Southeast Asia specialist at Cornell University, to respond to Nixon's arguments. The passages below are excerpts from Kahin's Cambodia: The Administration's Version and the Historical Record, *published in 1970.*

Referring to Vietnamese communist sanctuaries in Cambodia, President Nixon stated on April 30: "For five years neither the U.S. nor South Vietnam moved against those enemy sanctuaries because we did not wish to violate the territory of a neutral nation."

The Historical Record

In July 1965 the International Control Commission (I.C.C.) reported on evidence of border crossings into Cambodia by South Vietnamese forces, stating that there were 375 such incidents in 1964 and 385 in the first five months of 1965 alone. The commission unanimously concluded that "None of those incidents were provoked by the Royal Government of Cambodia." From that time on there were repeated reports of border incursions and air attacks against border areas inside Cambodia chiefly by South Vietnamese but also by American forces. . . .

On January 22, 1968, the U.S. acknowledged that a U.S.-South Vietnamese patrol had made a limited intrusion into Cambodia following fire from Vietnamese communist units on the Cambodian side. (NYT [*New York Times*] January 23, 1968)

In April 1969, U.S. air and artillery attacks were launched against communist bases inside Cambodia. (NYT April 26, 1969)

On May 8, 1969, U.S. B-52 bombers raided communist supply dumps and camps within Cambodia. (NYT May 9, 1969)

October–December, 1969, Sihanouk protested continuing U.S. bombing of Cambodian border areas. . . .

If, as the Administration has repeatedly stated, the Vietnamization program was designed to reduce American commitments in Southeast Asia and to facilitate the achievement of a negotiated settlement of the war, the Cambodian adventure is impossible to justify. By enlarging the area of conflict and the scope of American commitments and by increasing the number of disputing parties, it adds enormously to the length and complexity of any agenda for negotiations. With the U.S. and the Vietnamese now enmeshed in a Cambodian civil war a virtually insoluble Cambodian problem is added to the already intractable Vietnamese problem. It is no longer enough to settle the war in Vietnam and Laos; we are assuming a responsibility for settling a Cambodian war as well.

stantly during the coming year? Will Saigon forces stay in Cambodia—a throwback to the days when the French employed Vietnamese to supervise the Cambodian and Laotian parts of their Indochinese empire? The American offensive has proven to Hanoi the necessity of launching a revolutionary movement in Cambodia, and Sihanouk is on hand to lend ballast. Will we prop up Lon Nol and revolutionarily develop and pacify and napalm in Cambodia too?

By striking at the sanctuaries, said Mr. Nixon, the U.S. is striking at "the heart of the trouble." But why isn't "the heart of the trouble" in North Vietnam with its one-million-man army? With his air strikes, Secretary [of Defense Melvin] Laird more or less admitted as much. Of course, the heart of the trouble could as well be China, since North Vietnam is surely no threat to—as the President puts it—"the Pacific." And in the days when we bolstered French colonialism and Dean Rusk knew for a fact that Peking was only Moscow's cat's paw, then the heart of the trouble was Russia. The chill so many Americans felt at hearing Mr. Nixon's announcement was partly due to what they sensed behind this heart-of-the-trouble argument—the old rationale for preventive war, eerily suggested in the Orwellian term devised to cover our aggression against North Vietnam: "protective reaction."

Southeast Asia is filled with too many people who are determined to rule and be ruled in ways Washington does not approve, and too few equally determined to follow the American prescription The former refuse to play by the rules we righteously establish so that they can lose the game. The latter persist in looking like thieves, tyrants and massacrers. Our choice is to crush the former and prop up the latter, or to limit the losses and leave. The "heart of the problem" is in the United States of America. That is the last place our leaders will look.

Viewpoint 5

"The means used by the United States in this war have long since passed the point when they could be justified by the end."

The Christmas Bombing of Hanoi Was Indefensible

Anthony Lewis (b. 1927)

As the United States steadily withdrew troops from Vietnam under President Richard M. Nixon's plan of Vietnamization, the U.S. military relied on air power to support South Vietnam and to strengthen America's position in peace negotiations in Paris, France. When North Vietnam launched a large invasion of South Vietnam in April 1972, the United States, rather than commit ground troops, launched massive and sustained bombing attacks against North Vietnam and mined Haiphong Harbor to prevent supplies from the Soviet Union from reaching North Vietnam. The bombing campaign lasted until October 23, 1972, when North Vietnam and the United States, in secret talks, seemed on the verge of reaching a peace agreement. Negotiations foundered after the South Vietnamese government voiced objections, however, and Nixon ordered another campaign of bombing raids in Hanoi in December 1972. The "Christmas bombing," as it came to be known, was the most intensive air attack of the war and was sharply criticized by many in America and the rest of the world.

The following viewpoint is taken from a column by Anthony Lewis, a newspaper columnist for the *New York Times* who was one of the most prominent critics of the American war effort in

Vietnam. In the column, first published on December 23, 1972, a few days after the Christmas bombing was halted when North Vietnam agreed to resume peace talks, Lewis decries the bombing of North Vietnam as a "crime against humanity" that cannot be tactically or morally justified.

When the Lord told Abraham that He was going to destroy Sodom for its sins, as it is said in Genesis, Chapter 18, Abraham asked, "Wilt thou also destroy the righteous with the wicked?" The Lord agreed that if there were 10 righteous men in Sodom, "then I will spare all the place for their sakes." But there were not 10.

In that episode the Bible gave early expression to an idea fundamental to Western civilization: the worth of the individual. The story teaches also that the individual has an inescapable moral responsibility to his society, for on him may depend the salvation of all.

One of the terrible aspects of the massive recent American bombing campaign against North Vietnam has been the inertness of the response in many quarters. Worst of all has been the failure of a single person in the United States government to break with a policy that many must know history will judge a crime against humanity.

The Purpose of Bombing Is Terror

To send B-52s against populous areas such as Haiphong or Hanoi could have only one purpose: terror. It was the response of a man so overwhelmed by his sense of inadequacy and frustration that he had to strike out, punish, destroy.

An English newspaper that has taken a moderate line on the war, the *Guardian*, asked this week: "Does Mr. Nixon want to go down in history as one of the most murderous and bloodthirsty of American presidents?" But it no longer matters what he wants. The facts assure that he will be so recorded.

The American imagination has evidently ceased to be stirred by the facts of bombing. When people have not lived under bombs, as few Americans have, they perhaps cannot imagine the continuous fear. They may not understand that bombs dropped in cities and villages kill human beings indiscriminately, the innocent with the wicked. They do not see themselves caught even hundreds of yards from the center of a B-52 raid, the concussion crushing their lungs or spewing out their insides.

The bombing that most notably evoked the sympathy of Ameri-

The caption to this 1970 Paul Conrad cartoon read: "It became necessary to destroy (a) South Vietnam, (b) Laos, (c) Cambodia, (d) Thailand, (e) all of the above—to save Southeast Asia."

cans was the Nazi Blitz on Britain in World War II. How we admired the pluck of the British under those terrible raids.

In the nearly six years of World War II, less than 80,000 tons of bombs fell on the British Isles. In November alone, when American bombing was restricted because of the peace talks, US planes dropped 100,000 tons on Indochina. The total through the Johnson and Nixon administrations is now more than 7 million tons.

Whatever the cause, whatever the rights or wrongs of the parties in Vietnam, the means used by the United States in this war have long since passed the point when they could be justified by the end. Our war has failed the old and essential principle of proportionality, the moral doctrine that, in fighting, we must not do worse than the evil we oppose.

But what is the cause? It is no longer even arguably to "contain China," or roll back communism, or make the peasants of Vietnam free. It is only, Henry Kissinger says, to make sure the American departure is "honorable." For that we have caused, are causing and presumably will continue to cause the most terrible destruction in the history of man.

Human Indifference

Human indifference in the face of cruelty to others is hardly a new phenomenon. Supposedly civilized men and women said nothing while Hitler humiliated, tortured and eventually mur-

dered millions of Jews. Freud made us see that there is an inerad-
icable violence in us all.

Still, it does seem remarkable that no one in the United States
government has now made himself a witness against what his
country is doing. No members of the White House staff, no one in
the Pentagon, no Air Force pilot. Not ten, not five, not one.

Public men always tell themselves that they do more good trying to moderate an evil policy from the inside, but at some point
that self-deception has to stop. They say also that one man cannot
make a difference. That may be true, but it may not; and in any
case it does not relieve anyone from the responsibility of trying.
That is what we learn from the story of Abraham and Sodom.

"It was decided to try to bring home, really to both Vietnamese parties, that the continuation of the war had its price."

The Christmas Bombing of Hanoi Was Justified

Henry A. Kissinger (b. 1923)

On December 18, 1972, the United States launched a massive bombing attack on Hanoi in response to stalled peace negotiations. The "Christmas bombing" created much shock and anger in the United States and was denounced as an immoral terrorist act against the North Vietnamese civilian population. (Civilian casualties of the twelve-day campaign have been estimated at about fifteen hundred; the number was relatively low because American pilots took measures to minimize such casualties and the North Vietnamese government had evacuated much of Hanoi and other areas prior to the bombing.) At that time neither President Richard M. Nixon nor members of his administration made any public defense or explanation of the December bombing campaign.

The following viewpoint on the Christmas bombing of Hanoi and other parts of North Vietnam is taken from an interview by television journalist Marvin Kalb with Henry A. Kissinger on February 1, 1973. As national security adviser to Nixon, Kissinger shaped foreign policy more than any other person save Nixon himself. Beginning in 1969, while public peace negotiations were being held in Paris between delegations representing the governments of North Vietnam, South Vietnam, the National Liberation Front (NLF) rebels in South Vietnam, and the United States, Kissinger engaged in secret talks with a series of North Vietnamese envoys, including Le Duc Tho. These talks eventually resulted in the Paris Peace Accords, signed by the four official negotiating parties on January 27, 1973. The accords called for the United States to withdraw all of its military forces and marked the end of American participation in the Vietnam War. In his interview with Kalb, Kissinger defends the December 1972 bombings as part of the effort to convince both North and South Vietnam of the desirability and necessity for a peace agreement.

KALB: Dr. Kissinger, let's move the clock back about one month, at a time when the United States was engaged in a very extensive bombing program in the Hanoi-Haiphong area. We've never heard any explanation about why that was really necessary. Could you give us your own feeling on that?

KISSINGER: The decision to resume bombing in the middle of December was perhaps the most painful, the most difficult and certainly the most lonely that the President has had to make since he is in—has been in office. It was very painful to do this at that particular season, when the expectation for peace had been so high, and only six weeks before his inauguration. It was very difficult to do it under circumstances when the outcome was not demonstrable. There were really three parts to it. One: should we resume bombing? Two: if we resume bombing, with what weapons? That involved the whole issue of the B-52. And three: should we talk to the American people?—which was really implied in your question: there's never been an explanation.

With respect to the first part—why did the President decide to resume bombing—we had come to the conclusion that the negotiations as they were then being conducted were not serious; that for whatever reason, the North Vietnamese at that point had come to the conclusion that protracting the negotiations was more in their interest than concluding them. It was not a case that we made certain demands that they rejected. It was a case that no sooner was one issue settled than three others emerged, and as soon as one approached a solution, yet others came to the forefront. At the same time, the more difficult Hanoi was, the more rigid Saigon grew, and we could see a prospect, therefore, where we would be caught between the two contending Vietnamese parties with no element introduced that would change their opinion, with a gradual degeneration of the private talks between Le Duc Tho and me into the same sort of propaganda that the public talks . . . had reached. And therefore it was decided to try to bring home, really to both Vietnamese parties, that the continuation of the war had its price. And it was not generally recognized that when we started the bombing again of North Vietnam, we also sent General [Alexander] Haig to Saigon to make very clear what—that this did not mean that we would fail to settle on the

Critics Were Wrong

In his 1982 book Why We Were in Vietnam, *writer Norman Podhoretz argues that critics of the December 1972 bombings of Hanoi and North Vietnam have been wrong. Civilian casualties were not as high as critics claimed, he writes, and the bombing did not scuttle peace negotiations.*

One thing about the bombing *is* certain, however: practically all the comment it elicited in the United States was wrong. . . . The casualties and civilian damage were amazingly light (about 1,500 killed, according to Hanoi's own figures, as against the 35,000 in Dresden and 84,000 in Tokyo during the World War II raids with which it was compared, and fewer than the North Vietnamese themselves had just killed by their artillery bombardment of An Loc). Yet Senator George McGovern in an interview on NBC called it "the most murderous aerial bombardment in the history of the world," "the most immoral action that this nation has ever committed in its national history," and "a policy of mass-murder that's being carried on in the name of the American people." Senator Harold Hughes concurred: "It is unbelievable savagery that we have unleashed on this holy season; the only thing I can compare it with is the savagery at Hiroshima and Nagasaki." Anthony Lewis of the *New York Times* added his note to this temperate chorus, characterizing the bombing not only as "a crime against humanity" but "the most terrible destruction in the history of man." An editorial in the *Washington Post* agreed: the bombing, it declared, was "the most savage and senseless act of war ever visited, over a scant ten days, by one sovereign people upon another."

In addition to being wrong about the destruction the bombing was causing and about the moral weight that could legitimately be assigned to it in comparison with such horrors as Auschwitz and Hiroshima even by those who considered it unjustified, the critics (although that seems too tame a word to describe the people who used such language as I have just quoted) were wrong in their predictions. McGovern said that the bombing had "destroyed any immediate hopes for peace." Senator Mike Mansfield declared: "I think that bombing will just put steel in their backbones and prolong the war." Senator Jacob Javits said: "The North Vietnamese have not been induced into a settlement, and there is nothing to indicate that our renewed air strikes are going to have that effect now." Yet whether or not the bombing caused the North Vietnamese to resume negotiations, it certainly did *not* have the effect these three senators, and most of the editorialists and columnists, so confidently asserted it would.

terms that we had defined as reasonable. So we really moved in both directions simultaneously.

Once the decision was made to resume bombing, we faced the fact that it was in the rainy season and that really the only plane that could act consistently was the B-52, which was an all-weather plane. The—You mentioned the Hanoi-Haiphong area. But major efforts were made to avoid residential areas, and the casualty figures which were released by the North Vietnamese of something like a thousand tend to support that many—that this was the case, because many of these casualties must have occurred in the target areas and not in civilian residential areas.

KALB: Yet a lot of the civilian areas were hit, apparently. There were pictures of that and—

KISSINGER: Well, you can never tell when a picture is made how vast the surrounding area of destruction is, but of course some civilian areas must have been hit. And I'm—I don't want to say that it was not a very painful thing to have to do.

Now, why did the President decide not to speak to the American people? The President can speak most effectively when he announces a new departure in policy and indicates what can be done to bring that particular departure to a conclusion. He could have done only two things in such a speech—which was considered. One is to explain why the negotiations had stalemated, and two, to explain under what circumstances he would end the bombing. The first would have broken the confidentiality of the negotiations, even more than was the case anyway through the exchanges that were going on publicly. And the second would have made the resumption of talks an issue of prestige and might have delayed it. And therefore the President decided that if this action succeeded, then the results would speak for themselves in terms of a settlement, and if a settlement was not reached, then he would have to give an accounting to American people—to the American people of all the actions that led to the continuing stalemate. Now, whatever the reason, once the Viet—once the talks were resumed a settlement was reached fairly rapidly. And I have—we have never made an assertion as to what produced it, but you asked why was the decision made to resume bombing, and this was the reasoning that led to it.

KALB: Dr. Kissinger, isn't the assumption that you're leaving with us that without that kind of heavy bombing the North Vietnamese would not have become serious—your term—and that therefore one could conclude that it was the bombing that brought the North Vietnamese into a serious frame of mind? I ask the question only because they've been bombed so repeatedly and for so many years and still stuck to their guns and their position. What was so unique about this?

KISSINGER: Well, that it came at the end of a long process—

KALB: Mm-hmm.

KISSINGER:—in which they too had suffered a great deal. But I don't think—at this moment, when I am preparing to go to Hanoi—it would serve any useful purpose for me to make any—to speculate about what caused them to make this decision. . . . And at this moment, I think, it is important to understand that the decision was not made lightly, that it was made in the interest of speeding the end of the war, and that now that the war has ended, I think, it is best to put the acrimony behind us.

CHAPTER 5

Protesters and Soldiers

Chapter Preface

For the United States, the Vietnam War consisted of two wars in one. One war was the military conflict in Vietnam, in which nearly three million Americans eventually participated and in which fifty-eight thousand lost their lives. The other war was the struggle within the United States over Vietnam. "Every American war, going back to the American Revolutionary War of 1776, has had some opposition among the civilian population," notes writer and political activist Sydney Lens in his book *Vietnam: A War on Two Fronts*.

> Sometimes the dissent was negligible, as in the Korean "police action" or World War II, sometimes it was active and vocal, as in the Mexican War of 1846. But opposition to the Vietnam War was so strong and sustained that it took on an unprecedented dimension, becoming known as The War at Home.

Although a small group of pacifists and others opposed the Vietnam War prior to 1965, most Americans either supported or were unaware of America's growing involvement in that conflict. As late as 1964 only 8 percent of poll respondents expressed opposition to U.S. policy in Vietnam. Over the next several years the increasing U.S. role in Vietnam was mirrored by growing public discontent. For example, in April 1965 Students for a Democratic Society (SDS) sponsored an antiwar demonstration in Washington, D.C.; the organizers were surprised by the unexpectedly large number of people (25,000) who participated. By 1967, a similar gathering in Washington, D.C., was attended by 250,000. Demonstrations nationwide in October and November of 1969 drew several million participants.

It is somewhat misleading to view the antiwar movement as a cohesive operation. People who opposed the Vietnam War often differed sharply with each other on tactics, rhetoric, and goals. Out of the many divisions within the antiwar movement, a general schism emerged between its liberal and radical wings. Liberals focused on stopping the war, which they believed was unnecessary and harmful to the United States. They did not aim to remake U.S. society and generally used peaceful and legal means of protesting the war. On the other hand, radicals saw the Vietnam War as emblematic of a fundamentally unjust and imperialist society that needed radical reconstruction. A minority of antiwar activists supported the cause of the Vietcong revolutionaries and spoke of the need for violent revolution in "Amerika" itself.

In his book about the Vietnam War, Lens writes that a key feature of the antiwar movement was "its decentralized nature. There was no formal leadership. Someone would get an idea and put it into practice; if it was a good idea, it caught on." Among other activities, participants in the antiwar movement attended teach-ins (academic gatherings at which students and faculty debated and questioned America's Vietnam policy), signed "voter pledges" promising to vote only for candidates who favored a cease-fire, refused to pay federal taxes, disrupted the production and transportation of napalm and other war materials, ran newspaper advertisements expressing opposition to the war, held vigils and formed picket lines outside draft board meetings, wrote letters to the press and to Congress, and, in a famous 1967 incident, held a mass exorcism of the Pentagon. The antiwar movement was inextricably linked with other social movements and ideas of the 1960s, especially the civil rights movement, with its philosophy of civil disobedience, and the youth counterculture, which questioned fundamental American values.

The "war at home," like the war in Vietnam, had its casualties. Antiwar demonstrators risked abuse and beatings from onlookers and police. Imitating Buddhist protesters in Vietnam, Norman Morrison and a few other activists took their own lives in self-immolation as a statement against the war. In 1970 four students were killed by National Guard soldiers during an antiwar rally at Kent State University; ten days later, during a demonstration at Jackson State College in Mississippi, state police fired into a dormitory, killing two students.

Reactions to those who actively protested against the Vietnam War varied widely. Former president Dwight D. Eisenhower wrote in 1968 that "their action is not honorable dissent. It is rebellion, and it verges on treason." Spiro T. Agnew, vice president of the United States from 1969 to 1973, made speeches around the country attacking antiwar protesters as "an effete corps of impudent snobs" and as "malcontents, radicals, incendiaries, and civil and uncivil disobedients." On the other hand, Senator J. William Fulbright, who became one of the leading critics of the Vietnam War, wrote admiringly of a "regenerative counterforce of protests from Americans who are willing to act in defense of the principles they were brought up to believe in."

The Vietnam War and the antiwar movement had special relevance for young men of the era. Those who received draft notices during the war were confronted with the unavoidable and intensely personal question of whether or not to support the war—whether to be a soldier or an active resister. Thousands of men resisted or evaded the draft by various means, including deliberately flouting the draft laws and standing for arrest, fleeing to Canada and other countries, and utilizing a variety of exemptions or deferments in the draft rules. It is impossible to measure the proportion of draft resisters who acted out of genuine religious and moral opposition to the Vietnam War (or all war) versus those who acted for reasons of self-preservation. However, it became clear over time that particular methods of evading the draft—such as student deferments and medical excuses—proved easier for members of the middle and upper classes. Therefore the draftees who fought in Vietnam were disproportionately lower class and members of minority groups.

Disagreements about the Vietnam War spread to the U.S. military itself. Many who fought in the Vietnam War had volunteered for patriotic reasons or because they strongly believed in the American cause in Vietnam. But a significant number of soldiers participated in antiwar activities, especially during the war's later years. Both discharged veterans and soldiers on active duty marched in protests and demonstrations. Organizations such as Vietnam Veterans Against the War worked to end U.S. involvement in Vietnam. Desertions from the military increased, and some enlisted and drafted soldiers refused orders sending them to Vietnam. News reports from Vietnam related a growing number of incidents of combat refusal (soldiers' refusal to obey orders that might get them killed in combat) and of "fraggings" (assassinations of officers considered excessively zealous by their subordinates).

The divisions found in the military in the later years of the Vietnam War reflected the disparities of opinion within the general American population and indicated how divisive the Vietnam War had become. The following viewpoints provide a sampling of opinions on the war in Vietnam and the "war at home."

VIEWPOINT 1

*"This proposed legislation to make it illegal to
knowingly destroy or mutilate a draft card is only one
step in bringing some legal control over those who
would destroy American freedom."*

Burning One's Draft Card Is a Cowardly and Despicable Act

William G. Bray (1903–1979)

During the Vietnam War the U.S. armed forces relied heavily on
military conscription to fill their ranks. Draft calls grew from
100,000 in 1964 to 400,000 in 1966. Men between the ages of eigh-
teen and twenty-six who received induction notices faced the decision of whether to obey, resist, or evade the draft. Some Americans applied for conscientious objector (CO) status on the basis of
their religious beliefs; they were sent to Vietnam as noncombat-
ants or did alternative service in social service agencies in the
United States or Vietnam. But there were many other ways to
avoid being drafted and sent to Vietnam. Some Americans enlisted in the navy or air force to avoid being drafted by the U.S.
Army. Some deferred their draft eligibility by remaining in college or in certain occupations. Others took steps to deliberately
fail physical examinations or fled to Canada or other countries. A
minority risked prison sentences by openly refusing to cooperate
with all aspects of military conscription.

Draft resistance thus was a major component of the antiwar
movement. At many protests during the Vietnam War it was
common to see young men publicly burning or destroying their
draft cards—the identification cards draft-eligible men were re-

William G. Bray, statement before the U.S. House of Representatives, *Congressional Record*,
89th Cong., 1st sess. (August 10, 1965).

quired to carry at all times. On August 10, 1965, L. Mendel Williams, a Democrat from South Carolina and chairman of the House Armed Services Committee, introduced a bill making the "willful destruction" of one's draft card a federal offense punishable by five years in jail. In the following viewpoint, William G. Bray, a Republican lawyer and veteran of World War II who represented Indiana in Congress from 1951 to 1975, expresses his support for this bill. He condemns draft resisters and antiwar activists and argues that their defiance of the nation's laws impairs the integrity and viability of the Selective Service System and threatens America as a whole.

The House of Representatives passed the bill by a vote of 393 to 1; it was passed by the Senate two days later and signed by President Lyndon B. Johnson. In 1968 the U.S. Supreme Court upheld the law's constitutionality over the objections of those who argued that it violated the First Amendment's right of free speech.

M̲r. Speaker [of the House], the bill that we have before us today is simple and easy to understand. H.R. 10306 is an amendment to our selective service law providing that it is illegal to knowingly mutilate or destroy a draft card. It is already illegal to alter, forge, or change such a card.

Contempt for America

The need of this legislation is clear. Beatniks and so-called "campus-cults" have been publicly burning their draft cards to demonstrate their contempt for the United States and our resistance to Communist takeovers. Such actions have been suggested and led by college professors—professors supported by taxpayers' money.

At Rutgers University, Prof. Eugene Genovese, who prides himself on being a Marxist, publicly said that he "welcomed a Communist Vietcong victory." The board of governors refused to dismiss him.

Just yesterday such a mob attacking the United States and praising the Vietcong attempted to march on the Capitol but were prevented by the police from forcibly moving into our Chambers. They were led by a Yale University professor. They were generally a filthy sleazy beatnik gang; but the question which they pose to America is quite serious.

These so-called "student" mobs at home and abroad make demands and threats; they hurl rocks and ink bottles at American buildings; they publicly mutilate or burn their draft cards; they

181

even desecrate the American flag. Chanting and screaming vile epithets, these mobs of so-called "students" and Communist "stooges" attempt to create fear and destroy self-confidence in our country and its citizens and to downgrade the United States in the eyes of the world.

Such organized "student" groups in the United States have sent congratulations and money to Ho Chi Minh and have made anonymous and insulting calls to families of our servicemen killed in Vietnam.

The protests of the antiwar movement inspired some counter-demonstrations. A "March for Victory" in Washington, D.C., on October 3, 1970, included prowar demonstrators who urged the United States to expand its war effort in Vietnam.

Wide World Photos

This proposed legislation to make it illegal to knowingly destroy or mutilate a draft card is only one step in bringing some legal control over those who would destroy American freedom. This legislation, if passed, will be of some assistance to our country if the officers and courts charged with the enforcement of the law will have the energy, courage, and guts to make use of it.

The growing disrespect for our law and institutions in America holds a real threat to our country and to our freedom. Just 5 short years ago no one would have believed that disrespect for our country could have grown to the proportions that it has today.

Disrespect for our American heritage and anti-American demonstrations are all a part of the cold war in some way directed by those who would destroy us. The Communist world is aware that it cannot destroy the effectiveness of the United States by the use of its economic and military strength, because we are far stronger in these fields than it is and we outdistance it more every year.

Then how is the Communist victory to be brought about? The Communists are planning to use the "Judas goats" to lead those who are free to defect from freedom. So-called "students" and Communist stooges here and abroad, by demonstrations of anti-American feeling, by belittling, and by vilification are to downgrade the United States in the eyes of the world and shake the confidence and faith of our citizens in our democratic way of life. They hope to attain victory over freedom by subversion within the United States and by erosion of our national pride and confidence in the greatness of America and our national heritage.

America's Greatness

One of America's greatest sources of strength in discouraging these demonstrations is to pause and consider the greatness of America—to appreciate what our country has done for the benefit of mankind. Let us have a rebirth of patriotism. Let us be proud, possessed not of an arrogant pride, but a humble pride in our greatness, in our heritage.

Aside from becoming the strongest country economically and militarily during the last quarter century, this country, without any desire to gain a square foot of territory, has been the principal force in overthrowing the armed might of Hitler and Japan. The strength of the United States saved both Europe and Asia from the despotic rule of tyrants. We asked nothing in return. We asked no gain for this victory brought about by American dollars, American production and American youth. The people of the United States have unselfishly contributed more to the feeding, care, welfare and rehabilitation of the world than has all of the rest of the world combined. All of this has been done without any thought of gain except the reward of the deed itself.

The United States, without hope of personal gain, blocked the Communist takeover of South Korea and today is assuming the major role of blocking Communist slavery in southeast Asia. Yet there are today those in America who are weak at heart, those of little faith in the greatness of America and freedom, those who are naive and refuse to face up to the realities of Communist aggression. There are those who in various degrees and for various reasons ask our Government to yield more and more to Communist aggression.

Subversion

Our Government, through fear of the public opinion at home and abroad of our enemies, is failing to adequately enforce our laws on subversion and anti-governmental attacks. That is exactly as our enemies have planned it. In the exercise of our great ideals of fairness and tolerance, we seem to forget that it is axiomatic that a government must protect its citizenry against illegal acts and against mob violence. When decent, productive people are forced to support and coddle criminals and other dregs and drones of society, chaos, degradation, and ruin are inevitable.

Tolerance ceases to be a virtue when it condones evil. Governmental tolerance ceases to be a virtue when it allows mob violence on the law-abiding members of its society—when it winks at unlawful disrespect to its institutions and the flag. This is true whether this tolerance is the result of apathy, a maudlin sympathy, or a fear of the opinions of enemies.

When the mob once learns that its actions will lead to granting of its demands and its actions are condoned, there is a multiplication both of its demonstrations, riots, and wanton destruction, and of its demands.

If these "revolutionaries" are permitted to deface and destroy their draft cards, our entire Selective Service System is dealt a serious blow.

Mr. Speaker, I strongly urge all my fellow Members to support this legislation.

VIEWPOINT 2

"To destroy one's draft card, to place one's conscience before the dictates of one's government, is in the highest tradition of human conduct."

Burning One's Draft Card Is a Courageous and Moral Act

Martin Jezer (b. 1940)

On April 15, 1967, as part of the Spring Mobilization, one of the largest antiwar protests up to that time, about 170 draft-eligible men publicly burned their draft cards at Sheep Meadow in Central Park, New York City. The mass burning was controversial both outside and within the antiwar movement; some antiwar leaders sought to prevent the burning because they thought it was too radical.

One of those who chose to protest the Vietnam War in this fashion was Martin (Marty) Jezer. He was then an editor of *WIN Peace & Freedom Through Nonviolent Action*, a magazine published by the Workshop in Nonviolence (WIN), part of the War Resisters League, a pacifist group. Jezer was one of the contributors to *We Won't Go: Personal Accounts of War Resisters*, a collection of writings that was published in 1968. In his account for that book, excerpted here, Jezer describes how he felt on April 15 and explains how he came to believe that such open resistance to American draft laws was necessary. Jezer defends his draft-card burning as a moral and conscientious act, arguing that only through such civil disobedience can the conflict in Vietnam be stopped.

Excerpted from Martin Jezer, "Sheep Meadow Graduation," in *We Won't Go: Personal Accounts of War Objectors*, edited by Alice Lynd. Copyright 1968 by Alice Lynd. Reprinted with permission.

Up until the night before April 15th, no one was sure how many people would burn their draft cards at the Mobilization; indeed, we were not at all sure whether the action would even take place. About 120 people had signed the pledge to burn their cards if 500 others did it at the same time, so the pledge was not binding. Moreover, the Spring Mobilization Committee had disowned the draft card burners and were pressuring them to postpone or cancel their plans. Many Mobilization leaders support civil disobedience, but they were afraid that a radical act like draft card burning would scare away many people new to the Movement.

At a meeting the night of April 14th, we decided to burn our cards in the Sheep Meadow at 11 A.M. despite the Mobilization's opposition. We also decided that 50 would be the minimum number of burners to make it an important political act. There was a tense moment when Bruce Dancis asked, "How many will burn their cards if 50 do it at the same time?" Hands shot up around the room. The count was 57. We were in business.

That night I hardly slept. I recalled how it was the night before my graduation from college. . . . That was a celebration of my ability to get good grades and to conform, intellectually, to the current catechism of uncritical Americanism. Although I was something of the campus radical, by contemporary standards I was just a good, harmless white liberal, impressed with and convinced of my own powerlessness, prepared to allow politicians, generals, and corporate managers to make decisions over my life. . . . Burning a draft card, I thought, would be a more meaningful graduation. I had finally begun to be educated, to see through the myths of the American propaganda machine.

The Act

The next morning we gathered on the rocks in the Sheep Meadow. Friends of ours, veterans, women, and pacifists, linked arms and attempted to clear space for us. There were no uniformed police in sight. Soon the press, FBI men, and all kinds of ill-mannered people began pushing, shoving, pressing through the protective circle. Confusion reigned; an orderly demonstration seemed impossible. So we began burning our cards. Someone held up an empty tin can of Maxwell House Coffee with flaming paraffin inside. We lit our cards with matches, cigarette lighters, and from the flames of each other's cards. It was a pretty sight, draft cards—burning. Gary Rader, from Illinois, materialized from out of the crowd and set his card aflame. It was a wonderfully courageous act. He's an Army Reservist and was wearing his "green beret" uniform. Photographers trampled us to get his picture. He seemed very happy; smiling, shaking hands with those near him. Then, to bring some order to the demonstration, we all sat down.

The photographers fell back, our protective circle was restored. We began singing freedom songs and chanting, "Resist! Resist!" and "Burn Draft Cards, Not People." People in the audience were applauding us, shouting encouragement. Then some guys began to come out of the audience with draft cards in hand. They burned them. Alone, in pairs, by threes they came. Each flaming draft card brought renewed cheering and more people out of the crowd. Someone passed us daffodils. "Flower Power," we cried happily. . . . Some of the draft card burners were girls, wives or girlfriends of male card burners. . . . It lasted this way for about half an hour. About 175 people burned their cards. This was more than had signed the pledge. . . .

Burning my draft card was a recognition that I had finally learned something. But that I decided to commit what the U.S. government considers a heinous crime is due to a large degree to those responsible for my education. They instilled in me a sense of values, principle, and morality. They taught me that we were a peace-loving democracy, and I believed them. The education of Martin Jezer is the realization that if this *is* to be a peace-loving democracy, functioning on principled, moral values, it is for us, for me, to make it so.

A Radical Education

My education from one graduation to another, from college grad to draft resister, began slowly but accelerated after 1964. I spent a year and a half in graduate school studying journalism because I wanted to write, and didn't want to go into the army. I abandoned my thesis to go to Hazard, Kentucky, with a friend who was doing a book on the wildcat coal mine strikes. The trip had a decisive impact on my life. For the first time, and at first hand, I identified with the struggles of the oppressed. But though shaken, I was still in the liberal bag. The only hope, I thought, was for massive federal aid. The miners, I felt, couldn't do it for themselves.

I returned to New York, got married, and worked as a copy-writer and then as an encyclopedia editor. . . . I came to identify more and more with the Movement.

Quitting graduate school led to my being classified I-A [available for military service] and then I-Y [available for military service in times of war or national emergency] for medical reasons. I knew nothing about principled draft refusal or noncooperation. I would not have known how to go about filing a CO [conscientious objector] application. . . . I thought you had to be a Quaker or a Mennonite to become a noncombatant. I also knew nothing about pacifism. I thought the kids boarding Polaris submarines [to protest the nuclear arms race] were kooks. So if drafted I'd have gone, believing that in fighting communism I was fighting a noble cause. I'd not have liked it though. A brief experience in ROTC [Reserve Officers Training Corps] and my own anarchical tendencies make militarism anathema to me.

Radicalization

I campaigned for Lyndon Johnson in 1964. The complete acquiescence of Congress, the press, and all informed public opinion to his obvious violation of all his campaign promises shocked me. From the Gulf of Tonkin to the Sheep Meadow, my radicalization was fast and furious. The American government completely alienated itself from my concept of common human decency.

Many young men protested the Vietnam War by burning their draft cards, an act that was banned by federal legislation in 1965.

In progressive order I wrote my Congressmen, the Vice President and the President. The *New York Post* published my irate letters to the editor. I marched in my first peace parade, walked picket lines, leafletted and vigilled. When the U.S. resumed its bombing of North Vietnam in February 1966 , I sat down in Times Square and got busted for the first of three times. I finally came to the conclusion that only mass civil disobedience could stop the war. My own position became clear. To do nothing, or to fiddle around with petitions, peace candidates, and other respectable means of protest while Vietnam burns and we plunge madly on in our insanity, is intolerable. I have to resist in the most direct way possible, for myself, and to set an example for others. When the call for a mass draft card burning on April 15th arrived from the organizers at Cornell, I signed it at once. I had no doubt that this is what I had to do, even if the proposed 500 draft card burners did not show up. Not to have burned a draft card April 15th would have been tantamount to living in Boston in 1773 and not to have dumped tea in Boston harbor. I'd not have missed it.

Facing One's Fear

Despite my enthusiasm for the action and my personal commitment to go through with it no matter what, I was filled with fear. I agree with Thoreau that there are times when the only place for an honest man is a jail, and I accept the dictum that walls do not a prison make. But out of fear, and also for personal and selfish reasons, I did not want to go to jail. . . . My life was changing for the better. This was no time to interrupt it with a long jail sentence. But *any time* is the wrong time to go to jail, and I knew full well that to give in to my selfishness would be a far greater sacrifice than two or three years of my life. Moreover, all my friends supported my intention to burn my draft card. By April 15th I was positive I was doing right and events that followed have reinforced this view. But, of course, there are times, as I wait to be indicted, that I am scared—and selfish. . . .

When I burned my draft card, I thought that this was enough of a witness. I would publicize my act to encourage others and face up to the consequences. Now I believe that it is politically necessary for some of us to carry resistance into the courts and into jail, if necessary. The one weapon the government holds over us is prison. To be effective we must overcome our fear of jail. The civil rights movement helped shake this fear; it is for us to destroy it. For once imprisonment becomes an honorable alternative to the military, something to be sought rather than avoided, resistance to the draft can become massive. In order to strike at this fear, some of us will have to face imprisonment with joyous defiance.

Changing People's Lives

. . . The most important effect of the draft card burning was that it changed the lives of those who took part. I've been told many times that the Movement can't succeed, that you can't change people's hearts, that social change is gradual, and that we New Leftists are doomed to become frustrated, old, radicals. This is not true, for to the degree that the Movement has led its participants to change their lives, it has been successful. It has given people the insight to drop out of a brutal and dehumanized society, and it has given people the strength to devote their lives toward the creation of a community where love of one's fellow replaces the profit motive as the highest value. . . .

To destroy one's draft card, to place one's conscience before the dictates of one's government, is in the highest tradition of human conduct. This country was not created by men subservient to law and government. It was created and made great by civil disobedients like Quakers who refused to compromise their religion to suit the Puritan theocracy; by Puritans who openly defied British authority; by provo-type Sons of Liberty who burned stamps to protest the Stamp Act and who dumped tea in Boston harbor; by abolitionists who ignored the Fugitive Slave law, by slaves who refused to act like slaves; by workingmen who insisted, despite the law, on their right to organize; by black Americans who refused to ride in the back of the bus; and by the more than one

Resisting the War Machine

The mass draft-card burning in which Martin Jezer participated on April 15, 1967, in New York's Central Park was organized in part by We Won't Go, an antiwar group based at Cornell University in Ithaca, New York. The group sent out "A Call to Burn Draft Cards" on March 2; it is reprinted here.

The armies of the United States have, through conscription, already oppressed or destroyed the lives and consciences of millions of Americans and Vietnamese. We have argued and demonstrated to stop this destruction. We have not succeeded. Murderers do not respond to reason. Powerful resistance is now demanded: radical, illegal, unpleasant, sustained.

In Vietnam the war machine is directed against young and old, soldiers and civilians, without distinction. In our own country, the war machine is directed specifically against the young, against blacks more than against whites, but ultimately against all.

Body and soul, we are oppressed in common. Body and soul, we must resist in common. The undersigned believe that we should *begin* this mass resistance by publicly destroying our draft cards at the Spring Mobilization. WE URGE ALL PEOPLE WHO HAVE CONTEMPLATED THE ACT OF DESTROYING THEIR DRAFT CARDS TO CARRY OUT THIS ACT ON APRIL 15, WITH THE UNDERSTANDING THAT THIS PLEDGE BECOMES BINDING WHEN 500 PEOPLE HAVE MADE IT.

The climate of anti-war opinion is changing. In the last few months student governments, church groups, and other organizations have publicly expressed understanding and sympathy with the position of individuals who refuse to fight in Vietnam, who resist the draft. We are ready to put ourselves on the line for this position, and we expect that these people will come through with their support.

We are fully aware that our action makes us liable to penalties of up to five years in prison and $10,000 in fines. We believe, however, that the more people who take part in this action the more difficult it will be for the government to prosecute.

hundred young Americans already in prison for refusing to acquiesce in the misguided actions of their government.

So when people tell me that I have no respect for law and order and that I do not love my country, I reply: "Jefferson, Tom Paine, Garrison, Thoreau, A.J. Muste, the Freedom Riders, these are my countrymen whom I love; with them I take my stand."

"No longer will we tolerate 'law and order' backed up by soldiers in Vietnam and pigs in the communities and schools; a 'law and order' that serves only the interests of those in power."

The Antiwar Movement Should Seek Radical Change in America

Students for a Democratic Society (SDS)

Confrontations between antiwar activists and law enforcement officers sometimes resulted in violence, most notably in Chicago in 1968. Several thousand antiwar protesters sponsored by various peace and youth groups—including the Youth International Party (Yippies) and the National Mobilization Committee to End the War in Vietnam (MOBE)—gathered in Chicago in August during the Democratic National Convention. On several occasions the local police clubbed and beat marchers and onlookers; their actions were seen on national television in conjunction with the proceedings of the convention.

The violent confrontations in Chicago, combined with other events of 1968, including the continuation of the war in Vietnam, the assassinations of Robert Kennedy and Martin Luther King Jr., and the election of Richard M. Nixon as president in November, led many antiwar activists to conclude that the Vietnam War would not stop unless American society underwent radical change. The following viewpoint is taken from a "National Action Brochure" by Students for a Democratic Society, which was the leading radical white student organization for much of the 1960s. The brochure argues that the American economic and po-

Excerpted from "National Action Brochure" by the Students for a Democratic Society, August 1, 1969, in *Vietnam Documents: American and Vietnamese Views of the War*, edited by George Katsiaficas; ©1992 by M.E. Sharpe, Inc. Reprinted by permission of M.E. Sharpe, Inc.

litical system is corrupt and in decline, expresses support for a Communist victory in Vietnam, and links American "imperialism" in Vietnam to the poor treatment of minorities in America. SDS calls for young people to gather in Chicago in October 1969 to commemorate the 1968 protests, to express solidarity with the Chicago Eight (eight activists charged in federal court with conspiracy to incite the 1968 violence), and to fight the police and in other ways "bring the war home" to the American people.

Several hundred people gathered in Chicago on October 11, 1969, a number far less than the thousands some SDS leaders were hoping for. Over the next four "Days of Rage" they succeeded mainly in smashing windows before being overwhelmed, beaten, and arrested by the police.

———————

It has been almost a year since the Democratic Convention, when thousands of young people came together in Chicago and tore up pig city for five days. The action was a response to the crisis this system is facing as a result of the war, the demand by black people for liberation, and the ever-growing reality that this system just can't make it.

This fall, people are coming back to Chicago: more powerful, better organized, and more together than we were last August.

SDS is calling for a National Action in Chicago on October 11. We are coming back to Chicago, and we are going to bring those we left behind last year.

The War Goes On

Look At It: America, 1969.

The war goes on, despite the jive double-talk about troop withdrawals and peace talks. Black people continue to be murdered by agents of the fat cats who run this country, if not in one way, then in another: by the pigs or the courts, by the boss or the welfare department. Working people face higher taxes, inflation, speed-ups, and the sure knowledge—if it hasn't happened already—that their sons may be shipped off to Vietnam and shipped home in a box. And young people all over the country go to prisons that are called schools, are trained for jobs that don't exist or serve no one's real interest but the boss's, and, to top it all off, get told that Vietnam is the place to defend their "freedom."

None of this is very new. The cities have been falling apart, the schools have been bullshit, the jobs have been rotten and unfulfilling for a long time.

What's new is that today not quite so many people are con-fused, and a lot more people are angry: angry about the fact that the promises we have heard since first grade are all jive; angry that, when you get down to it, this system is nothing but the total economic and military put-down of the oppressed peoples of the world.

And more: it's a system that steals the goods, the resources, and the labor of poor and working people all over the world in order to fill the pockets and bank accounts of a tiny capitalist class. (Call it imperialism.) It's a system that divides white workers from blacks by offering whites crumbs off the table, and telling them that if they don't stay cool the blacks will move in on their jobs, their homes, and their schools. (Call it white supremacy.) It's a system that divides men from women, forcing women to be subservient to men from childhood, to be slave labor in the home and cheap labor in the factory. (Call it male supremacy.) And it's a system that has colonized whole nations within this country—the nation of black people, the nation of brown people to enslave, op-press, and ultimately murder the people on whose backs this country was built. (Call it fascism.)

Solidarity with the Vietcong

In a speech delivered at a peace rally on November 15, 1969, in San Francisco, antiwar leader Rennie Davis expresses support for the National Liberation Front (NLF).

I want [Vice President] Spiro Agnew to know that I bring this assembly a message of greetings and solidarity to the American people from the "Vietcong" (NLF).

I want Agnew to know that this generation is establishing its own diplomatic relations, because we are not at war with the people of Vietnam or Korea or China or Cuba. Our war is with the Pentagon, Wall Street and Spiro T. Agnew.

But the lies are catching up to America and the slick rich people and their agents in the government bureaucracies, the courts, the schools, and the pig [police] stations just can't cut it anymore.

Black and brown people know it.

Young people know it.

More and more white working people know it.

And you know it.

Last Year, There Were Only about 10,000 of Us in Chicago.

The press made it look like a massacre. All you could see on TV were shots of the horrors and blood of pig brutality. That was the line that the bald-headed businessmen were trying to run down—"If you mess with us, we'll let you have it." But those who were there tell a different story. We were together and our power was felt. It's true that some of us got hurt, but last summer was a victory for the people in a thousand ways.

Our actions showed the Vietnamese that there were masses of young people in this country facing the same enemy that they faced.

We showed that white people would no longer sit by passively while black communities were being invaded by occupation troops every day.

We showed that the "democratic process" of choosing candidates for a presidential election was nothing more than a hoax, pulled off by the businessmen who really run this country.

And we showed the whole world that in the face of the oppressive and exploitative rulers—and the military might to back them up—thousands of people are willing to fight back.

SDS Is Calling the Action This Year.

But it will be a different action. An action not only against a single war or a "foreign policy," but against the whole imperialist system that made that war a necessity. An action not only for immediate withdrawal of all U.S. occupation troops, but in support of the heroic fight of the Vietnamese people and the National Liberation Front for freedom and independence. An action not only to bring "peace to Vietnam," but beginning to establish another front against imperialism right here in America—to "bring the war home."

Remove All Troops

We are demanding that all occupational troops get out of Vietnam and every other place they don't belong. This includes the black and brown communities, the workers' picket lines, the high schools, and the streets of Berkeley. No longer will we tolerate "law and order" backed up by soldiers in Vietnam and pigs in the communities and schools; a "law and order" that serves only the interests of those in power and tries to smash the people down whenever they rise up.

We are demanding the release of all political prisoners who have been victimized by the ever-growing attacks on the black liberation struggle and the people in general. . . .

We are expressing total support for the National Liberation Front and the newly formed Provisional Revolutionary Government of South Vietnam. Throughout the history of the war, the NLF has provided the political and military leadership to the people of South Vietnam. The Provisional Revolutionary Government, recently formed by the NLF and other groups, has pledged to "mobilize the south Vietnamese armed forces and people" in order to continue the struggle for independence. The PRG also has expressed solidarity with "the just struggle of the Afro-American people for their fundamental national rights," and has pledged to "actively support the national independence movements of Asia, Africa, and Latin America."

We are also expressing total support for the black liberation struggle, part of the same struggle that the Vietnamese are fighting, against the same enemy.

We are demanding independence for Puerto Rico, and an end to the colonial oppression that the Puerto Rican nation faces at the hands of U.S. imperialism.

We are demanding an end to the surtax, a tax taken from the working people of this country and used to kill working people in Vietnam and other places for fun and profit.

We are expressing solidarity with the Conspiracy 8 who led the struggle last summer in Chicago. Our action is planned to roughly coincide with the beginning of their trial.

And we are expressing support for GIs in Vietnam and throughout the world who are being made to fight the battles of the rich, like poor and working people have always been made to do. We support those GIs at Fort Hood, Fort Jackson, and many other army bases who have refused to be cannon fodder in a war against the people of Vietnam.

It's Almost Hard to Remember When the War Began.

But, after years of peace marches, petitions, and the gradual realization that this war was no "mistake" at all, one critical fact remains: the war is not just happening in Vietnam.

It is happening in the jungles of Guatemala, Bolivia, Thailand, and all oppressed nations throughout the world.

And it is happening here. In black communities throughout the country. On college campuses. And in the high schools, in the shops, and on the streets.

It is a war in which there are only two sides; a war not for domination but for an end to domination, not for destruction, but for liberation and the unchaining of human freedom.

And it is a war in which we cannot "resist"; it is a war in which we must fight.

On October 11, tens of thousands of people will come to Chicago to bring the war home. Join us.

All power to the people!

VIEWPOINT 4

"The [antiwar movement] leadership must be willing to talk about Vietnam in terms that will appeal to Middle America."

The Antiwar Movement Should Seek to Influence Mainstream America

Sam Brown (b. 1943)

Activists who opposed the Vietnam War often argued among themselves over the strategy, tactics, and general goals of the antiwar movement. One question that divided the movement was whether or not activists should work within existing political channels to end the war. Many activists came to believe that their efforts to voice their opposition through conventional means such as electoral politics and petitioning their government leaders were futile. They concluded that American democracy was a sham and that Americans needed to be confronted with the necessity of revolutionizing the "System." However, others argued that embracing radical ideas would alienate potential support from the majority of Americans and retard the antiwar movement.

An example of the latter perspective is found in the following viewpoint, excerpted from a 1970 article by Sam Brown, one of the leaders of the antiwar movement. A former Harvard Divinity School student, Brown coordinated young volunteers for the 1968 presidential campaign of Eugene McCarthy, who ran on a platform of opposition to the Vietnam War. Brown was also one of the organizers of the Vietnam Moratorium, a nationwide protest held on October 15, 1969. In his 1970 article, Brown contends that America must immediately extricate itself from Vietnam and con-

Reprinted from "The Politics of Peace" by Sam Brown, *Washington Monthly*, August 1970, by permission of the *Washington Monthly*.

demns President Richard M. Nixon (elected in 1968) for failing to end the war. To bring about America's withdrawal, he argues, the peace activists must broaden their appeal and ensure that the debate over Vietnam is not framed as "the Silent Majority versus the Loud-Mouth Militants." He maintains that older and respected figures should replace the young students as leaders of the anti-war movement.

The outline of a successful anti-war strategy, it seems to me, is clear: the appeal must be made in such a way that Middle Americans will not ignore the substance of the argument because of an offensive style. Support for such an appeal exists. After all, immediate withdrawal is not a radical proposal in this country today, and careful analysis of the polls shows that all political stances on the war must be couched in terms of reaching the quickest possible termination. This indicates that a quick political settlement or immediate withdrawal can become a majority position if the message is presented in a strong but palatable fashion.

Nixon's Commitment to War

While peace activists should not underestimate potential support for an anti-war position, we should also avoid underestimating President Nixon's commitment to some sort of victory in Southeast Asia. I believe that the President's "new" image as a cool, neutral majority-maker, a consummate politician who responds and shapes rather than leads, considerably understates his ego commitment to the war. We are dealing with a man who has a full-time awareness of himself as history—the first President ever to name his own doctrine, the Nixon Doctrine, which I suspect was motivated as much by the simple desire to place his name on the books as to enunciate whatever its meaning is. We are dealing with a man who felt called upon by the world to issue a "State of the World" message, to dwell upon its historic primacy, and to quote himself 27 times in the document while citing all other human beings in history only three times (all three of these quotations were of Secretary of State [William] Rogers agreeing with the President). The President has read the history books and knows that the great Presidents of the United States won wars. He even knows what room of the White House was used to announce the great wartime decisions.

These ego commitments are very harsh terms in which to describe a crucial motive for the Administration's continuation of the war, but I find no others which make as much sense. There is no more plausible way to explain why the President did not end the war right after he came into office, with little or no political risk. Nor can I otherwise explain his total aversion to Congressional moves toward sharing the political responsibility for ending the war.

The President's personal commitment to the war helps explain why he goes for the political groin to justify his actions. He uses patriotism and the flag, which are deep-seated loyalties for most Americans, to stimulate support for a war which clearly calls forth no such loyalties. He uses the media presence of the Presidency to characterize the opposition as near traitors. I think the President has won a large part of the Vietnam debate in the past merely by naming the teams. When it's the Silent Majority versus the Loud-Mouth Militants, the Silent Majority wins every time. He and the Vice President have also managed to sell the incredible notion that the press of the United States is left-wing. People who believe that have obviously never attended a convention of the American Society of Newspaper Editors, where the sentiment is overwhelmingly conservative, verging on outright jingoism.

Since the country drifts toward impatience for withdrawal as the war drags on, the President will have to continue seeking the jugular if he clings to the victory wish. This is one of the greatest dangers to the peace movement; for when the dialogue over the war is degraded past a certain point, it ends. (Liberals should remember the converse: that when the dialogue is elevated to a certain level of generality, involving, for example, petty squabbles over doctrinal minutiae, then the talk goes on forever without action.) People can no longer talk to each other, and confrontations based on tribal sign language become the norm. In all political likelihood, most of Middle America would line up with the President in any such jungle warfare.

The atmosphere of debate over Vietnam is already so debased that it will be very difficult to take the high road—to offer the American people the kind of positive tone and hope which would stand out by contrast with the President's increasingly defensive and visceral statements. It will be impossible to do so without very strong leadership. I suppose that is the heart of my feelings about the peace movement—that the strategy can be devised, that the constituency is there, but that these assets are useless without strong, non-student leadership. The money will follow evidence of leadership. If my analysis of President Nixon's objective in Vietnam is on the right track, the task will be very difficult, but all the more imperative.

The leadership must have the media presence to counter the President's enormous TV influence. Someone must respond to his smears on the patriotism of doves. A figure like [Iowa senator] Harold Hughes would have great impact if he said in effect: "Look here, Mr. President, we're not talking about campus bums. We're talking about whether Vietnam is worth continued killings and maimings. I fought through Europe in World War II and con-

Advice for Peace Activists

Ralph K. White, a psychology professor at George Washington University in Washington, D.C., wrote the following words of advice to would-be peace activists in the 1970 book Vietnam and the Silent Majority.

Dissociate yourself, in every way that you honestly can, from the distorted public stereotype of the peace demonstrator. The potency of this distorted stereotype was evident as the United States approached the 1970 Congressional elections. For example, Senator [Ralph] Yarborough, a staunch liberal, had lost to an opponent whose most effective technique was to show on television a film depicting unkempt, long-haired students demonstrating for Eugene McCarthy in Chicago, to link them with Yarborough by quoting a statement of his supporting McCarthy, and then to ask: Is this the sort of person you want in Washington? Other candidates had taken Yarborough's experience to heart. . . .

What meaning can be drawn from such recent signs? Their most immediate import is simply to remind us that the great majority of the American people are intensely antagonistic to what they conceive to be the typical student peace demonstrator. Even antiwar people are usually hostile toward organized public protest against the war. The reader need only recall that most of the public sided with the National Guard in the Kent State episode.

The sources for this antagonism are many, but it is not our purpose to explicate the generation gap or to explain, condemn, or defend this antagonism. That goes well beyond our task. The connection between the peace movement and the more general culture conflict between the "hip" and the "straight" styles of life may be largely a historical accident of the time period in which Vietnam took place (though the connection is more complicated than that). Our only concern is to point out that such a connection may do the peace movement little good.

On the other hand, the vast talent and energy of American youth is probably the greatest single potential resource that the peace movement possesses. The way out of this dilemma lies in recognizing that if student support is to be as positive an asset as it can be, those involved have some hard decisions to make. The first of these is a decision about the purpose of the whole operation. For those who have undertaken to work as members of a team to elect a peace candidate, the essential purpose should be clear. It is not—except in the long run—to stop the war. It is to get a certain candidate elected.

sider myself as American as anyone, but that was 25 years ago. And the fact is that Vietnam stands between us and everything America hopes to become." The leadership must be willing to talk about Vietnam in terms that will appeal to Middle America—to rename the teams so that we start on ground zero with the hawks, rather than at an emotional disadvantage.

The Silent Majority Myth

Part of the new message must be the destruction of the silent majority myth. The only clear lesson of the polls is that most Americans want an end to the war. If the President were to use television to justify withdrawal on the grounds that we had done all we could or that the South Vietnamese government was corrupt and unworthy of support, I believe he would receive 70 percent support. The silent majority is largely produced by the American propensity to defer to the President. In March of 1968, for example, the Gallup poll showed 40 percent for and 51 percent against stopping the bombing of North Vietnam. After President Johnson stopped the bombing, the polls showed 64 percent for and 26 percent against his decision. The silent majority appears quite malleable.

Not only must the silent majority argument be exposed as a sham, but the popular characterization of doves as militant, long-haired kids and the silent majority as middle-aged and middle-class must be dispelled. Young people as a group are *not* more dovish than old people, nor do over-educated eggheads tend to be more dovish than "the folks." In fact, the polls show that college-educated people in their twenties are consistently more hawkish than older non-college graduates, by a significant margin of about 20 percent.

In addition to establishing a tone acceptable to Middle America, renaming the teams, and destroying Presidential myths, the peace leadership should use the media to make becoming a dove more psychologically attractive to Middle Americans. Prior emphasis on the moral aspects of the war has meant that the first psychological step toward an anti-war position has of necessity been the admission that the United States is somehow evil. Since many people are unable to make that jump, an admission of American guilt should not be asked of all potential supporters. To the extent that we in the peace movement have played down the pragmatic arguments for peace, we have weakened our case—and lessened our chances of ending the war. It is in no way inconsistent with our moral opposition to the war to lay much greater stress than most of us have as yet on the great practical benefits of peace.

This new peace leadership should be composed of Senators, Congressmen, governors, mayors, businessmen—all the straight people who are willing to make a firm and unequivocal commitment against the war. The spokesmen should be those most visible and most attractive to Middle America, those who can speak intelligently about the war with strength rather than condescension or aloofness. . . .

The new peace leadership must make it clear that it is in for the duration—until the end of American involvement in Indochina. The cyclical activity of the anti-war movement has had a double disadvantage in the past: during periods of upswing, the peace movement has overestimated its effect and thus paved the way for subsequent acute frustration and resignation; during the downswing, the government has underestimated latent anti-war sentiment, and this has possibly contributed to adventurism.

The Role of Young People

If the focus of the peace movement could be shifted to the new and long-awaited leadership, young people would be far more effective politically. I don't think we have to hide who we are, or even what we say. We should merely recognize the fact that the political balance on the war is held by people with different life styles. Students could be a left, moral pressure on the coat-and-tie leadership. Students could make it clear to Richard Nixon that *they* will write his history and that all wars are not heroic. They could make it clear that there are *costs* held against those who wage this war. Those who wage the war should be constantly reminded that they are responsible for a moral horror—like the British Viceroy in colonial India. Every time the Viceroy showed his face in public, he saw a silent Indian holding a sign which read "Assassin." Lyndon Johnson and Richard Nixon should be subject to the same treatment. We should make them aware that there are large numbers of people in this country who hold them responsible for criminal activities and who believe that those who wage the war cannot cast off the responsibility merely by leaving office.

There is no assurance at present that a new peace leadership is forthcoming, although recently several prospective leaders have been leaning toward conscience and away from conservative careerism. If these people were to emerge, I believe that it is quite possible to build a peace constituency and create a national atmosphere in which it would not be possible to wage war. This would be partly a matter of national mood, which is highly volatile. . . .

A renewed peace movement would also exercise political clout, apart from its impact on the nation's war temperature. The National Rifle Association is an unpleasant model; but if a tiny fraction of the population can stop gun control with organization and the bullet vote, then the peace movement can stop the war. The new constituency would have obvious potential in 1972.

The American System

All these ruminations have been predicated on certain traditional assumptions: that people's political opinions should count, that democracy can be made to work, that there is enough good will left in the country to make it work, and that given a choice between rational alternatives, Americans will choose the most humane course. At the same time, the American people have shown that they will not respond favorably to violence committed in the name of ending the war, or to a version of democracy that romanticizes about participation of the poor and the black but ignores the middle, or to peace advocates who think demonstrations are a substitute for the sustained work of peaceful persuasion.

But the "system" should not be applauded even if the war were to end tomorrow. For five years, it has provided no real way for people to express their views on a war which was presented to them as a test of manhood. The system provided no public debate over whether we should enter the war, but instead permitted our leaders to involve us by stealth. This critical failure gave inertia to the propagation of the Vietnam war and sneaked the flag onto the battlefield—leaving the peace movement at an enormous political disadvantage. The system has provided poor information to voters and little active leadership for a position of obvious principle.

If the war is now ended by political action, as I believe it can be, some will undoubtedly argue that the system has vindicated itself. That argument, however, is self-deceiving; for in many crucial respects our system has already failed and requires radical reconstruction.

VIEWPOINT 5

"If Presidents could grant amnesty for the more serious offense of armed insurrection, why should amnesty be withheld from men who were apparently motivated by humanitarian opposition to war?"

A General Amnesty Should Be Granted to Draft Evaders

John M. Swomley Jr. (b. 1915)

A highly controversial issue during the Vietnam War was the question of whether to grant legal forgiveness, or amnesty, to the thousands of men who left the country or in other ways illegally evaded the draft and those who went to prison rather than comply with conscription orders. In the following viewpoint, taken from an article first published in 1969 and adapted and reprinted in 1972, John M. Swomley Jr. presents the case for amnesty. Swomley, a professor of ethics at St. Paul School of Theology, Kansas City, Missouri, had long been active in various political and social causes, including the desegregation of the U.S. military, the abolishment of universal military conscription, and the civil rights movement.

In the article, Swomley defines amnesty and describes instances in which it had been granted in world and U.S. history. He argues that granting amnesty to those who refused to serve in Vietnam would help the United States heal social divisions, end the suffering of draft resisters and their families, and rid the country of the onus of housing what he asserts are essentially political prisoners.

Revised and reprinted from "Memo to Nixon: Why Not an Amnesty?" *National Catholic Reporter*, January 1, 1969. Reprinted by permission of the author.

> "... it appears to me no less consistent with the public good than it is with my personal feelings to mingle in the operations of Government every degree of moderation and tenderness which the national justice, dignity and safety may permit." From George Washington's proclamation of amnesty, July 10, 1795.

Thousands of young men are either in prison or exile because of military conscription in the United States. Some of these men are sincere conscientious objectors to all war who were not recognized as such by their draft boards. Other young men did not pass the religious test imposed by Congress.

Some men are in prison because they are objectors to the war in Vietnam, but not to all war. Traditional Roman Catholic theology provides criteria for just wars, and hence for unjust wars. Similarly some non–Roman Catholics could not conscientiously participate in the war in Vietnam even though they are not prepared to declare their opposition to all war. They felt they could not maintain personal integrity and participate in a war they believed was unjust or served no defensive purpose.

Other men went to prison because they believed conscription itself to be wrong—a type of involuntary servitude. They refused to cooperate by keeping a draft card or by accepting induction as conscientious objectors. A few ministers who objected to "special privileges" not granted to laymen took this position.

Most of those who went to Canada to take up immigrant status there either felt they could not get "justice" from their draft board or were not prepared to spend a term in prison because they could not meet the religious test or claim objection to all war.

What Is Amnesty?

The word "amnesty" comes to us from ancient Greek, where it meant "oblivion" or "not remembering." It was an intentional overlooking of an offense. Today it means "a general overlooking or pardon of past offenses by the ruling authority" [from the Oxford English Dictionary]. It differs from a typical pardon in that it involves a whole class of offenders rather than one or a few individuals. It may result in the commutation of sentences of those already convicted, as well as a blanket pardon for those who have not been brought to trial.

The United States Constitution gives the President "power to grant reprieves and pardons for offenses against the United States, except in cases of impeachment." The framers of the Constitution borrowed the idea from England, for this has been firmly imbedded in Anglo-Saxon law for centuries. Amnesties may also be declared by act of Congress, but the traditional and most expedient is by presidential proclamation.

The first recorded amnesty was in about 40 B.C., when Thrasybulus in Athens forbade any additional punishment of citizens for their past political acts and exacted an oath of amnesty so as to eliminate civil strife from legal memory. . . .

There have been a number of amnesties following wars granted both to enemies and to a nation's own citizens. For example, France, Norway, Germany, Belgium, Japan, and the Netherlands granted amnesties for persons engaged in compromising activities during the Second World War.

George Washington on July 10, 1795, granted "a full, free and entire pardon" to those involved in an insurrection in Pennsylvania against the United States. In explaining this to Congress he said:

> For though I shall always think it a sacred duty to exercise with firmness and energy the constitutional powers with which I am vested, yet it appears to me no less consistent with the public good than it is with my personal feelings to mingle in the operations of Government every degree of moderation and tenderness which the national justice, dignity and safety may permit.

John Adams in May 1800 granted an amnesty for another "wicked and treasonable insurrection" in Pennsylvania that occurred a year earlier. James Madison also proclaimed in 1815 "a free and full pardon of all offenses . . . touching the revenue trade and navigation" in the vicinity of New Orleans.

During the Civil War, Abraham Lincoln on December 8, 1863, offered a full pardon to those who "participated in the existing rebellion" who were prepared to take a prescribed oath. Certain classes of persons were excepted. Lincoln also directed the War Department in February 1864 to see to it "that the sentence of all deserters who have been condemned by court-martial to death . . . be mitigated to imprisonment during the war. . . ."

Following the Civil War Andrew Johnson proclaimed a partial amnesty in 1865, another in 1867, and on July 4, 1868, a full pardon to everyone who "participated in the late insurrection of rebellion" except for those under indictment for treason or other felony. Finally, on December 25, 1868, he granted a Christmas "amnesty for the offense of treason against the United States. . . ." President Johnson's first proclamation states his reasons for pardon. He believed that

> a retaliatory or vindictive policy, attended by unnecessary disqualification, pains, penalties, confiscations and disfranchisements, now as always could only tend to hinder reconciliation among the people and national restoration, while it must seriously embarrass, obstruct and repress popular energies and national industry and enterprise. . . .

There were no general amnesties following World Wars I and II. Woodrow Wilson, who was vindictive and considered critics of the war as traitors, refused his own attorney general's recommendation for commuting the sentence of the sixty-five-year-old Eugene Debs. Only after the Senate ratified the peace treaty with Germany did President Warren G. Harding release Debs from prison. On December 23, 1921, Harding announced that Debs and twenty-three other political prisoners would be released on Christmas Day. He did not, however, grant the general amnesty for which hundreds of thousands of Americans had asked. . . .

Following World War II President Harry Truman was under great public pressure to grant an amnesty. He appeared to comply with the demand while avoiding it, by appointing an amnesty board of persons hostile to the idea [the Roberts Board]. On their recommendation, 1523 of the 15,805 who had been convicted under the Selective Service Act were pardoned on December 23, 1947. In general, Truman's phony 1947 amnesty excluded Jehovah's Witnesses, political prisoners, and willful violators of the law who had walked out of the conscientious objector camps. Earlier, on Christmas in 1945, Truman granted full pardon to all former prisoners who had served honorably in the Armed Forces for at least a year. Former criminals were thus pardoned, but men whose convictions led them to violate the Selective Service Act were not.

Why Amnesty Now?

Amnesty is generally granted only for political or military offenses against a state. In each of the presidential pardons prior to World War I described above, the offense involved actual insurrection or war against the United States, which the Constitution calls treason. The men in prison or exile today are not charged with military action or insurrection against the United States. Their offense is either that they valued freedom too highly to submit to conscription or that their consciences did not permit them to prepare for, participate in, or even indirectly contribute to the war in Vietnam. Americans may rightly differ about the wisdom of their actions, but it is quite clear that their acts in no way involved the destruction of life or armed revolt against the United States. If Presidents could grant amnesty for the more serious offense of armed insurrection, why should amnesty be withheld from men who were apparently motivated by humanitarian opposition to war?

One major purpose of amnesty is to heal the wounds and divisions of war, to restore confidence in government on the part of those who have been alienated by the war. It is obvious that former Presidents of the United States had such healing in mind

207

The Sacrifices Made by Exiles

The U.S. National Student Association, in a statement submitted to Congress in 1972, calls for universal amnesty and recognition of the debt the United States owes to draft resisters.

But there is a moral imperative involved here, too, and it far outweighs the politics of expediency. And that is why we support a universal amnesty that is unconditional, automatic and non-punitive. We call for universal amnesty for all those who resisted the Vietnam War in whatever form. Let there be no mistaking precisely what this means: to call for universal amnesty is not to "forgive and forget." To forgive and forget is to reject the responsibility that we as a nation must bear for the brutality and destruction we have perpetrated on the peoples of Southeast Asia. To forgive and forget is to leave open the possibility that this nation might again embark on a disastrous foreign policy such as the one which dictated American involvement in this war. And we must never allow such a war to be waged.

On the contrary, we must force this nation to recognize and accept its responsibility for the war and its aftermath, and to understand that part of its aftermath is a generation of political exiles: exiles because they refused to participate in a war against which their individual consciences argued, and against which most of the American peoples sentiments have turned. Exiles because they refused induction, or fled the country, or deserted the military, or were dismissed from service with a less than honorable discharge, or otherwise violated civil or military codes in protesting the war. Exiles because the American government persists in prosecuting and imprisoning them. Exiles because employers reject them, communities harass them, and the American people refuse to accept their collective responsibility and insist on placing the sole legal responsibility for the war on the very people who refused to wage it.

And we cannot forget that these people, at very great personal sacrifice, awakened the conscience of the American people. They maintained the war as an issue before the eyes of the public. They countered every instance of Administrative duplicity with their own personal statements, quiet or dramatic, of the truth. In the 1960's, while many of us trembled to put even our personal or political credibility on the line to oppose the war, they put everything on the line—their homes, their families and friends, their careers, their freedom, their honor. We would betray their convictions if we proposed to the American people that they forgive and forget. On the contrary, we insist that a universal amnesty would have such far-reaching ramifications that, far from obliterating their records and forgetting the crisis of conscience through which the war forced them, the whole society would be compelled to bear the burden of conscience these men and women now carry.

after the armed uprisings in the 1790s and the 1800s. The division in the United States today is just as real. It is not based on sectional grievances, nor is it confined to any part of the United States. Rather it is chiefly defined by age—draft age—or by the kind of idealism that expected the United States to behave differently from other nations. Still, the fact must be acknowledged that the United States' war in Vietnam has been opposed and condemned by many highly respected citizens in all walks of life and of all age groups. Whatever one may think of the phrase "credibility gap," it does express a loss of faith in their government by thousands of Americans. An act of amnesty now would go a long way toward restoration of that faith.

Another purpose of amnesty is to bring back into useful citizenship those who are now barred by legal restrictions. Many of those sentenced for draft resistance as unrecognized conscientious objectors will be barred by state laws from voting or running for public office. Others may find it difficult or impossible to enter certain professions, such as law, with a technical felony on their records. Needless to say, the thousands in exile from the United States would be valuable assets to American society were they able to return with freedom from imprisonment.

Amnesty would also put an end to the emotional and economic suffering of the families of those who resisted the draft. These families, together with their friends and neighbors, represent a larger segment of the American community than the draft resisters themselves, and in varying degrees are affected by the imprisonment or exile of persons they have known intimately as children and young adults. The renewal or increase of their confidence in government would be a by-product of amnesty.

Amnesty by any government is generally a sign of governmental strength and always a sign of magnanimity. *The Encyclopedia of the Social Sciences* says that "the granting of an amnesty is nearly always a sign that the government feels its position secure . . . and that having disarmed its enemy in the field, it may proceed with the attempt at disarming hatred and resentment by an act of grace." Since modern limited wars seldom end in victory for either side, amnesty for those who refused to participate in the war would be an even greater indication of the security of the government that proclaims it.

Prisoners of war are sometimes freed during war and almost always at the end of the war in spite of their direct participation on the other side. There is an implied recognition that they did what duty and citizenship required of them. Governments ought similarly to recognize the devotion of some of their own citizens to a higher moral duty or citizenship that makes them disobey an order for induction or the draft law itself. Amnesty for violators of the draft law would in effect be an acknowledgment by government that in the stress and strain of war some laws may have been administered too narrowly, and some boards may have been too war-minded to recognize conscientious objectors. It would be an act of humility and magnanimity to indicate that no government or law is so perfect that conscious or unconscious injustice cannot take place in its administration.

The Social Meaning of Amnesty

Millions of people in the United States and in other countries have been taught that forgiveness is a virtue. Most religions encourage their adherents to forgive those who seek forgiveness. Some proclaim the importance of forgiving those who wrong you even if they seek no reconciliation. It is assumed in this latter case that the act of forgiving is an expression of no malice by the recipient of the wrongdoing and even a gesture of acceptance of the wrongdoer in spite of the unacceptability of his deed. Amnesty is the political equivalent of such a religious act.

To those who understand that God is love there can be no human act or alienation that is unforgivable. Persons alienated from their fellow men and therefore from God are brought back from a fractured relationship into genuine community by the knowledge or faith that they are accepted in spite of any apparent unworthiness. It is the initiative taken by the person wronged that is always to some degree unexpected and therefore the more impressive. Christian theology holds that God's forgiveness is always present for the wrongdoer. Only when persons show by their own refusal to forgive their fellows that they have no faith in forgiveness are they denied forgiveness by their own rejection of it.

In political terms a government that cannot bring itself to proclaim amnesty for political offenses indicates its hardness of heart, its willingness to keep the nation divided in order to vindicate its own partisan judgments. By its own lack of faith in the process of forgiveness it prolongs and perhaps intensifies the resentment of those who could not cooperate with the war in the first place. It is willing to risk a build up of hostility, perhaps even continued violence, rather than take the step of initiating reconciliation. Only the government can take such a step because it alone speaks for the whole nation and because it has prosecuted or driven into exile, or stands ready to punish, those who are politically dissident.

Amnesty is an act of grace—clemency—by the President, restoring offenders against the draft or the war to their position in society without any legal stigma or impediments. It does not mean that their position has been vindicated. From the government's point of view it is forgiveness for an act that is still legally wrong.

Amnesty changes legal status only. It does not change society's social approval or disapproval of what happened. To some Americans the offenders against the draft are heroes, and to others, villains. Those who view them as heroes will be less able to view amnestied men as martyrs, and those who view them as villains may take some satisfaction from that fact, for they are less likely to be symbols of continuing opposition to government if they are amnestied. On the other hand, amnesty does not silence opponents of conscription or war; neither are they silenced now by penalties already imposed or about to be imposed. For many Americans, Eugene Debs' imprisonment during World War I was a greater reminder of the injustice of government than anything he would have said, had he been free to speak on the outside. Similarly, the fact of "good" men in prison today is a constant prod to many Americans who generally do not have friends or acquaintances in prison.

Political Prisoners

Americans generally have frowned upon imprisoning men for political reasons. Although violation of a conscription law is technically the same as violating any other law, it is not assumed by most Americans to involve the violation of other persons or personal property that is implied by assault or theft. Breaking the draft law is a political offense in that it challenges a political course of action that the government can implement only by taking away a man's freedom. Those who resist conscription at whatever level are political offenders and constitute the largest category of political prisoners in the United States today. In a sense the test of how democratic any government is depends upon the number of political prisoners it keeps behind bars. In the eyes of millions of people around the world the United States' reputation as a democracy would be enhanced rather than diminished by amnesty for those who are in prison for draft-related offenses as well as for those in exile or still awaiting trial.

There is probably very little public opposition to amnesty for those who resisted the draft by nonviolent means. After all, three-fourths of the American people have, at the time of this writing, according to public-opinion polls, registered their opposition to continuing the war in Vietnam. It is without doubt the most unpopular war in American history. The crucial questions about amnesty, therefore, relate to activity that is harder to explain than mere draft resistance. Such activity ranges from the destruction of government property such as draft board files or offices, to desertion and war-related acts of violence. These actions may seem extreme to those devoted to domestic tranquillity. Yet they can be understood as the result of frustration at the failure of people in general and government leaders in particular to respond to massive and orderly dissent. The nation engages in war not only against combatants but against noncombatant women and children. To some of those sensitive to this injustice, the destruction of property, desertion, and other extreme acts are ways of political opposition. It may be difficult to separate these politically inspired offenses from typical crimes, yet this is essential if there is a governmental intent to wipe the political slate clean and to seek to blot out the divisions and resentments caused by the war. It is assumed that totalitarian nations have political prisoners because freedom-loving or peace-loving people will oppose the regime. One assumption about democratic states is that there are no political prisoners because men are free to say "no" to their governments. The fact that men are not free to say "no" to conscription or to war and thus feel it necessary to resort to extreme acts puts any free society to the test. General amnesty is the way a free society can proclaim its acceptance of political offenders who are no longer "dangerous" to governments because the war that caused or precipitated their actions has been ended. They are not offenders against society or threats to the life and property of their fellow citizens. Their offense was war-inspired and war-directed. Therefore, there is no reason for their continued alienation, unless the nation continues to see itself as a largely war-motivated entity or as justified in punishing its conscientious protesters.

"Any wholesale amnesty . . . would make a mockery of the sacrifices of those men who did their duty, assumed the responsibilities in time of conflict, and—in many cases—were killed."

A General Amnesty Should Not Be Granted to Draft Evaders

John H. Geiger (b.1925)

On February 28 and 29 and March 1, 1972, a subcommittee of the Senate Judiciary Committee, chaired by Senator Edward M. Kennedy of Massachusetts, held public hearings on the issue of whether amnesty should be granted to those Americans who defied the law and refused to serve in Vietnam, either by evading or resisting the draft, by going absent without leave (AWOL), or by otherwise deserting their positions in the military. Among those who testified before the subcommittee was John H. Geiger, national commander of the American Legion, a membership association of American war veterans. Speaking for the organization, Geiger argues against any plan for a blanket amnesty for those who resisted or illegally avoided service in Vietnam, insisting instead that each case should be tried separately in the courts. A general amnesty, he asserts, would constitute an insult to those who died in Vietnam and would weaken the morale of American soldiers in Vietnam and elsewhere. He also rejects the assertion that America's role in Vietnam is immoral.

Excerpted from John H. Geiger, statement before the U.S. Senate Committee on the Judiciary, Subcommittee on Administrative Practice and Procedure, March 1, 1972.

The issue of amnesty continued to be debated after the 1973 Paris Peace Accords and the 1975 fall of South Vietnam. In 1977 President Jimmy Carter issued presidential pardons to approximately ten thousand draft evaders in exile in Canada and elsewhere.

Members of the subcommittee, I am appearing here today at your invitation to present the views of the American Legion on the question of executive clemency for those who have failed to comply with the statutory and regulatory requirements of the Selective Service Act and those who have deserted from military service during the Vietnam war.

You and the members of the subcommittee are to be commended for your efforts to develop information on this complex subject. As national commander, I am pleased that so many members of the subcommittee are veterans and members of the American Legion and are aware of our interest in defense and military matters. For the record, our current membership exceeds 2,700,000 honorably discharged former servicemen and women of World War I, World War II, Korea and Vietnam.

With the exception of World War II, the largest segment of our current membership, some half a million, based their eligibility on Vietnam era service. While the reason for belonging to our organization are many and varied, all of our members have a concern for our nation's well-being, particularly in the area of national defense.

This concern has, from the Legion's beginning in 1919 following World War I, manifested itself in the resolutions annually adopted at its national conventions.

The American Legion's Position

Today my appearance and the position I take on amnesty are based upon resolution 207 adopted at our 1971 National Convention.

A copy of this resolution is appended to this statement and I respectfully request that it be made a part of the official records of these hearings. The delegates who unanimously adopted resolution 207 represented every one of the 50 States and the District of Columbia. They were all honorably discharged veterans of wartime service and represented a cross-section of American ethnic, cultural, political and economical life. Resolution 207 also has unanimous support of the American Legion Auxiliary whose nearly 1 million members are the wives, mothers, sisters, and daughters of men who served their nation.

Like you, we Legionnaires are deeply concerned over the complex problems presented by the issue of amnesty. It is an emotional problem with overtones of justice, tempered with mercy and understanding. Amnesty is particularly difficult to consider today because of the profound and bitter division in our land over the Vietnam conflict—our longest war and—like the Revolutionary, Mexican and Civil Wars—a bitterly divisive one.

A large number of our young men are involved in the amnesty question—though far more were involved in this question in the Civil War. Today, our Vietnam casualties far outnumber our draft evaders. Over 70,000 by unofficial estimates are either military deserters or Selective Service evaders. For many, their excuse is the immorality of the participation of the United States in the conflict in Vietnam. Canada, Sweden, and, to a much lesser extent, other countries have given these young men asylum. Their cause is now being popularized and propagandized by many and diverse groups in the United States and abroad—including several candidates for high public office in our own country.

Let us hope that as a result of these hearings, earnest and full consideration will be given to all facets of the issue of executive clemency so that we shall be able to discover and follow that difficult line between the dictates of the law and the charity our moral heritage demands. The American Legion has an intense and direct interest in amnesty because of the fact that its members all were subject to the laws, regulations, pressures and responsibilities of military service in defense of the United States. . . .

We believe that we have a real and vital stake in this issue since it concerns basically the rights and responsibilities of the citizen to bear arms in defense of his nation.

In 1783, Gen. George Washington expressed clearly the responsibility of citizenship which I believe goes to the heart of the proposition under discussion. Washington said: "It may be laid down as a primary position and the basis of our system that every citizen who enjoys the protection of a free government owes not only a portion of his property, but even of his personal services to the defense of it." The American Legion was formed to help insure that these rights and responsibilities were carried out in civilian life by those comrades who have borne them in time of war.

Proponents of amnesty at the present time fall into two categories. One group advocates unconditional amnesty for all military deserters and draft evaders. This group reasons that the Vietnam conflict is an immoral war for the United States; that those who recognize this and follow their conscience ought not to suffer any legal penalties for being right while their country was wrong; and, therefore, amnesty should be a blanket recognition of this. . . .

The second group of proponents offer amnesty to draft evaders but not to military deserters providing that draft evaders prove their sincerity by performing alternate service for their country.

The American Legion believes that most draft evaders and deserters consciously decided to refuse to accept their responsibilities as citizens under the law; that they evaded their responsibilities by flouting our laws and legal remedies rather than by going through the available legal channels of redress; that their actions in declining to obey certain laws distasteful to them [are] contrary to sound legal and moral standards; and that the obligations of citizenship cannot be applied to some and evaded by others.

Exiles in Canada Made Their Choice

In a January 27, 1972, letter to the Chicago Sun-Times, *Mrs. Robert A. Merker, a mother of a soldier killed in Vietnam, objected to amnesty for draft resisters and those who had gone to Canada and other countries. The letter was later submitted as part of the record of the 1972 Senate hearings on amnesty.*

I do not favor any sort of amnesty to the draft resisters and deserters, either now or after the war is over. If anyone is truly a conscientious objector, they could have served in a non-combat capacity and still given time to their country. I feel that we will be at the mercy of foreign powers if they know our citizens are allowed to disregard their country by being unwilling to fight and die for it.

Our eldest son could have resisted the draft too. Instead he enlisted in the Army, became a Warrant Officer and a helicopter pilot. He was killed in action when his light scout helicopter was hit by small arms fire and crashed. He loved this country enough to die to contribute to the safety and well being of it and its citizens.

Why should anyone leading the soft, safe, life in Canada be given extra consideration for their cop-out on their responsibilities as citizens. Let them stay in Canada. This was their choice.

The American Legion resolved that: "We go on record as opposing any attempt to grant amnesty or freedom from prosecution to those men who either by illegally avoiding the draft or desertion from the Armed Forces failed to fulfill their military obligation to the United States." In other words, we of the American Legion firmly believe that giving any wholesale amnesty—whether conditional or unconditional—would make a mockery of the sacrifices of those men who did their duty, assumed the responsibilities in time of conflict and—in many cases—were killed, seriously wounded, or now lie in a prison camp somewhere in Indochina. Over 50,000 men have paid the supreme price of patriotism and citizenship: Another 302,602 have been wounded or injured. Over 1600 men are prisoners or missing in action in Vietnam, Laos, or Cambodia and the casualties have not ended.

How can any general amnesty be explained to these men? How can amnesty be explained to parents, wives, children—all those who have lost a son, husband, or a father in their country's service? How can we excuse ourselves to the prisoners of war, the missing in action, or to their suffering families for offering amnesty? Furthermore, what would be the effect on the morale of our Armed Forces if amnesty were granted to those who have violated the law and their oath of service by turning their backs and fleeing their country?

In our opinion, it could only badly undermine that morale and cheapen the value of honorable service to one's country—at the very moment these values are most in need of strengthening.

Amnesty might even be the last bitter pill to our servicemen now caught in a web of confusion and held in disdain by those who hate the war and would do anything to drive us out of it in dishonor, including destroying our Armed Forces on the field of battle and their spirit. Our men are fighting the enemy. They are fighting dangerous drugs, they are fighting hatred and misunderstanding at home. They are coping with racial problems and the problems involved in a transitional period in military life and discipline.

We cannot afford to add the issue of a general amnesty to those problems at this time. It is clear from the Legion's resolution that our official opposition to amnesty is not a total opposition to it but an opposition to any sort of amnesty—with or without conditions—to all draft evaders as a class. Our resolution asks that all draft evaders be prosecuted.

This means that we would like each case to be heard in court and tried on its merits. The courts can deal with the particulars of each case and exercise leniency or sternness, based on the actual facts brought out in hearings about each particular draft evader. Surely the courts will find those who are innocent, and who should be excused without any further conditions. It is also implicit in our resolution that those found guilty would still have open to them the right of appeal. Should appeal fail they would have recourse to the President's pardoning power, if, on review of the facts in each case he wishes to extend additional leniency beyond what the courts may extend.

This is implicit in our resolution, because any request for prosecution implies not only the possible finding of their guilt but the finding of innocence and the avenues for redress, appeal, and pardon are available to all persons who are prosecuted.

Our request that draft evaders be prosecuted does not deny to them their full rights under the law, or the opportunity for Executive clemency. Our resolution, in effect, opposes any form of blanket amnesty, and asks that each case be considered on its merits. The only other example in our history of amnesty for wartime draft evaders certainly bears out the wisdom of this approach—and, of course, it is consistent with the whole American system of justice which is based on hearing the charges and the facts in each case.

The World War II Precedent

After World War II, the Roberts Board tried to treat all 15,805 World War II draft evaders the same, as all proposals for blanket amnesty do. The board threw up its hands at the injustice of such an operation. It found sinners of all degrees, as well as innocent men, among the World War II draft evaders. In the end, with the aid of the Justice Department staff, it reviewed each case. That was not the easy way out but the Roberts Board shouldered the huge job of review rather than accept the onus of dispensing justice by the shovelful.

There are some in this country who would create the illusion that every Vietnam draft dodger was acting on high principle out of deep-seated convictions against war. When all cases were judged individually by the Roberts Board after World War II, nearly half were found to have been men wanted for murder, robbery, desertion of their families, and other serious crimes.

On the other hand, others were found to have been legally exempt from military service, or they fell afoul of the law through ignorance or illiteracy. President Truman gave a complete pardon to 1,523 and a conditional one to 1,518 while more than 12,000 did not merit such treatment. If the Vietnam draft evaders are all prosecuted, courts will be able to judge each case on it merits. They will again find a mixture of victims of error, deliberate conspirators, and professional criminals. The President could then have them screened and consider recommendations for clemency in each case. An act of Congress to provide an across the board 3-year stint of Government service in exchange for amnesty would offer that penance to some for whom it is too heavy a penalty and to others for whom it is too mild a punishment. The most flagrant offenders will get the best break and the least offenders the worst.

This is hardly equal justice under the law. At least 10 Presidents, from Washington to Truman, have handled the amnesty question under existing machinery. An act of Congress that decides all cases without a hearing is neither necessary nor desirable. There was no amnesty granted after the Korean War. It is therefore clear

218

that amnesty has not been lightly given by our modern American Presidents and it has been granted only after the shooting has stopped and the war is over.

An Immoral War?

Lastly, an argument much used by advocates of unconditional general amnesty is that the Vietnam conflict is immoral, therefore, no American should be prosecuted or punished for refusing to take part in any direct or indirect way in an immoral war. I am not aware of the precise moral standards used by those who would label our military assistance to the Republic of Vietnam immoral. It is rarely defined and the assumption that the Vietnam conflict is now, or was in the beginning, an immoral war is much in dispute.

We Legionnaires reject the simplistic labeling of our effort in Vietnam as immoral. We reject it on the grounds that such allegations are patently false. The United States' commitment to the government and the people of South Vietnam is just and moral. We are committed to providing South Vietnam a means whereby it can defend its independence and its right of self-determination. Our involvement in Vietnam was authorized under proper constitutional procedures and was sustained by the Congress.

The Vietcong were committing genocide in South Vietnam at the time we became heavily involved in that conflict—systematically slaughtering innocent civilians wholesale as a means of gaining political control. We knew this then and we know it now. Everyone within sound of my words knows it, but when discussion of the morality of the Vietnam war arises today, the fact that we intervened against genocide, when the United Nations would not, is simply omitted from the discussion.

One cannot admit it and still define our role in Vietnam as immoral. We hope and believe that the Congress will not decide such a moral question by closing its eyes to genocide. We cannot believe that the Congress will ever decide that those who violated the law have the superior moral position to the President, the Congress and to the men who served.

If Congress should decide that they do, we wonder who next will take up the pretext and use the precedent to claim a moral superiority over some fresh enactments of the Congress. We wonder what future legal dissemblance will be in store for us if we create such an extraordinary precedent as the Congress assenting to the rights of citizens to determine unilaterally which laws they will obey.

Any determination of amnesty based on the moral superiority of draft law violators is contrary to our concept of justice. Historically, the Congress, the President and the Judiciary have struggled to determine the extent of power of each. Should we now add a new dimension to this three-sided struggle—namely any citizen who claims that his unilateral view of morality is superior to the Congress, the courts and the President alike?

If we establish this as the correct view, the day will arrive when there will little further use for the Presidents, the courts, or the Congress.

In summary, the American Legion's position on amnesty is: one, we oppose any attempt to grant amnesty now. Two, after the conflict ends, peace is established, and our prisoners of war and missing-in-action have been repatriated or accounted for, each case should be reviewed under existing procedures available to the courts and the President.

"We believe that the will of the people says that we should be out of Vietnam now."

A Veteran Calls for Immediate Withdrawal

John Kerry (b. 1943)

From April 19 to April 23, 1971, one of the most effective anti-war demonstrations was staged in Washington, D.C. The participants—who camped on the National Mall, held a memorial ceremony at Arlington National Cemetery, and lobbied Congress and the Supreme Court to end the war—were notable not for their relatively small number (about eleven hundred), but because they were military veterans who had served in Vietnam. The protest was organized by Vietnam Veterans Against the War (VVAW), a group that was founded in 1967 and that by 1971 had grown to about twelve thousand members in the United States and fifteen hundred in Vietnam. At the culmination of the protest, on April 23, a group of veterans threw their war medals and ribbons onto the steps of the Capitol building.

The previous day, John Kerry, a spokesman for VVAW, testified before the Senate Foreign Relations Committee. A graduate of Yale University, Kerry served in the U.S. Navy from 1966 to 1969. In his statement, excerpted here, Kerry condemns the war in Vietnam and argues that delaying America's withdrawal will pointlessly cost more American lives. He contends that the justifications for the war given by U.S. leaders have had no relation to the situation in Vietnam as found by the soldiers. Kerry describes the "Winter Soldier" hearings that the VVAW sponsored in Detroit from January 31 to February 2, 1971, at which American soldiers

Excerpted from John Kerry, statement before the U.S. Senate Committee on Foreign Relations, April 22, 1971.

testified about acts of brutality they had committed or witnessed in Vietnam. He concludes that America has no moral purpose or standing to remain in that country.

Kerry later entered politics. In 1984 he was elected to represent Massachusetts in the U.S. Senate.

I would like to say for the record, and also for the men behind me who are also wearing the uniform and their medals, that my sitting here is really symbolic. I am not here as John Kerry. I am here as one member of the group of 1,000 which is a small representation of a very much larger group of veterans in this country, and were it possible for all of them to sit at this table they would be here and have the same kind of testimony. . . .

I would like to talk on behalf of all those veterans and say that several months ago in Detroit we had an investigation at which over 150 honorably discharged, and many very highly decorated, veterans testified to war crimes committed in Southeast Asia. These were not isolated incidents but crimes committed on a day to day basis with the full awareness of officers at all levels of command.

It is impossible to describe to you exactly what did happen in Detroit—the emotions in the room and the feelings of the men who were reliving their experiences in Vietnam. They relived the absolute horror of what this country, in a sense, made them do.

Stories of Atrocities

They told stories that at times they had personally raped, cut off ears, cut off heads, taped wires from portable telephones to human genitals and turned up the power, cut off limbs, blown up bodies, randomly shot at civilians, razed villages in fashion reminiscent of Genghis Khan, shot cattle and dogs for fun, poisoned food stocks, and generally ravaged the countryside of South Vietnam in addition to the normal ravage of war and the normal and very particular ravaging which is done by the applied bombing power of this country.

We call this investigation the Winter Soldier Investigation. The term Winter Soldier is a play on words of Thomas Paine's in 1776 when he spoke of the Sunshine Patriots and summer time soldiers who deserted at Valley Forge because the going was rough.

We who have come here to Washington have come here because we feel we have to be winter soldiers now. We could come back to this country, we could be quiet, we could hold our silence, we could not tell what went on in Vietnam, but we feel because of what threatens this country, not the reds, but the crimes which we are committing that threaten it, that we have to speak out.

I would like to talk to you a little bit about what the result is of the feelings these men carry with them after coming back from Vietnam. The country doesn't know it yet but it has created a monster, a monster in the form of millions of men who have been taught to deal and to trade in violence and who are given the chance to die for the biggest nothing in history; men who have returned with a sense of anger and a sense of betrayal which no one has yet grasped.

The State of the Army in Vietnam

Discontent with the Vietnam War manifested itself in several ways among U.S. troops stationed there. In a June 7, 1971, article in Armed Forces Journal, *Colonel Robert D. Heinl of the U.S. Marines argued that the U.S. armed forces in Vietnam were in a state approaching collapse.*

By every conceivable indicator, our army that now remains in Vietnam is in a state approaching collapse, with individual units avoiding or having refused combat, murdering their officers and noncommissioned officers, drug-ridden, and dispirited where not near-mutinous. . . .

"They have set up separate companies," writes an American soldier from Cu Chi, quoted in the *New York Times*, "for men who refuse to go out into the field. It is no big thing to refuse to go. If a man is ordered to go to such and such a place he no longer goes through the hassle of refusing; he just packs his shirt and goes to visit some buddies at another base camp. Operations have become incredibly ragtag. Many guys don't even put on their uniforms any more. . . . The American garrisons on the larger bases are virtually disarmed. The lifers have taken our weapons from us and put them under lock and key. . . . There have also been quite a few frag incidents in the battalion."

Can all this really be typical or even truthful?

Unfortunately the answer is yes.

As a veteran and one who feels this anger I would like to talk about it. We are angry because we feel we have been used in the worst fashion by the administration of this country.

In 1970 at West Point Vice President [Spiro T.] Agnew said "some glamorize the criminal misfits of society while our best men die in Asian rice paddies to preserve the freedom which most of those misfits abuse," and this was used as a rallying point for our effort in Vietnam.

But for us, as boys in Asia whom the country was supposed to support, his statement is a terrible distortion from which we can only draw a very deep sense of revulsion, and hence the anger of some of the men who are here in Washington today. It is a distortion because we in no way consider ourselves the best men of this country; because those he calls misfits were standing up for us in a way that nobody else in this country dared to; because so many who have died would have returned to this country to join the misfits in their efforts to ask for an immediate withdrawal from South Vietnam; because so many of those best men have returned as quadriplegics and amputees—and they lie forgotten in Veterans Administration Hospitals in this country which fly the flag which so many have chosen as their own personal symbol—and we cannot consider ourselves America's best men when we are ashamed of and hated for what we were called on to do in Southeast Asia.

In our opinion, and from our experience, there is nothing in South Vietnam which could happen that realistically threatens the United States of America. And to attempt to justify the loss of one American life in Vietnam, Cambodia or Laos by linking such loss to the preservation of freedom, which those misfits supposedly abuse, is to us the height of criminal hypocrisy, and it is that kind of hypocrisy which we feel has torn this country apart.

We are probably much more angry than that, but I don't want to go into the foreign policy aspects because I am outclassed here. I know that all of you talk about every possible alternative for getting out of Vietnam. We understand that. We know you have considered the seriousness of the aspects to the utmost level and I am not going to try to dwell on that. But I want to relate to you the feeling that many of the men who have returned to this country express because we are probably angriest about all that we were told about Vietnam and about the mystical war against communism.

What We Saw

We found that not only was it a civil war, an effort by a people who had for years been seeking their liberation from any colonial influence whatsoever, but also we found that the Vietnamese whom we had enthusiastically molded after our own image were hard put to take up the fight against the threat we were supposedly saving them from.

We found most people didn't even know the difference between communism and democracy. They only wanted to work in rice paddies without helicopters strafing them and bombs with napalm burning their villages and tearing their country apart. They wanted everything to do with the war, particularly with this foreign presence of the United States of America, to leave them alone in peace, and they practiced the art of survival by siding with whichever military force was present at a particular time, be it Viet Cong, North Vietnamese or American.

We found also that all too often American men were dying in those rice paddies for want of support from their allies. We saw firsthand how monies from American taxes were used for a corrupt dictatorial regime. We saw that many people in this country had a one-sided idea of who was kept free by our flag, and blacks provided the highest percentage of casualties. We saw Vietnam ravaged equally by American bombs and search and destroy missions, as well as by Viet Cong terrorism, and yet we listened while this country tried to blame all of the havoc on the Viet Cong.

We rationalized destroying villages in order to save them. We saw America lose her sense of morality as she accepted very coolly a My Lai and refused to give up the image of American soldiers who hand out chocolate bars and chewing gum.

We learned the meaning of free fire zones, shooting anything that moves, and we watched while America placed a cheapness on the lives of orientals.

We watched the United States falsification of body counts, in fact the glorification of body counts. We listened while month after month we were told the back of the enemy was about to break. We fought using weapons against "oriental human beings." We fought using weapons against those people which I do not believe this country would dream of using were we fighting in the European theater. We watched while men charged up hills because a general said that hill has to be taken, and after losing one platoon or two platoons they marched away to leave the hill for reoccupation by the North Vietnamese. We watched pride allow the most unimportant battles to be blown into extravaganzas, because we couldn't lose, and we couldn't retreat, and because it didn't matter how many American bodies were lost to prove that point, and so there were Hamburger Hills and Khe Sanhs and Hill 81s and Fire Base 6s, and so many others. . . .

Each day to facilitate the process by which the United States washes her hands of Vietnam someone has to give up his life so that the United States doesn't have to admit something that the entire world already knows, so that we can't say that we have made a mistake. Someone has to die so that President Nixon won't be, and these are his words, "the first President to lose a war."

To Die for a Mistake

We are asking Americans to think about that because how do you ask a man to be the last man to die in Vietnam? How do you ask a man to be the last man to die for a mistake? But we are trying to do that, and we see doing it with thousands of rationalizations, and if you read carefully the President's last speech to the people of this country, you can see that he says, and says clearly:

> But the issue, gentlemen, the issue is communism, and the question is whether or not we will leave that country to the Communists or whether or not we will try to give it hope to be a free people.

But the point is they are not a free people now under us. They are not a free people, and we cannot fight communism all over the world, and I think we should have learned that lesson by now. . . .

We are asking here in Washington for some action; action from the Congress of the United States of America which has the power to raise and maintain armies, and which by the Constitution also has the power to declare war.

We have come here, not to the President, because we believe that this body can be responsive to the will of the people, and we believe that the will of the people says that we should be out of Vietnam now.

We are here in Washington also to say that the problem of this war is not just a question of war and diplomacy. It is part and parcel of everything that we are trying as human beings to communicate to people in this country—the question of racism which is rampant in the military, and so many other questions such as the use of weapons; the hypocrisy of our taking umbrage at the Geneva Conventions and using that as justification for a continuation of this war when we are more guilty than any other body of violations of those Geneva Conventions; in the use of free fire zones, harassment interdiction fire, search and destroy missions, the bombings, the torture of prisoners, the killing of prisoners, all accepted policy by many units in South Vietnam. That is what we are trying to say. It is part and parcel of everything.

An American Indian friend of mine who lives in the Indian Nation of Alcatraz put it to me very succinctly. He told me how as a boy on an Indian reservation he had watched television and he used to cheer the cowboys when they came in and shot the Indians, and then suddenly one day he stopped in Vietnam and he said, "My God, I am doing to these people the very same thing that was done to my people," and he stopped. And that is what we are trying to say, that we think this thing has to end.

We are also here to ask, and we are here to ask vehemently, where are the leaders of our country? Where is the leadership? We are here to ask where are McNamara, Rostow, Bundy, Gilpatric and so many others? Where are they now that we, the men whom they sent off to war, have returned? These are commanders who have deserted their troops, and there is no more serious crime in the laws of war. The Army says they never leave their wounded. The Marines say they never leave even their dead. These men have left the real stuff of their reputation bleaching behind them in the sun in this country.

Finally, this administration has done us the ultimate dishonor. They have attempted to disown us and the sacrifices we made for this country. In their blindness and fear they have tried to deny that we are veterans or that we served in Nam. We do not need their testimony. Our own scars and stumps or limbs are witness enough for others and for ourselves.

We wish that a merciful God could wipe away our own memories of that service as easily as this administration has wiped away the memories of us. But all that they have done and all that they can do by this denial is to make more clear than ever our own determination to undertake one less mission—to search out and destroy the last vestige of this barbaric war, to pacify our hearts, to conquer the hate and the fear that have driven this country these last ten years and more, so when 30 years from now our brothers go down the street without a leg, without an arm, or a face, and small boys ask why, we will be able to say "Vietnam" and not mean a desert, not a filthy obscene memory, but mean instead the place where America finally turned and where soldiers like us helped it in the turning.

*"The setting of an arbitrary date for American
withdrawal can only hurt the cause of the South
Vietnamese people."*

A Veteran Opposes
Immediate Withdrawal

Melville L. Stephens (dates unknown)

American soldiers who served in Vietnam were, like other segments of American society, divided over the Vietnam War. The
1971 demonstrations by the Vietnam Veterans Against the War
(VVAW) were criticized by some who argued that the organization did not truly represent the views of Vietnam veterans. The
following viewpoint is excerpted from remarks before the Senate
Foreign Relations Committee by Melville L. Stephens, who, as a
lieutenant in the U.S. Navy from 1967 to 1970, spent much time in
Vietnam. He made his statement on April 28, 1971, partly as a response to VVAW spokesman John Kerry, who one week earlier
testified about American atrocities in Vietnam and urged an immediate U.S. withdrawal (see opposing viewpoint). Stephens expresses his support for ending the war, but argues against an immediate U.S. pullout from Vietnam. He asserts that the United
States still has a moral commitment not to abandon the South
Vietnamese, who he believes greatly fear the prospect of Communist rule. In response to Kerry's charge that Americans have committed war crimes in Vietnam, Stephens states that the Vietcong
have committed their share of war atrocities.

In addition to Stephens's statement, the following viewpoint
contains excerpts of a question by Republican senator Hugh Scott
of Pennsylvania on whether Stephens's views are shared by other
Vietnam veterans. Stephens responds that many other veterans
remain committed to the South Vietnamese.

Excerpted from Melville L. Stephens, statement before the U.S. Senate Committee on Foreign
Relations, April 22, 1971.

I would like to thank . . . members of the committee for the opportunity to be here. I particularly appreciate the opportunity to speak because I know that my views are not very popular these days.

However, my convictions are very strong and based on my own experience and what I believe is a realistic sense of the situation and the feelings of the Vietnamese people.

Experiences in Vietnam

I was in the Navy from June of 1967 until September of last year [1970] and spent nearly 34 months in the Southeast Asia combat zone. This nearly 3-year period included 10 months aboard a cruiser of the 7th Fleet in a gunfire support role, during which time I had an opportunity to visit various areas of I Corps [U.S. Army First Corps' South Vietnamese Area of Operations]; and almost 2 years in Vietnamese incountry tours. I worked extensively with the U.S. 9th Infantry Division and various units of the South Vietnamese armed forces including the Vietnamese Navy, the Vietnamese Marine Corps, the Vietnamese Army, the regional and popular forces, and the irregular defense groups. During my last tour, which ended in May of last year, I had an opportunity to travel extensively throughout the country of Vietnam, and view firsthand the process of American withdrawal and the Vietnamese forces moving in to take over the combat role.

During this time I feel very fortunate to have made a great many friends among the Vietnamese people. I cannot speak more highly of my personal regard and affection for these people, both as friends and as comrades. My concern and the reason that I asked to speak today, is to ask you to consider carefully your course, so that peace for Americans does not come at the cost of additional sacrifice for these people.

Against Unconditional Withdrawal

It seems, that since I returned to the States last spring, that the cries for unconditional withdrawal and the setting of an immediate date for ending American support have become very loud, and I know that you on the committee have listened very carefully.

I believe that these arguments have two principal weaknesses. First, they are based on questions which certainly should have been asked in the early 1960's, but which were not. We are there; we have been there for a long time. The questions of legality and specific strategy which were valid 10 years ago are no longer the relevant ones.

Second, the very truth that all war is terrible and brutal is especially true of this one in which the civilian population is so intimately involved. Only those of us who have been there and fought and lived with the Vietnamese people can know how very true this is. I certainly agree that this war has gone on too long and must come to an end. But I ask you to consider carefully the manner in which you intend to end it.

I want to assure you that after my nearly 3 years in Vietnam I am convinced that the overwhelming majority of the Vietnamese people are opposed to the Communists. A great many of them have taken their stand because of the American commitment to the Government of Vietnam. I would like to think that you and I and the American people have a responsibility to these Vietnamese who have had faith in us in the past, and have risked their lives for something they believe in. Peace for us must not come at the cost of their lives.

As I look around Washington today, and last week, I am very offended to see Americans carrying the flag of the VC. I fear that some Americans, in their passion for peace, have made heroes of the Vietcong. Let me assure you . . . that in South Vietnam, the Vietcong are not heroes.

I heard a great deal about atrocities last week, particularly from my fellow Vietnam veterans who were here. I certainly do not deny that some of them took place. But there is also another side which should be heard more often. I would like to tell you about two particular incidents, which I am personally aware of.

In the spring of 1969 near Can Tho in the southern part of the delta I was unfortunate enough to be a witness to the grenading of a Vietnamese school bus, which was clearly marked as a school bus, by the Vietcong. Two of the children were killed outright; several were wounded so severely that I doubt that they could possibly have survived; and three others were maimed in the most grotesque manner that you could imagine.

Earlier in my tour I became very close friends with a young Vietnamese boy of 11 named Tran who had been orphaned by the Vietcong. Tran told me that in the fall of 1967 his father had been elected to a local village office and Tran had been seized by the Vietcong in the area and had had his left arm cut off with a machete as an example to his father. His father had refused to resign even at this, but he, along with his mother, were killed in the Tet offensive of 1968.

Senator, as I say, I speak from personal experience. I speak of only a few incidents like this, but anyone who has spent any time in Vietnam will assure you of the brutality and the terror of the Communists. They, the Communists themselves, have been quite blunt in stating that terror and mass execution are their principal strategy. The South Vietnamese I lived with know this. They know that they take their lives in their hands when they support the Government of Vietnam and so they depend upon us for the support which we have promised.

I think I understand as well as any the passion of all of us in this country for an end to the war, but it is my firm conviction that peace at the price of these Vietnamese people is too expen-

What Vietnam Veterans Believe

Speaking at the same hearings at which John Kerry testified on behalf of Vietnam Veterans Against the War (VVAW), H.R. Rainwater, the commander of the organization Veterans of Foreign Wars, argues that Kerry's views are not shared by most Vietnam veterans.

Thank you for the opportunity you have given me to present my views as commander in chief of the more than 1.8 million members of the Veterans of Foreign Wars, including over 400,000 Vietnam veterans, concerning the ramifications of U.S. involvement in Indochina.

Our convictions are based on the combined experience of our members, and I hope to present a realistic picture of our true consensus of opinion. The majority of our membership is deeply concerned because the views of the minority of Vietnam veterans are being heard, and stressed, over the views of the majority. As you know, there have been in excess of 2½ million U.S. servicemen involved in the Indochina conflict. The Veterans of Foreign Wars has included in its membership almost 20 percent of that total U.S. commitment. The views expressed, and given such unproportionate news media coverage, by the Vietnam Veterans Against the War represented less than 1 percent of the Vietnam veterans; neither their alleged experiences nor opinions represent the average veteran. Furthermore, it is very questionable whether their demands for future U.S. policies would be those which the Nation might choose if it were given a free choice. . . .

We do not agree with those who espouse an immediate, unilateral, and unconditional withdrawal of U.S. forces from Indochina. We do not agree with those who desire the abandonment of our present judicial and expedient investigative policies concerning alleged war atrocities. We do not agree with those who call for our withdrawal of support for the legally elected Government of South Vietnam. We do not agree with those who believe that the only method for obtaining the release of U.S. prisoners of war is by complete abandonment of our present negotiation policies at the Paris peace talks. We do not agree with those who choose to isolate certain incidents which are aberrations of U.S. policy and use them as a basis for total condemnation of our efforts in Indochina. The all-encompassing and self-righteous finger of condemnation which they point at the heart of our Nation is leveled by a hand of betrayal.

sive, and it is a peace that I could not live with.

I want to tell you from my own sense, from my own personal experience from nearly 3 years in Vietnam, that the setting of an arbitrary date for American withdrawal can only hurt the cause of the South Vietnamese people, and that I am firmly convinced that the current program, which I was a part of, and which I have watched since I left, is as progressive and ambitious as I believe the situation could permit.

When I speak of my fear for the Vietnamese people, I certainly don't speak of the generals and the admirals, of the high ranking officials. Frankly, I am quite sure that in a situation they can handle themselves. I do refer to the junior officers and the troops who I knew, to the merchants and to the farmers and to the local officials, those who we would call the average citizens of the country.

I think, sir, that the issue of ending this war is not the issue of our saving face; but the issue of our responsibility, as a nation and as individuals, to these citizens of South Vietnam. Many of them have committed themselves, because we very literally asked them to. I hope and urge that in our urgency for peace that we do not abandon them. . . .

A Majority Sentiment?

Senator [Hugh] Scott: Lieutenant Stephens, yours is a calm, quiet voice, and yet it is just as important surely that your views and your voice be heard in the media, on television and on radio. It is more difficult for you to draw the cameras to you because you are speaking rationally and reasonably and out of a very deep concern. . . .

You have talked to other veterans. By various estimates, approximately 1,500 veterans were here. There have been over 2.5 million who have served in Southeast Asia, and you have, of course, talked with many of them. Is it your opinion that you are reflecting a general sentiment or a majority sentiment of those veterans with whom you are familiar and with whom you have served?

Mr. Stephens: Mr. Scott, even among the 1,500 veterans here last week in the protest, there were very few who did not have very close Vietnamese friends whom they hold very dearly and when they think about the issue objectively, they know that we have a responsibility to them, and they look for an answer which will not abandon them.

I can understand that from war develops a passion for peace, but that passion sometimes makes people less than objective, and I feel that I speak for the majority of the people—no, I don't, I don't want to presume to speak for the majority or for anyone

232

else except myself, but my sense of being there and being with other Americans and South Vietnamese, is that there is a lot of respect for the South Vietnamese and a commitment to them. . . .

I certainly understand the urgency of the American people, and of those in this room particularly for a quick end to the war. I mean it has gone a long time for us also.

But the reason I came here to speak today is because I am afraid that in this urgency that we will lose our objectivity, and we will forget the commitment which we made in the past and which the Vietnamese depend upon.

CHAPTER 6

A Debate over the Media's Role in Vietnam

Chapter Preface

More than two decades have passed since the fall of South Vietnam in 1975, but the Vietnam War remains a source of controversy and unanswered questions. People continue to differ on whether the United States should have intervened at all, whether sending troops was the right sort of intervention, whether different strategies and tactics would have resulted in an American victory, and whether antiwar opposition should be blamed (or credited) for America's defeat. The two viewpoints in this chapter focus on a specific aspect of the Vietnam War that was controversial both during and after the conflict: the role of media coverage and how it affected American public opinion and the war's outcome.

Because America never officially declared war on Vietnam, journalists were able to operate there without the military censorship rules that had governed coverage of prior wars, such as World War II. This did not prevent the relationship between the American military and journalists from becoming strained, however. Military and government officials often complained that news reports sharply differed from optimistic official accounts, and they accused journalists of undermining public support for the war effort by exaggerating setbacks and atrocities. Journalists responded by complaining of a "credibility gap" between what they observed and what the government was telling them and the American people.

One component of media coverage of the Vietnam War that had not been a major factor in previous American wars was television. "War has always been beastly," historian Guenter Lewy explains, "but the Vietnam war was the first war exposed to television cameras and seen in practically every home, often in living color." Historians differ as to how the daily dose of televised war affected the views of American citizens. Lewy, among others, believes this new aspect of media coverage had a major impact on public opinion, asserting that "this close-up view of destruction and suffering, repeated daily, strengthened the growing desire for peace." Historian George Moss, however, argues that analyses of television coverage of the Vietnam War reveal a different picture:

> Television coverage . . . depicting American soldiers in combat over many years, which did not show much live action, which rarely showed dead or wounded soldiers, and which was usually framed by a melodramatic, black-and-white interpretation of our good guys against their bad guys, would more likely

have the effect of legitimizing combat in Vietnam than delegitimizing it. The evidence suggests that television coverage of the war more often elicited popular support for the conflict than caused people to reject or oppose it.

Moss and others contend that television coverage reflected—rather than shaped—diminishing public support for the war, maintaining that television reports became more critical of the war only after public opinion had already turned against it.

Critics of television and the media give special concern to the Tet Offensive of 1968, now widely considered to be the turning point of the war. As 1968 began, the U.S. Army and the Army of the Republic of Vietnam (ARVN) were reporting increasing success in the Vietnamese countryside and the establishment of secure control of South Vietnam's cities. The American military commander, William C. Westmoreland, made several public statements claiming that the enemy could no longer conduct large-scale offensive operations and that victory was in America's grasp. But on January 30, 1968, at the beginning of a Vietnamese holiday (Tet) that had traditionally been a time of truce, Vietcong and North Vietnamese units attacked five of South Vietnam's six cities and most of its provincial and district capitals. In Saigon, Communist forces attacked the presidential palace and broke into the U.S. embassy compound. The massive offensive was ultimately beaten back, having achieved few of its goals; the heavy casualties (estimated to be around forty thousand) essentially decimated the Vietcong as a military force.

Despite the fact that the Tet episode resulted in an American tactical victory on the battlefield, it was widely seen as a setback for the United States and South Vietnam. Some critics have since blamed media coverage, especially of the first few days of the offensive, for this perception. Westmoreland wrote in his memoirs of the impact of television on American opinion:

> Nobody in Saigon to my knowledge anticipated remotely the psychological impact the offensive would have in the United States. Militarily, the [Tet] offensive was foredoomed to failure, destined to be over everywhere, except in Saigon and Hué and Khe Sanh, in a day or so. . . . No one to my knowledge foresaw that, in terms of public opinion, press and television would transform what was undeniably a catastrophic military defeat for the enemy into a presumed debacle for Americans and South Vietnamese, an attitude that still lingers in the minds of many.

Norman Podhoretz, in his book *Why We Were in Vietnam*, maintains that the media failed in their coverage of Tet in many different areas:

> On every point the situation was misrepresented by misleading stories and pictures and in some cases by outright falsehood.

Thus the media continued to harp on the successes of Hanoi even after the assault on the cities had already been blunted; they spoke of rural areas having fallen under Communist control which where in fact being held by American and South Vietnamese forces; they said that the South Vietnamese troops in the provinces were refusing to fight when in fact they were refusing to cave in; they spoke of the "wily" North Vietnamese commander General [Vo Nguyen] Giap as a genius, although he had in fact made serious errors of military judgment.

Such mistakes in the media coverage convinced the American public that the Tet episode was a U.S. defeat and poisoned American public support for Vietnam, Podhoretz asserts. He contends that this mishandling of the Tet Offensive effectively established the television networks and major newspapers and magazines as "members of the antiwar movement."

Others, however, disagree that media coverage of the Tet Offensive was a decisive factor in turning American public opinion against the Vietnam War. Many have argued that it was not the media, but the prospect of continued war and American casualties—without hopes for immediate victory—that caused antiwar sentiment to grow. According to these commentators, it was the fact that the enemy was able to even attempt an operation like the Tet Offensive, despite the pronouncements of Westmoreland and others of impending victory, that shocked most Americans. Moss writes:

> It was not that journalists or the American people thought that the Communists were winning the Tet battles. That was not the problem. The public was shocked by the fact that the Tet offensive had occurred. . . . Tet-68 exploded all the official reassurances that the U.S. was winning the war, that the Vietcong were on their way out, and that the war would end soon. To most Americans, Tet confirmed what many of them already suspected, that the Johnson administration had not been telling the truth, that America had become involved in an endless war that was consuming ever-rising numbers of lives and dollars.

The debate over the media coverage of the Tet campaign, and of the Vietnam War in general, reflects deeper divisions over the conflict. Critics of the media insist or imply that the United States could possibly have succeeded in its objectives of preserving an independent and non-Communist South Vietnam if not for unfavorable media coverage that caused the American people to prematurely lose faith in the war effort. But others have questioned this assumption, arguing that the failure of the United States in Vietnam stemmed from much more profound problems in its understanding of Vietnam and its people, the strategy it pursued, and the limits of the government of South Vietnam. The viewpoints in this chapter debate the issue of media coverage of Vietnam and in the process raise many other questions regarding the Vietnam War.

"For the first time in modern history, the outcome of a war was determined not on the battlefield, but on the printed page and, above all, on the television screen."

Media Coverage Was a Significant Cause of the U.S. Defeat in Vietnam

Robert Elegant (b. 1928)

Robert Elegant worked in Vietnam as a foreign correspondent for *Newsweek* and the *Los Angeles Times/Washington Post* News Service and was, in his words, "a participant as well as an observer in the Viet Nam imbroglio from 1955 to 1975." He holds an M.A. in Asian Studies and has written fifteen books, both fiction and nonfiction, about Asia. The following viewpoint is excerpted from a 1981 article in which Elegant strongly criticizes television and print journalists in Vietnam for what he describes as their shallow, biased, and inaccurate reporting. Their descriptions of the war, he argues, shaped public opinion and created political pressures in the United States that ultimately led to American withdrawal and defeat in Vietnam.

The question of the relationship between public opinion and the media, Elegant later wrote, could be "best put in the form of syllogism: American and world public opinion judged the war in Viet Nam on the basis of the information they received. Almost all that information came from the independent media. Therefore the media vitally influenced American and world public opinion. If not the media, who?"

Adapted from Robert Elegant, "How to Lose a War," *Encounter*, August 1981. Reprinted by permission of the author.

In the early 1960s, when the Viet Nam War became a big story, most foreign correspondents assigned to cover the story wrote primarily to win the approbation of the crowd, above all their own crowd. As a result, in my view, the self-proving system of reporting they created became ever further detached from political and military realities because it instinctively concentrated on its own self-justification. The American press, naturally dominant in an "American war," somehow felt obliged to be less objective than partisan, to take sides, for it was inspired by the *engagé* "investigative" reporting that burgeoned in the US in these impassioned years. The press was instinctively "agin the Government"—and, at least reflexively, for Saigon's enemies.

During the latter half of the 15-year American involvement in Viet Nam the media became the primary battlefield. Illusory events reported *by* the press as well as real events *within* the press corps were more decisive than the clash of arms or the contention of ideologies. For the first time in modern history, the outcome of a war was determined not on the battlefield, but on the printed page and, above all, on the television screen. Looking back coolly, I believe it can be said (surprising as it may still sound) that South Vietnamese and American forces actually won the limited military struggle. They virtually crushed the Viet Cong in the South, the "native" guerrillas who were directed, reinforced, and equipped from Hanoi; and thereafter they threw back the invasion by regular North Vietnamese divisions. None the less, the War was finally lost to the invaders *after* the US disengagement because the political pressures built up by the media had made it quite impossible for Washington to maintain even the minimal material and moral support that would have enabled the Saigon régime to continue effective resistance. . . .

"You could be hard about it and deny that there was a brotherhood working there, but what else could you call it?" This is a question that Michael Herr asked in his *Dispatches,* a personally honest, but basically deceptive book.

> But . . . all you ever talked about was the war, and they could come to seem like two different wars at the same time. Because who but another correspondent could talk the kind of *mythical* war you *wanted* to hear described?

I have added the italics; for in the words "mythical" and "wanted" the essential truth is laid bare. In my own personal experience most correspondents *wanted* to talk chiefly to other correspondents to confirm their own *mythical* vision of the war. Even newcomers were pre-committed, as the American jargon has it, to the collective position most of their colleagues had already taken.

What I can only call surrealistic reporting constantly fed on itself; and did not diminish thereby, but swelled into ever more grotesque shapes. I found the process equally reprehensible for being in no small part unwitting. . . .

Most correspondents were isolated from the Vietnamese by ignorance of their language and culture, as well as by a measure of race estrangement. Most were isolated from the quixotic American Army establishment, itself often as confused as they themselves were, by their moralistic attitudes and their political prejudices. It was inevitable, in the circumstances, that they came to write, in the first instance, for each other. . . .

It was my impression that most correspondents were, in one respect, very much like the ambitious soldiers they derided. A tour in Viet Nam was almost essential to promotion for a US Regular Army officer, and a combat command was the best road to rapid advancement. Covering the biggest continuing story in the world was not absolutely essential to a correspondent's rise, but it was an invaluable cachet. Quick careers were made by spectacular reporting of the obvious fact that men, women, and children were being killed; fame or at least notoriety rewarded the correspondent who became part of the action—rather than a mere observer—by influencing events directly.

Journalists, particularly those serving in television, were therefore, like soldiers, "rotated" to Viet Nam. Few were given time to develop the knowledge, and indeed the intellectual instincts, necessary to report the War in the round. Only a few remained "in country" for years, though the experienced Far Eastern correspondents visited regularly from Hong Kong, Singapore, and Tokyo. Not surprisingly, one found that most reporting veered farther and farther from the fundamental political, economic, and military realities of the War, for these were usually *not* spectacular. Reporting Viet Nam became a closed, self-generating system sustained largely by the acclaim the participants lavished on each other in almost equal measure to the opprobrium they heaped on "the Establishment," a fashionable and very vulnerable target.

For some journalists, perhaps most, a moment of truth through self-examination was never to come. The farther they were from the real conflict, the more smugly self-approving they now remain as commentators who led the public to expect a brave new world when the North Vietnamese finally "liberated" South Viet Nam. Even those correspondents who today gingerly confess to some errors or distortions usually insist that the true fault was not theirs at all, but Washington's. The enormity of having helped in one way or another to bring tens of millions under grinding totalitarian rule—and having tilted the global balance of power—appears too great to acknowledge. It is easier to absolve one's self by blaming exclusively Johnson, Nixon, and Kissinger. . . .

Journalistic institutions are, of course, rarely afflicted by false modesty. They have not disclaimed credit for the outcome of the war, and their representatives have taken public bows for their successful intervention. The multitude of professional prizes bestowed upon the "big-story" coverage of Viet Nam certainly implied approval of the general effort.

One-Dimensional Coverage

In his 1978 book America in Vietnam, *historian Guenter Lewy argues that television coverage that emphasized the brutalities of South Vietnam's government while failing to cover atrocities of Vietnamese Communists contributed to public disillusionment with the war.*

The coverage of the war by television was a crucial factor. . . . The VC [Vietcong] were notoriously uncooperative in allowing Western cameramen to shoot pictures of the disemboweling of village chiefs or other acts of terror, while scenes of South Vietnamese brutality, such as the mistreatment of prisoners, were often seen on American TV screens. Television stresses the dramatic and contentious, and the Vietnam war offered plenty of both. The result was a one-dimensional coverage of the conflict—apparently meaningless destruction of lives and property in operations which rarely led to visible success. War has always been beastly, but the Vietnam war was the first war exposed to television cameras and seen in practically every home, often in living color. Not surprisingly this close-up view of devastation and suffering, repeated daily, strengthened the growing desire for peace. The events of Tet and the siege of Khe Sanh in 1968, in particular, shook the American public. The nightly portrayal of violence and gore and of American soldiers seemingly on the brink of disaster contributed significantly to disillusionment with the war. Gallup poll data suggest that between early February and the middle of March 1968 nearly one person in five switched from the "hawk" to the "dove" position.

However, the media have been rather coy; they have not declared that they played a *key* role in the conflict. They have not proudly trumpeted Hanoi's repeated expressions of gratitude to the mass media of the non-Communist world, although Hanoi has indeed affirmed that it could not have won "without the Western press." The Western press appears either unaware of the direct connection between cause (its reporting) and effect (the Western defeat in Viet Nam), or strangely reluctant to proclaim that the pen and the camera proved decisively mightier than the bayonet and ultra-modern weapons.

Nor have the media dwelt upon the glaring inconsistency between the expectation they raised of peaceful, prosperous development after Saigon's collapse and the present post-War circumstances in Indo-China. . . .

. . . Any searching analysis of fundamental premises has remained as unthinkable to "the critics" as it was during the fighting. They have remained committed to the proposition that the American role in Indo-China was totally reprehensible and inexcusable, while the North Vietnamese role—and, by extension, the roles of the Khmer Rouge in Cambodia and the Pathet Lao in Laos—was righteous, magnanimous, and just. Even the growing number who finally deplored the repressive consequences of the totalitarian victory could not bring themselves to re-examine the premises that led them to contribute so decisively to those victories. Thus William Shawcross, before his sententious book, *Sideshow*, wrote of the Communists' reshaping of Cambodian society: "The process is atrociously brutal." Although "the Khmer people are suffering horribly under their new rulers," this is how Shawcross unhesitatingly assigned the ultimate blame:

> They have suffered every day of the last six years—ever since the beginning of one of the most destructive foreign policies the United States has ever pursued: the "Nixon-Kissinger doctrine" in its purest form.[1] . . .

Most correspondents on the scene were not quite as vehement. But they were moved by the same conviction of American guilt, which was so fixed that it resisted all the evidence pointing to a much more complex reality. Employed in the service of that crusading fervor was, for the first time, the most emotionally moving medium of all.

Television

Television, its thrusting and simplistic character shaping its message, was most shocking because it was most immediate. The Viet Nam War was a presence in homes throughout the world. Who could seriously doubt the veracity of so plausible and so moving a witness in one's own livingroom?

At any given moment, a million images were available to the camera's lens in Saigon alone—and hundreds of millions throughout Indo-China. But TV crews naturally preferred the most dramatic. That, after all, was their business—show business. It was not news to film farmers peacefully tilling their rice-fields, though it might have been argued that nothing happening *was* news when the American public had been led to believe that almost every Vietnamese farmer was regularly threatened by the

---

1. Author's note: Shawcross has subsequently told people, including Elegant, that he misassessed the war in Vietnam.

Viet Cong, constantly imperilled by battle, and rarely safe from indiscriminate US bombing.

A few hard, documented instances. A burning village was news, even though it was a deserted village used in a Marine training exercise—even though the television correspondent had handed his Zippo lighter to a noncommissioned officer with the suggestion that he set fire to an abandoned house. American soldiers cutting ears off a Viet Cong corpse was news—even if the cameraman had offered the soldiers his knife and "dared" them to take those grisly souvenirs. (Since the antics of the media were definitely *not* news, the network refrained from apologizing for the contrived "event" when a special investigation called the facts to its attention.) Cargo-nets full of dead South Vietnamese soldiers being lowered by helicopters were news—even if that image implicitly contradicted the prevailing conviction that the South Vietnamese never fought, but invariably threw away their weapons and ran. . . .

Equally lamentable was the failure of the Western press to cover with any thoroughness the Army of the Republic of South Viet Nam, which over the long run was doing most of the fighting. Correspondents were reluctant to commit their safety to units whose resolution they distrusted—sometimes for good reason, more often because of a kind of racist contempt—in order to get stories that interested their editors so little. Coverage of Vietnamese politics, as well as social and economic developments, was sporadic—except for military coups and political crises, and those were often misreported.

Distorted Reporting

Examples of misdirected or distorted reporting could be amassed almost indefinitely. The War, after all, lasted some twenty years. A former *Washington Post* and *New York Times* correspondent, Peter Braestrup, has published a two-volume study of the coverage of the Tet Offensive of 1968. Quite significantly, it attracted little interest compared to, say, William Shawcross's *Sideshow* or Michael Herr's *Dispatches*.

Nowadays, Jean Lacouture, Anthony Lewis, and William Shawcross (among some other "Viet Nam veterans") clearly feel deceived or even betrayed by the Communists of Indo-China; yet surely, they voluntarily adopted the ideological bias that allowed Hanoi to deceive them. The Vietnamese Communists—unlike their Cambodian confrères—had, after all, openly *declared* their intention of imposing totalitarian rule upon the South. Why, then, were the "critics of the American war" so genuinely surprised by the consequences? More crucially, why did a virtual generation of Western journalists deceive itself so consistently as to the nature of the "liberation" in Indo-China? Why did the correspondents *want* to believe in the good faith of the Communists? Why did they so *want* to disbelieve the avowed motives of the United States? Why did so much of their presumably factual reporting regularly reflect their ideological bias?

The obvious explanation is not as ingenuous as it may appear: the majority of Western correspondents and commentators adopted their idiosyncratic approach to the Indo-China War precisely because other journalists had already adopted that approach. To put it more directly, it was fashionable (this was, after all, the age of Radical Chic) to be "a critic of the American war."

Decisive in the case of the Americans, who set the tone, was the normally healthy adversary relationship between the US press and the US government. American newspapermen have often felt, with some justification, that if an Administration affirmed a controversial fact, that fact—if not *prima facie* false—was at the least suspect. As the lies of successive Administrations regarding Indo-China escalated, that conviction became the credo of the press. The psychological process that began with the unfounded optimism of President John F. Kennedy's ebullient "New Frontiersmen," who were by and large believed, ended with the disastrous last stand of Richard Nixon's dour palace guard, who were believed by no one.

The reaction against official mendacity was initially healthy, but later became distorted, self-serving, and self-perpetuating. A faulty syllogism was unconsciously accepted: Washington was lying consistently; Hanoi contradicted Washington; therefore Hanoi was telling the truth.

The initial inclination to look upon Hanoi as a fount of pure truth was intelligently fostered by the Communists, who selectively rewarded "critics of the American war" with visas to North Viet Nam. A number of influential journalists and public figures (ranging from former cabinet officers to film actresses) were fêted in North Viet Nam. They were flattered not only by the attention and the presumed inside information proffered by the North Vietnamese, but by their access to a land closed to most Americans. The favored few—and the aspiring many—helped establish a climate in which it was not only fashionable but, somehow, an act of courage to follow the critical crowd in Saigon and Washington while praising Hanoi. The skeptical correspondent risked ostracism by his peers and conflicts with his editors if he did not run with "the herd of independent minds," if he did not support the consensus.

The larger reason for the tenacity of the consensus went much deeper. It welled from a new view of *this* War, which was quite different from the press's view of other wars—and from a new messianic approach to the role of the press in wartime.

The Main Question

The main question persists. Why was the press—whether in favor of official policy at the beginning or vehemently against the War at the end—so superficial and so biased?

Chief among many reasons was, I believe, the politicization of correspondents by the constantly intensifying clamor over Viet Nam in Europe and America. Amateur (and professional) propagandists served both sides of the question, but the champions of Hanoi were spectacularly more effective. They created an atmosphere of high pressure that made it exceedingly difficult to be objective.

In Korea, senior officers who were incensed by unfavorable reports would sometimes demand: "Who are you for—the Communists or us?" Most correspondents were detached and could answer honestly: "Personally for the UN and the US, but professionally for neither side. Just trying to tell the true story. . . ." In Viet Nam that response was virtually impossible amid growing Western horror at the "dirty, immoral war." Correspondents were almost compelled to become partisans, and most became partisans for Hanoi, or, at least, *against* Saigon and Washington.

Revulsion in Europe and America sprang as much from the nature of the correspondents' reporting as it did from the belligerents' direct manipulation of public opinion. Some of my senior colleagues had learned wisdom on a hundred battlefields, having covered World War II, the Chinese Civil War, the Viet Minh campaign against the French, and the Indonesian revolt against the Dutch. I had at least been through Korea, the Malayan "Emergency," and the fighting between Chinese Nationalists and Chinese Communists for Quemoy. But most correspondents had never seen war before their arrival in Indo-China. Many confused the beastliness of all war with the particular war in Indo-China, which they unthinkingly concluded was unique in human history because it was new to them.

This much must be said: the best of their reporting accurately conveyed the horror of war—all war. Yet it presented the suffering, barbarism, and devastation as somehow peculiar to Indo-China. It almost made it appear that other wars had been fought by mailed champions on fields remote from human habitation, while in Indo-China, for the first time, carnage brutally involved both massed military formations and the civilian populace. Since a guerrilla war is inherently not as destructive as a conventional war, human suffering and material devastation had, in reality, been markedly greater in Korea than in Viet Nam—and much, much greater on both Asian and European fronts in World War II.

Because Viet Nam did not attract many senior correspondents

for extended tours, at any given time a majority of the correspondents were new to the complexities of Indo-China. Some could not even look after themselves in combat, the *sine qua non* of a successful—and surviving—war correspondent.

One afternoon in May 1968, when the Viet Cong were attacking the outskirts of Saigon, six young correspondents piled into a single mini taxi to drive to the shifting "front." They were startled when advised to take two or three taxis so that they could get out faster if they came under fire. A tall, rotund neophyte wearing a scarlet shirt paraded up and down the road the Viet Cong were attacking. He was dismayed by the pained abhorrence with which South Vietnamese paratroops regarded him, until it was explained that he was drawing rocket fire. The six clustered around a 24-year-old US 1st lieutenant, just out of the Military Academy at West Point, who was struggling to communicate with the Vietnamese major commanding and, simultaneously, to direct the gunships that swooped low, firing their machine-guns. While shells burst around them, the correspondents tried to interrogate the lieutenant on the morality of the US presence in Indo-China. . . .

The "Viet Nam Syndrome" is compounded of a variety of symptoms, none unique in itself, but unprecedented in combination and devastating in their totality. Wars have been badly reported in the past. Facts have been mis-stated, and their interpretation has been biased. Emotions have been deliberately inflamed, and reporters have ridden to fame on waves of misrepresentation. But never before Viet Nam had the collective policy of the media—no less stringent term will serve—sought by graphic and unremitting distortion the victory of the enemies of the correspondents' own side. Television coverage was, of course, new in its intensity and repetitiveness; it was crucial in shifting the emphasis from fact to emotion. And television will play the same role in future conflicts—on the Western side, of course. It will not and cannot expose the crimes of an enemy who is too shrewd to allow the cameras free play.

"The thesis that the media, particularly television, were responsible for losing the Vietnam war . . . is groundless and untenable, for many reasons."

Media Coverage Did Not Cause the U.S. Defeat in Vietnam

George Moss (b. 1935)

George Moss is a professor of history at City College in San Francisco and the author of several books on the history of the United States, including *America in the Twentieth Century* and *The Rise of Modern America*. The following viewpoint is excerpted from his book *Vietnam: An American Ordeal*. Moss argues against the thesis that media coverage of the Vietnam War played a major role in America's defeat. He contends that while U.S. involvement in Vietnam was escalating during the 1960s, media coverage was generally uncritical of the American war effort. Americans, he asserts, turned against the war *before* media coverage became increasingly negative. According to Moss, the United States lost the Vietnam War because flawed political and military strategic thinking had trapped it in a costly stalemate that would never have sustained popular support.

Vietnam was America's first televised war, the first war to be shown night after night in American living rooms. For years, color video brought Americans the sights and sounds of men at war. The Vietnam war was also the first major war that the United States ever lost. Many Americans believe that television was a major cause of the American defeat in Southeast Asia. That is, they believe that America lost history's first televised war precisely because it was televised.

General [William C.] Westmoreland and others, including journalist Robert Elegant, have insisted that America lost a war in Vietnam that it could have won. They have blamed the defeat on the mass media, particularly the television networks, for turning American public opinion against the war and eventually forcing a U.S. withdrawal from Vietnam, which allowed the Communists to overwhelm the South Vietnamese defenders and to take over the entire country in the spring of 1975.

Westmoreland has stated that the news media, especially television, snatched defeat from the jaws of victory in the aftermath of Tet-68, just when the allies had a battered enemy on the ropes and ready for the kill. He has asserted that a golden opportunity to mobilize U.S. military resources for a maximum effort to win the Vietnam war in a year or two was lost because television news coverage of the Tet campaigns turned the public against the war in early 1968 and prevented Johnson from escalating the conflict. Westmoreland's stab-in-the-back thesis, that powerful and hostile media, particularly television news coverage, were primarily responsible for the American strategic defeat in Vietnam, is embraced by many Americans who hold that the U.S. military intervention in Southeast Asia was a noble cause that could and should have been successful.

The thesis that the media, particularly television, were responsible for losing the Vietnam war, or were a major cause of the American defeat in Vietnam, is groundless and untenable, for many reasons. Most historians of the Vietnam war and most analysts of mass media dismiss it as without merit. Television news coverage of the Vietnam war up to the time of Tet was overwhelmingly favorable; television journalists consistently represented American soldiers as fighting aggressively and winning every major battle en route to inevitable victory in the war. During the first few years of television coverage of the war, the networks rarely showed American soldiers getting killed or wounded. Remarkably little American blood got spilled on television prime-time news. Typical video sequences of combat action showed U.S. troops moving across rice paddies or an air strike from a distance. Sometimes one heard the muted sounds of rifle fire or the rhythmic whir of helicopter rotors.

The only public opinion poll that ever asked people how watching television news coverage of the Vietnam war influenced their attitudes toward the war found that 83 percent of the respondents said they felt more hawkish after watching the news. At the time this poll was taken—July 1967—other polls showed that 50 percent of Americans believed that U.S. entry into the war had been a mistake. These polls showed that opposition to the Vietnam war and to Johnson's war policy was massive despite, not because of, television news coverage, which was highly favorable at the time. Many Americans had turned against the war and had distrusted Johnson's leadership long before Tet.

Television news coverage of the war became more critical during the Tet battles, and, for the first time, television provided viewers with a steady diet of live-action coverage of the carnage. Viewers witnessed the destructiveness and brutality of war, of American soldiers fighting and dying in the streets of Saigon and Hue. But evidence from public opinion polls taken soon after the Tet attacks have undermined Westmoreland's thesis. At a time when the media exaggerated the tactical gains made by the enemy, portrayed Tet as a great shock and disaster for America, and showed American soldiers being killed in combat, public opinion polls registered temporary rises in popular support.

Proponents of the stab-in-the-back thesis often cite Peter Braestrup's writings to substantiate their charges. Braestrup, a former Marine officer, Vietnam journalist, and media scholar, produced a massive study of the media coverage of Tet. He found that during the first few days of the Tet Offensive the public was misled into thinking that the Vietcong were winning when in fact they were losing, and losing badly, almost everywhere. He has criticized journalists for their inaccurate and misleading stories. To Westmoreland, Braestrup's critique proved that distorted media coverage misled Americans and turned them against the war; biased reportage turned a tactical victory into a major defeat that eventually cost America a war.

But a careful reading of Braestrup's study has shown that he furnishes the proponents of the stab-in-the-back thesis neither aid nor comfort. Braestrup himself did not embrace the thesis and has challenged those who did. Braestrup took pains to make clear that he did not charge either print or television journalists with biased coverage during Tet. He has never said that Tet-68 coverage by either the print or television journalists, however deficient in the early stages, turned public opinion against the Vietnam war. In fact, he believed that such claims were impossible to substantiate: "No empirical data exist to link news coverage with changes in public opinion."

Braestrup contended that skewed media coverage of the Tet campaigns exacerbated a growing political crisis in Washington that would have occurred even if those journalistic accounts had been clinically accurate. He believed that it was Johnson's indecisive leadership in the weeks following Tet that caused the falloff of popular support for the war that occurred in March. For Braestrup, changes occurring in public opinion of the Vietnam war in the weeks following Tet were caused by failures of political leadership and not by television news or by the other media coverage of the battles. Ironically, the administration's propaganda efforts in the fall of 1967, which were aimed at convincing Americans that the United States was winning the war and that it would end soon, magnified the public shock and disillusionment that occurred during the Tet campaigns and widened the credibility gap.

The Media Were Supportive of the War

In an essay in A Vietnam Reader, *George Moss cites* The Uncensored War *by political scientist Daniel C. Hallin in refuting the "myth" that the media caused U.S. defeat.*

The scholar who has mounted the most telling critique of the myth in a series of articles and a thoroughly researched book, *The Uncensored War*, is Daniel C. Hallin. Drawing upon the complete body of *New York Times* coverage of the war from 1961 to 1965, and from over 1,500 television newscasts of the war from 1965 to 1973, Hallin delineates the many ideological and institutional restraints operating to prevent the national television news networks from functioning as adversaries of governmental policy. Using content analyses of television news programs, he shows how television provided mostly favorable coverage of the war through its first three years. Sometime in 1969, about the time President Nixon began withdrawing American troops, television coverage of the war became more negative, but only after public opinion and many government leaders had turned against the war. Even during these later years when television coverage was more critical, the Nixon administration was usually able to manipulate the news networks, control the flow of war news, and retain public support for its war policies. Hallin proves that television news did not play any important part in undermining popular support for the war.

When trends in public opinion on the Vietnam war have been matched with trends in television news coverage of the conflict, it has been shown that a majority of the American people turned against the Vietnam war before television news coverage of the conflict became predominantly negative. Despite more negative emphasis in their television coverage of the war during and after Tet, on the whole, the network television news coverages continued to be more positive than negative until the fall of 1969. A majority of Americans had developed dovish views on the Vietnam war long before then. Television coverage of the war normally lagged behind public opinion.

A Response to Public Opinion

The increasingly critical television coverage of the war that occurred at the time of Tet and after represented a response by media journalists to public opinion, not an effort to shape it. The stab-in-the-back theorists, in their confusion and their haste to make the media into a scapegoat, have inverted the relationship between television news coverage of the Vietnam war and public opinion concerning the war and presidential leadership. Westmoreland, Elegant, and many others failed to understand that it was public opinion that influenced television coverage of the war much more than it was television coverage that influenced public opinion on the war.

As public support for the war dropped, television news coverage became more critical. The news networks were merely catching up to what their viewers were already thinking about the war and the U.S. leadership; they were not telling them what to think. When Walter Cronkite, the most popular and influential television anchor during the Vietnam war era, declared at the end of his newscast on the evening of February 27, 1968, that the war was a stalemate, the erstwhile hawk was aligning his views with those of his Middle American constituents. Numerous public opinion polls show that Cronkite told Americans nothing that most of them did not already believe.

The stab-in-the-back theorists also faced another difficulty. Westmoreland's insistence that victory was within the U.S. grasp following Tet, if Johnson had only sent the requested troops and taken the other escalatory steps called for at the time, was dubious. At the time, [Secretary of Defense] Clark Clifford and most Pentagon analysts had concluded that Hanoi had both the political will and the military assets to match any and all U.S. post-Tet escalations. Hanoi could also count on the Chinese, who would probably have intervened militarily if the North Vietnamese ever faced national extinction. Had Johnson escalated the war after Tet, he most likely would not have achieved strategic victory within a year or two. Most likely Johnson would have attained only continuing military stalemate at a far higher level of costs and casualties. Such a continuing costly stalemate in Vietnam would have brought intensified opposition, political polarization, and violent conflict within the United States that could have undermined American political stability.

The basic problem with the stab-in-the-back thesis is that it represents a lamentable failure of historical understanding. Powerful economic, political, and strategic forces determined the outcome of the Vietnam war and caused the eventual American strategic defeat. The role of the media, including television news coverage, in determining that outcome was peripheral, minor, trivial, in fact, so inconsequential it is unmeasurable. It was the course taken by the Vietnam war—the United States had locked itself into a stalemated conflict of rising casualties and costs—coupled to a loss of confidence in the integrity and competence of the government, all of which were highlighted and intensified by the Tet Offensive, that turned public opinion against the Vietnam war.

Public opinion turned the media, particularly television news, against the war. Had the cathode ray tube never been invented, and had censorship been imposed on Vietnam war news or had all the journalists covering the war in Southeast Asia been cheerleaders for the allied side, public opinion would have turned against the Vietnam war just as it did against the Korean war. The Korean war was popular when the UN [United Nations] forces appeared to be rolling toward an easy victory over the North Koreans in the fall of 1950. Following the surprise Chinese intervention in late November 1950, and the subsequent stalemated warfare that went on for years, public opinion polls consistently showed that a majority of Americans did not support the Korean war. Yet television news was in its infancy, most U.S. households did not have television sets, war news from Korea was heavily censored, and U.S. war correspondents were all supportive of the UN effort. Those who blame the television networks for the American defeat in Vietnam promulgate a myth that may serve hidden political and ideological agenda, but they do not explain why the United States lost the war.

Glossary

AID   The Agency for International Development.

Annam   The name given by France to the central section of Vietnam; a French protectorate from 1883 to 1954.

ARVN   The Army of the Republic of Vietnam (South Vietnam).

Associated States   *See* **French Union**.

B-52   A high-altitude, long-range strategic bomber.

Bao Dai   The last emperor of Vietnam; he served under the French as emperor of **Annam** from 1932 to 1945 and as chief of state of the **State of Vietnam** from 1949 to 1955.

Binh Xuyen   An organized criminal gang that controlled portions of Saigon until crushed by **Ngo Dinh Diem** in 1955.

Cai Dai   A religious sect formed in 1925 in southern Vietnam.

CIA   The Central Intelligence Agency.

Cochinchina   The name given by France to the southern section of Vietnam; a French colony from 1863 to 1954.

Dien Bien Phu   The site in northwestern Vietnam, close to Laos, where the French suffered a major defeat in 1954, which led to their withdrawal from Vietnam and the end of the **Indochina War**.

DMZ   Demilitarized Zone; the border between North and South Vietnam at the seventeenth parallel.

DRV   Democratic Republic of Vietnam (North Vietnam); created by **Ho Chi Minh** on September 2, 1945.

fragging   The murder of an officer by a soldier in his charge, usually with a fragmentation grenade.

French Indochina   *See* **Indochina**.

French Union   The name given to the French empire from 1946 to 1958; its nominally independent **Associated States** included Vietnam, Cambodia, and Laos.

Geneva Accords   The product of the 1954 international conference in Geneva, Switzerland, that ended the **Indochina War** and by which Vietnam was divided into northern and southern regions.

GVN   The Government of Vietnam (South Vietnam).

Hanoi   The capital of North Vietnam.

Hoa Hao   A religious sect founded in southern Vietnam in 1939.

Ho Chi Minh   The founder of the Indochinese Communist Party in 1930 and president of the **Democratic Republic of Vietnam** from 1945 to 1969.

253

Ho Chi Minh Trail   A series of paths and roads from North Vietnam to South Vietnam used by the North Vietnamese to transport soldiers and supplies; parts of it ran through Cambodia and Laos.

ICC   The International Control Commission; created by the 1954 **Geneva Accords** to supervise unification elections in Vietnam.

Indochina   The peninsula in Southeast Asia that includes the countries of Vietnam, Laos, Cambodia, Thailand, Myanmar (Burma), and West Malaysia; the term also refers to the eastern part of the peninsula under the colonial control of France until 1954.

Indochina War   The war between France and the **Vietminh** that lasted from 1946 to 1954.

Khe Sanh   The site of a U.S. Marine base in Vietnam near the Laotian border that was under heavy siege by the Communists from 1967 to 1968.

Khmer Rouge   The Communist revolutionaries who took over Cambodia in 1975.

Le Duc Tho   The North Vietnamese official who helped negotiate the 1973 **Paris Peace Agreement**.

MAAG   Military Assistance Advisory Group; the name of the group of American military advisers in South Vietnam from 1955 to 1964 and the forerunner of **MACV**.

MACV   Military Assistance Command, Vietnam; the headquarters of the American military mission in Vietnam from 1962 to 1973.

Manila Pact   *See* **SEATO**.

MIA   missing in action.

Montagnards   The French term used to describe minority tribal populations in Vietnam who typically inhabited mountainous areas.

My Lai   The Vietnamese village that was the site of a massacre of civilians by U.S. soldiers in March 1968.

Ngo Dinh Diem   The leader of South Vietnam from 1954 to 1963, when he was overthrown and killed in a military coup.

Ngo Dinh Nhu   The brother of and chief adviser to **Ngo Dinh Diem**.

Nguyen Cao Ky   The Vietnamese air force general who served as prime minister of South Vietnam from 1965 to 1967 and vice president from 1967 to 1971.

Nguyen Khanh   The **ARVN** major general who ruled South Vietnam for parts of 1964 and 1965.

Nguyen Van Thieu   The Vietnamese general who served as president of South Vietnam from 1967 to 1975.

NLF   National Liberation Front; formed December 1960 in South Vietnam to take charge of the growing insurgency against the **GVN**.

NVA   North Vietnamese Army (same as **PAVN**).

OSS   The Office of Strategic Services; the World War II forerunner of the **CIA**.

Paris Peace Agreement   The 1973 cease-fire agreement under which the United States withdrew from Vietnam.

PAVN   People's Army of Vietnam (same as **NVA**).

Pentagon Papers   The secret military study of the Vietnam War that was leaked to the press in 1971.

POW   prisoner of war.

PRG   Provisional Revolutionary Government; formed by the **NLF** in 1969.

Rolling Thunder   The American operation of sustained bombing of North Vietnam; it lasted off and on from 1965 to 1968.

ROTC   Reserve Officers Training Corps.

RVN   Republic of Vietnam (South Vietnam).

RVNAF   Republic of Vietnam Armed Forces, including **ARVN**.

Saigon   The capital of South Vietnam; renamed Ho Chi Minh City in 1975.

SDS   Students for a Democratic Society.

SEATO   Southeast Asia Treaty Organization; created by the **Manila Pact** in 1954, its signatories—including the United States, Great Britain, France, Australia, New Zealand, Pakistan, the Philippines, and Thailand—agreed to "meet and confer" if attacked; it was used to justify American intervention in South Vietnam.

Special Forces   U.S. Army units trained for counterinsurgency (and often covert and unconventional) operations.

State of Vietnam   The name given to the 1949–55 government of **Bao Dai**.

strategic hamlets   Fortified villages in which, in a program begun in 1962, Vietnamese peasants were relocated in order to separate and protect them from **Vietcong** rebels.

SVN   South Vietnam.

Tet   Vietnamese lunar new year holiday.

Tonkin   The name given by France to the northern section of Vietnam; a French protectorate from 1883 to 1954.

USARV   United States Army, Vietnam.

VCI   **Vietcong** infrastructure; the political leaders of the **Vietcong**.

Vietcong (VC)   The name given to the Communist rebels in South Vietnam.

Vietminh   The shortened name for the Vietnam Doc Lap Dong Minh Hoi—the League for the Independence of Vietnam, founded by **Ho Chi Minh** in 1941.

Vo Nguyen Giap   The chief military commander and strategist of North Vietnam.

VVAW   Vietnam Veterans Against the War.

For Discussion

Chapter One

1. What exactly is Ho Chi Minh asking of the United States? On what basis does he believe the United States might support his cause? What sort of reply do you think the United States could have (or should have) made to his requests?
2. According to the U.S. State Department report, what future does the United States envision for Indochina? Is there anything in the document that implies or ordains America's subsequent decisions to intervene? Explain.
3. John Foster Dulles speaks of the need "to clarify further the United States position." Does he succeed in doing so? Why or why not? What position does he stake out?
4. What differences are there in the way John Foster Dulles and John F. Kennedy characterize the nature and causes of the conflict in Indochina and the character and loyalties of Ho Chi Minh? How are these different views reflected in their respective analyses on whether U.S. intervention in Vietnam is in America's interest? Explain.

Chapter Two

1. David Hotham asserts that Ngo Dinh Diem has been the beneficiary of "Western propaganda" portraying his rise as a success story. In your opinion, does the article by William Henderson fall in this category? Why or why not?
2. How are David Hotham's assessments of the impact of U.S. aid, the Communist threat in South Vietnam, and the performance of Ngo Dinh Diem different from those of William Henderson? What do the two articles suggest about the limits of what an outsider such as the United States could accomplish in South Vietnam? Explain.
3. According to Mike Mansfield, what questions about Vietnam and American interests in Southeast Asia must be answered before the United States deepens its involvement in Vietnam? Do you believe these questions are adequately answered in the report by Robert S. McNamara and Dean Rusk? Why or why not?
4. Mike Mansfield was a strong supporter of Ngo Dinh Diem in the 1950s. Does that background add credence to his arguments? Why or why not?
5. What sources of information does the *Time* article rely on for its assessment? What sources does Sol W. Sanders use? How might these different sources account for their disparate judgments on the progress of the war in Vietnam?
6. Of the three choices laid out by Sanders at the end of his article, which one most closely approximates the Rusk-McNamara proposals? Which most resembles subsequent American intervention in Vietnam? Explain.

Chapter Three

1. What alternatives do soldiers in the U.S. Army have, according to the Vietnam Day Committee? Is the Vietnam Day Committee recommending that U.S. soldiers commit treason? Explain your answer.

2. Are Robert S. McNamara's recommendations consistent with the idea expressed by John F. Kennedy in 1963 that "in the final analysis, it is their war. They [the Vietnamese] are the ones who have to win it or lose it"? Why or why not?

3. What fundamental questions about U.S. policy in Vietnam does George Ball raise? Which of these questions, if any, are ignored by Robert S. McNamara?

4. William C. Westmoreland's speech was made a few months before the Tet Offensive, in which Vietcong and North Vietnamese units launched a massive surprise attack on South Vietnam's cities before being driven back with heavy losses. Does Westmoreland anticipate or acknowledge the possibility of such an attack in his speech? In your opinion, does the fact that the Tet Offensive occurred weaken or invalidate all or parts of his analysis? Why or why not?

5. What basic criteria does Westmoreland use in measuring progress in the war? What criteria does Robert F. Kennedy use in his arguments? Do Kennedy and Westmoreland differ in their assessments of the same criteria or in what kinds of criteria they choose to emphasize? Explain.

Chapter Four

1. What reasons does Richard M. Nixon give for opposing U.S. withdrawal from Vietnam? How are they similar to or different from those expressed by President Johnson in 1965 (see chapter three)?

2. Nixon argues that Vietnamization represents a fundamental shift in U.S. policy towards Vietnam. George S. McGovern argues that Vietnamization is essentially a continuation of past U.S. policy under a new name. Who is correct, in your opinion? Explain your answer.

3. Nixon also argues that the operation against Cambodia was "not an invasion." In your opinion, is this assertion reasonable or misleading/deceptive? Explain your answer.

4. What were the true reasons for the Cambodian operation, according to the editors of *Commonweal*? In assessing the ramifications of the incursion, where do the editors place the event in the context of the history of the war?

5. Historians generally have agreed that although the Christmas bombing of Hanoi and Haiphong did kill some civilians, relatively few were killed in comparison with the thousands that perished in the bombings of Tokyo and Dresden during World War II. Stanley Karnow wrote in *Vietnam: A History* that "the B-52s were programmed to spare civilians, and they pinpointed their targets with extraordinary precision. Nevertheless, some bombs did stray, with ghastly results." Do these facts affect your assessment of the viewpoints by Anthony Lewis and Henry Kissinger? Why or why not?

Chapter Five

1. What argumentative tactics and language does William G. Bray use to discredit antiwar protesters? Do you find his arguments effective? Why or why not?
2. How does Martin Jezer defend his actions as "American"? What links does he make between his draft resistance and various episodes and individuals in American history?
3. What elements of the Students for a Democratic Society (SDS) document provide the clearest examples of what Sam Brown says activists should not do? Describe the fundamental differences between radicals, such as the authors of the SDS document, and less extreme antiwar activists, such as Brown.
4. What moral issues regarding amnesty does John M. Swomley emphasize? What practical reasons does he give for amnesty? Does John H. Geiger separate moral and practical reasons for his opposition to amnesty? Which arguments do you find the strongest? Explain.
5. What personal experiences of Vietnam and its people do John Kerry and Melville L. Stephens describe? How do they use their stories of Vietnam to buttress their views on American policy there?

Chapter Six

1. Do both Robert Elegant and George Moss argue that the media presented a skewed picture of the Vietnam War to America? If so, what did the media fail to include in their reporting, according to the authors?
2. Elegant, who was a journalist on the scene in Vietnam, draws heavily from his own experiences. Moss is a history professor who was not in Vietnam and who utilizes a variety of sources for his arguments. What are the strengths and weaknesses of each perspective in examining the question of media coverage and its effect on the war? Who do you believe makes the more convincing case? Explain.

General

1. How did the rationale for American intervention in Vietnam evolve from 1945 to 1975? Did the goals change along with the growth and decline of direct U.S. involvement? Explain.
2. Most proponents and opponents of the Vietnam War claimed to be in agreement with fundamental American values. What are some of these values that you find emphasized by supporters of the war? By its opponents?
3. Using the viewpoints in this volume, identify some key points at which American policy makers could have made different decisions regarding Vietnam than they did. What alternatives existed? How do you think the history of the Vietnam War might have been different if these alternatives had been chosen?

Chronology

1930	Ho Chi Minh and associates organize the Indochinese Communist Party. The party opposes French colonial rule.
1932	Bao Dai returns from school in France to reign as emperor of Vietnam under French tutelage.
September 1939	World War II begins in Europe; France falls to Germany in June 1940.
September 1940	Japanese troops occupy Indochina but allow France's colonial administration to continue.
May 1941	Ho Chi Minh returns to French Indochina to found the Vietminh, a nationalist coalition group.
1943–1945	Americans attached to the Office of Strategic Services (OSS) work with the Vietminh on espionage and sabotage missions against the Japanese in Vietnam. On September 26, 1945, A. Peter Dewey of the OSS becomes the first American soldier to die in Vietnam.
March 1945	Japan, facing defeat in World War II, takes over the administration of Vietnam; Bao Dai cooperates with the Japanese.
August 1945	While Japan surrenders to the Allies, the Vietminh launch a general uprising throughout Vietnam; Bao Dai abdicates.
September 2, 1945	Ho Chi Minh proclaims the formation of the Democratic Republic of Vietnam (DRV) under his leadership.
1946	In France, Ho Chi Minh attempts to negotiate independence from French rule. The discussions fail to produce a full agreement. In November, the French shelling of Haiphong Harbor, which kills over six thousand Vietnamese civilians, ignites open war between France and the Vietminh.
March 1949	French president Vincent Auriol and Bao Dai sign an agreement making Vietnam an "associated state" of the French Union.
July 1949	Bao Dai decrees the establishment of the Government of Vietnam (GVN).
October 1949	The Communist takeover of China helps convince the Truman administration to move toward greater

involvement in defending French interests in Indochina.

January 14, 1950	Ho Chi Minh announces that the Democratic Republic of Vietnam is the only legal government of Vietnam.
January 18, 1950	The People's Republic of China recognizes the DRV as the legal government of Vietnam; it begins to supply weapons to the Vietminh.
January 30, 1950	The Soviet Union extends diplomatic recognition to the Democratic Republic of Vietnam; the Truman administration concludes that Ho Chi Minh's primary allegiance is to communism.
February 7, 1950	The United States and Great Britain recognize Bao Dai's government in Vietnam.
May 8, 1950	The United States signs an agreement with France to provide military assistance to the French Associated States of Indochina (Cambodia, Laos, and Bao Dai's regime in Vietnam).
June 26, 1950– July 27, 1953	The Korean War begins when North Korea invades South Korea. President Truman, without consulting Congress, commits American troops to defend South Korea under UN auspices. The war ends with an armistice signed after Dwight D. Eisenhower replaces Truman as president.
August 3, 1950	A U.S. Military Assistance Advisory Group (MAAG) of thirty-five men arrives in Saigon.
December 23, 1950	A Mutual Defense Assistance Agreement is signed by the United States, Vietnam, France, Cambodia, and Laos; by the end of the Truman administration the United States is bearing one-half of the cost of the French war effort in Vietnam.
September 30, 1953	President Dwight D. Eisenhower approves $785 million for military aid to Bao Dai's regime.
April 1954	Eisenhower enunciates the "domino theory." He considers but rejects direct American military intervention to relieve French forces trapped at Dien Bien Phu.
May 7, 1954	The French surrender at Dien Bien Phu, one day before an international conference in Geneva, Switzerland, is scheduled to open discussions on the Indochina situation.
June 18, 1954	Bao Dai selects Ngo Dinh Diem as prime minister of his government.
July 21, 1954	The Geneva Accords temporarily divide Vietnam at the seventeenth parallel and give Ho Chi Minh's regime control of North Vietnam and Bao Dai's regime control of South Vietnam; reunification

elections are scheduled for 1956. Bao Dai's government denounces the Geneva agreement and the United States refuses to sign it, but the American representative, Walter Bedell Smith, declares that the United States will refrain from either threatening or using force to prevent its implementation.

September 8, 1954   The Southeast Asia Treaty Organization (SEATO) is formed by the United States, France, Britain, Australia, New Zealand, Pakistan, Thailand, and the Philippines; a separate protocol extends the defensive umbrella to Indochina, including "the free territory under the jurisdiction of Vietnam" (South Vietnam).

October 24, 1954   In a letter to Ngo Dinh Diem, President Eisenhower pledges U.S. support to Diem's government and military forces.

April 1955   Diem's government survives challenges from a coalition of political enemies with the help of CIA operative Edwin Lansdale.

October 26, 1955   After defeating Bao Dai in a rigged election, Ngo Dinh Diem proclaims the existence of the Republic of Vietnam with himself as president; the government is recognized by the United States and its allies, including France.

April 28, 1956   The last French troops leave Vietnam; the United States assumes full responsibility for training South Vietnam's military forces.

July 20, 1956   The Geneva deadline for reunification elections passes; the United States supports Diem in his refusal to hold them.

May 5–19, 1957   President Diem makes a triumphant visit to the United States, addressing a joint session of Congress and receiving a declaration of support from President Eisenhower.

October 1957   Hostilities erupt between Diem's forces and Vietminh forces still in South Vietnam.

May 1959   North Vietnam takes steps to increase the infiltration of troops and supplies into South Vietnam via the Ho Chi Minh trail; U.S. advisers are assigned to the regimental level of the Army of the Republic of (South) Vietnam (ARVN).

December 20, 1960   With North Vietnam's support, the National Liberation Front (NLF) is formed in South Vietnam to overthrow Diem's government; Diem calls the NLF the "Vietcong" (Vietnamese Communists).

January 6, 1961   Soviet premier Nikita Khrushchev announces his support for "wars of national liberation" around the world; his pronouncement influences the incoming administration of President John F. Kennedy to block Communist advances in Vietnam.

May 1961	Kennedy approves sending Special Forces troops to South Vietnam and authorizes clandestine warfare against North Vietnam, including operations in Laos.
June 1961	Kennedy and Khruschchev, meeting in Vienna, agree to a neutral and independent Laos; Kennedy rejects a similar agreement for Vietnam.
October 1961	Kennedy dispatches Gen. Maxwell Taylor and foreign-policy adviser Walt Rostow to South Vietnam; they recommend sending an eight-thousand-man "logistical task force" to assist in the guerrilla war against North Vietnam.
December 8, 1961	The U.S. State Department claims in a public report that South Vietnam is threatened by a "clear and present danger" of Communist aggression.
December 31, 1961	The number of U.S. military personnel serving in South Vietnam has increased from 900 to 3,205 over the preceding year.
February 8, 1962	The Military Assistance Command, Vietnam (MACV) is established in Saigon; its first commander is Paul D. Harkins; the number of U.S. troops in Vietnam reaches four thousand.
December 1962	The number of American military personnel in Vietnam reaches nine thousand; Democratic senator Mike Mansfield visits South Vietnam and gives President Kennedy a pessimistic report on the state of the military effort.
January 1963	South Vietnamese troops are defeated by a much smaller Vietcong force despite considerable American assistance at the battle of Ap Bac.
May 8, 1963	In Hue, South Vietnam, government troops fire on twenty thousand Buddhist protesters, killing nine and creating a political crisis for the Diem regime.
November 1, 1963	South Vietnamese generals, led by Tran Van Don and Duong Van Minh, and with the foreknowledge and encouragement of the United States, stage a military coup that overthrows the Diem government; Diem and his brother Ngo Dinh Nhu are captured and executed.
November 24, 1963	Two days after the assassination of President Kennedy, new U.S. president Lyndon B. Johnson reaffirms American support for the government of South Vietnam. By year's end 16,500 American soldiers are stationed in Vietnam.
January 2, 1964	President Johnson approves covert military operations against North Vietnam, to be carried out by

South Vietnamese and Asian mercenaries.

January 30, 1964 Gen. Nguyen Khanh replaces Duong Van Minh as head of South Vietnam in a bloodless military coup.

August 1–4, 1964 A series of reported attacks on American destroyers in the Gulf of Tonkin prompts President Johnson to ask Congress to authorize "all necessary measures" to repel armed attacks against American forces in the area; the Gulf of Tonkin Resolution is passed almost unanimously by Congress on August 7.

October 1964 Gen. Khanh resigns as head of South Vietnam and is replaced by Tran Van Huong, a civilian; Khanh returns to power on January 28, 1965.

February 7, 1965 North Vietnamese attacks on American bases in South Vietnam lead to retaliatory American air strikes against North Vietnam.

February 13, 1965 President Johnson authorizes a sustained bombing campaign against North Vietnam, to begin on March 2. Called Operation Rolling Thunder, it lasts, with occasional pauses, until October 31, 1968.

February 25, 1965 Gen. Khanh is forced out of power by Air Marshal Nguyen Cao Ky.

March 8, 1965 Thirty-five hundred American marines land at the city of Da Nang. They are the first U.S. combat troops sent to Vietnam.

March 24, 1965 The first "teach-in" against the Vietnam War is held at the University of Michigan in Ann Arbor.

April 6, 1965 President Johnson authorizes U.S. military personnel in Vietnam to undertake offensives in support of ARVN (Army of the Republic of Vietnam) operations.

April 7, 1965 President Johnson offers a billion-dollar economic development program for the Mekong Delta region of Vietnam if the North Vietnamese will participate in "unconditional discussions." North Vietnamese prime minister Pham Van Dong rejects Johnson's proposal the next day.

April 17, 1965 The first major antiwar march on Washington takes place.

May 1965 President Johnson presents Congress with a request for $400 million to support American military operations in Vietnam.

June 8, 1965 The U.S. State Department publicly authorizes American troops in Vietnam to participate in combat.

July 21–28, 1965 After meeting with his advisers, President Johnson makes several decisions that escalate American involvement in Vietnam; they include sending fifty thousand soldiers to Vietnam, with the promise of additional increases if they are needed; expanding the air war against North Vietnam; and raising draft calls to thirty-five thousand per month.

October 15–16, 1965   The National Coordinating Committee to End the War in Vietnam sponsors nationwide demonstrations against the war.

December 31, 1965   The number of U.S. military personnel in South Vietnam grows to 184,000 from 23,000 at the year's start.

January–February 1966   Sen. J. William Fulbright of Arkansas holds hearings of the Senate Foreign Relations Committee to investigate the background and future of the war in Vietnam.

January 31, 1966   Johnson announces the resumption of the bombing of North Vietnam after a thirty-seven-day pause that failed to lead to peace negotiations.

May 1966   Four California housewives in San Jose, California, obstruct shipments of napalm to protest its use in Vietnam.

June 1966   President Johnson approves a force level of 431,000 troops, to be reached by mid-1967. The Black Anti-Draft Union and Afro-Americans Against the War in Vietnam are organized by black activists.

December 1966   The Student Mobilization Committee (SMC), the first national student antiwar coalition, is formed; the number of U.S. military personnel in Vietnam reaches 385,000.

January 8–26, 1967   In Operation Cedar Falls, the largest American offensive of the war to date, sixteen thousand U.S. troops attempt to disrupt Vietcong operations northeast of Saigon.

January 10, 1967   President Johnson requests a 6 percent income-tax surcharge to finance U.S. involvement in Vietnam.

April 15, 1967   More than one hundred thousand people in New York and San Francisco demonstrate against the war in Vietnam, including civil rights leader Martin Luther King Jr.

June 1, 1967   Vietnam Veterans Against the War is formed.

September 1967   Elections in South Vietnam bring to power President Nguyen Van Thieu and Vice President Nguyen Cao Ky; Thieu will remain in power until 1975.

October 16–21, 1967   Nationwide antiwar demonstrations are held, including a large march on the Pentagon; President Johnson's approval rating for his handling of the

	war falls to 28 percent.
December 1967	Defense secretary Robert McNamara resigns; more than a half-million American troops are in Vietnam.
January 30–31, 1968	In what will be called the Tet Offensive, Communist forces launch massive and coordinated surprise attacks on South Vietnamese cities.
February 28, 1968	Gen. Earle Wheeler, chairman of the Joint Chiefs of Staff, asks President Johnson for 206,000 additional troops for Vietnam, a step that would require the United States to call up the reserves. Johnson delays his decision and asks new secretary of defense Clark Clifford to conduct a thorough review of U.S. policy in Vietnam.
March 12, 1968	Antiwar presidential candidate Eugene McCarthy wins 43 percent of the vote at the New Hampshire primary; four days later, Robert Kennedy announces he will run for president.
March 16, 1968	Two platoons of American soldiers kill hundreds of unarmed Vietnamese civilians in the hamlet of My Lai-4; the incident is kept secret.
March 25–26, 1968	The "Wise Men," a group of distinguished former public officials convened by President Johnson and Secretary of Defense Clifford, counsel against any more troop increases in Vietnam.
March 31, 1968	In a televised address, President Johnson announces a partial halt to the U.S. bombing of North Vietnam, a call to North Vietnam to begin peace talks, and his decision not to seek reelection.
April 4, 1968	Martin Luther King Jr. is assassinated.
May 13, 1968	Formal peace talks between the United States and North Vietnam open in Paris.
June 5, 1968	Robert Kennedy is shot and killed shortly after winning the California primary.
August 1968	The Republican Party nominates Richard M. Nixon for president at its national convention in Miami, Florida, and calls for an honorable negotiated peace in Vietnam. Vice President Hubert Humphrey is nominated by the Democratic Party, while police and radical antiwar demonstrators clash in the streets of Chicago.
October 31, 1968	President Johnson announces a complete halt to the bombing of North Vietnam.
November 5, 1968	Richard M. Nixon is elected president.
March 15, 1969	Nixon orders the bombing of Vietcong sanctuaries in Cambodia; the bombing is kept secret from the American public.

May 1969	With American troop commitment at its peak of 543,000, President Nixon announces his first major troop withdrawal and pledges to replace the Selective Service System with a lottery.
June 8, 1969	Nixon announces that twenty-five thousand U.S. troops will be withdrawn and replaced by South Vietnamese soldiers.
June 10, 1969	The NLF announces the formation of a Provisional Revolutionary Government (PRG) to challenge the political legitimacy of South Vietnamese leader Thieu.
September 3, 1969	Ho Chi Minh dies at the age of seventy-nine.
September 23, 1969	Eight radical activist leaders go on trial in Chicago for their part in organizing the August 1968 antiwar demonstrations in that city.
October 15, 1969	More than a million people participate in antiwar demonstrations in cities across the country in the "October Moratorium."
November 3, 1969	In a televised address, President Nixon appeals to the "silent majority" of Americans to support his plan for "Vietnamization" and gradual American withdrawal from the war.
November 13, 1969	The U.S. public learns of the March 1968 My Lai incident.
November 15, 1969	In the largest single antiwar demonstration to date, 250,000 people gather in Washington, D.C.
December 31, 1969	U.S. troop levels in Vietnam stand at 479,000.
April 29, 1970	U.S. troops invade Cambodia to attack North Vietnamese and Vietcong sanctuaries.
May 4, 1970	Ohio National Guardsmen kill four Kent State University students during a campus antiwar demonstration.
June 24, 1970	The Senate repeals the 1964 Gulf of Tonkin Resolution by a vote of 82-1.
December 31, 1970	335,000 U.S. military personnel remain in South Vietnam.
January 1, 1971	Congress forbids the use of U.S. troops in Cambodia or Laos.
February 21–27, 1971	President Nixon makes a historic visit to China.
March 6–24, 1971	ARVN forces invade Laos to cut off enemy supply routes; they are beaten back and incur heavy losses.
March 29, 1971	U.S. Army Lt. William Calley is convicted for his role in the murder of South Vietnamese civilians at My Lai.
April 19–23, 1971	Vietnam Veterans Against the War stages demonstrations in Washington, D.C.

May 1971	National Security Adviser Henry Kissinger secretly promises North Vietnam that the United States will withdraw all troops within six months if American POWs are returned.
June 13, 1971	The *New York Times* begins publication of leaked portions of the *Pentagon Papers*—the forty-seven-volume Pentagon analysis of U.S. policy in Vietnam through 1967.
December 31, 1971	The number of U.S. military personnel in Vietnam has fallen to under 157,000.
March 1972	North Vietnam begins a major invasion of South Vietnam at a time when only ninety-five thousand American troops remain; Americans intensify bombing attacks to support the South Vietnamese.
May 1972	President Nixon resumes B-52 bombing raids of North Vietnam and orders the mining of Haiphong Harbor and a naval blockade of North Vietnam.
October 8–11, 1972	In secret talks, Henry Kissinger and North Vietnamese negotiator Le Duc Tho reach a cease-fire agreement; South Vietnam's leader Thieu rejects the agreement on October 22.
November 7, 1972	Nixon is reelected by a wide margin over his Democratic challenger, Sen. George McGovern, who had campaigned for immediate American withdrawal from Vietnam.
December 18, 1972	Four days after peace negotiations have been broken off, Nixon announces the resumption of bombing and mining of North Vietnam, while promising $1 billion in military hardware to President Thieu of South Vietnam.
December 31, 1972	Twenty-four thousand U.S. troops remain in South Vietnam.
January 8, 1973	Peace negotiations resume in Paris.
January 27, 1973	The Paris Peace Accords go into effect; the United States promises to remove its remaining twenty-seven thousand troops within sixty days. The draft ends.
February 12–27, 1973	American POWs begin to come home.
February 21, 1973	A cease-fire formally ends the war in Laos.
March 29, 1973	North Vietnam releases sixty American prisoners of war, who leave Vietnam along with the last remaining U.S. troops aside from Defense Attaché units and marine embassy guards. Eighty-five hundred American civilians also remain.
June 4, 1973	Congress blocks all funds for continuing U.S. military activities in Indochina; the last bombing operation in Cambodia ends on August 15.

November 7, 1973	Congress passes the War Powers Act over President Nixon's veto; it requires a president to inform Congress within forty-eight hours of the deployment of American troops and obligates the withdrawal of those troops within sixty days if there is no congressional approval in the interim.
August 1974	Nixon resigns to avoid being impeached for his role in the Watergate scandal. Vice President Gerald Ford assumes office.
January 1975	North Vietnam begins a series of large-scale offensives preparatory to a "general offensive" in 1976.
January 28, 1975	President Ford asks for an additional $722 million in emergency aid for South Vietnam; Congress refuses his request.
April 16, 1975	The Cambodian government surrenders to the Communist Khmer Rouge.
April 17, 1975	The Senate Armed Services Committee rejects a final administration request for emergency aid to South Vietnam.
April 21, 1975	President Nguyen Van Thieu resigns; in his last speech he attacks the United States as "unfair . . . inhumane . . . irresponsible."
April 24, 1975	President Ford declares the war "finished."
April 30, 1975	The South Vietnamese capital of Saigon falls to invading North Vietnamese forces as the last Americans are evacuated by helicopter from the U.S. embassy.

Annotated Bibliography

Dean Acheson. *Present at the Creation.* New York: Norton, 1969. The memoirs of President Harry S. Truman's secretary of state, who helped make the decisions that committed the United States to France in its war against Ho Chi Minh and the Vietminh.

Sam Adams. *War of Numbers: An Intelligence Memoir.* South Royalton, VT: Steerforth Press, 1994. The memoirs of a young CIA analyst about his efforts to get the truth as he saw it into the hands of those who were fighting the war just prior to the Tet Offensive of 1968.

David C. Anderson, ed. *Shadow on the White House: Presidents and the Vietnam War, 1945–1975.* Lawrence: University Press of Kansas, 1993. A series of scholarly essays on how presidential decisions about Vietnam were made.

Anthony Austin. *The President's War: The Story of the Gulf of Tonkin Resolution and How the Nation Was Trapped in Vietnam.* Philadelphia: Lippincott, 1971. A journalistic account of the 1964 Gulf of Tonkin incident and the congressional resolution that resulted.

Loren Baritz. *Backfire: A History of How American Culture Led Us into Vietnam and Made Us Fight the Way We Did.* New York: Morrow, 1985. A cultural history of the background of the Vietnam War and of the impact of American culture on the American military.

David M. Barrett. *Uncertain Warriors: Lyndon Johnson and His Vietnam Advisers.* Lawrence: University Press of Kansas, 1993. A history of the evolution of Johnson's inner circle of Vietnam War advisers between 1965 and 1968.

Lawrence M. Baskir and William A. Strauss. *Chance and Circumstance: The Draft, the War, and the Vietnam Generation.* New York: Knopf, 1978. A study that argues for general amnesty for those who evaded the draft during the Vietnam War.

Larry Berman. *Lyndon Johnson's War.* New York: Norton, 1989. An examination of U.S. war policies between 1965 and 1968 that is critical of President Johnson.

Larry Berman. *Planning a Tragedy: The Americanization of the War in Vietnam.* New York: Norton, 1982. An in-depth examination of President Lyndon B. Johnson's decision in July 1965 to escalate American involvement in Vietnam.

Melanie Billings-Yun. *Decision Against War: Eisenhower and Dienbienphu.* New York: Columbia University Press, 1988. The definitive study of the diplomacy and decision of the Eisenhower administration in 1954 in response to France's request for military support in its war against the Vietminh.

Lucien Bodard. *The Quicksand War: Prelude to Vietnam.* Boston: Little, Brown, 1967. A history of French Indochina from 1946 to 1950 by a French war correspondent who argues that the roots of American involvement can be traced to those years.

Peter Braestrup. *Big Story: How the American Press and Television Reported and Interpreted the Crisis of Tet 1968 in Vietnam and Washington.* Boulder, CO: Westview Press, 1977. A detailed history of the immediate aftermath of the 1968 Tet Offensive that argues that it was, contrary to American media reports, a military defeat for North Vietnam.

Bob Brewin and Sydney Shaw. *Vietnam on Trial: Westmoreland vs. CBS.* New York: Atheneum, 1987. A case history of the libel suit that Gen. William C. Westmoreland brought against the CBS television network for accusing him of deliberately underestimating enemy troop strength in Vietnam.

Malcolm W. Browne. *The New Face of War.* Indianapolis: Bobbs-Merrill, 1965. An account of the Vietnam War between 1961 and 1965 by an Associated Press correspondent who, although discouraged by American military prospects, still argues that the United States must not retreat from its stand to preserve South Vietnam.

William Broyles. *Brothers in Arms.* New York: Knopf, 1987. The reflections of a marine lieutenant who served in Vietnam in the late 1960s and who returned in 1984.

Wilfred Burchett. *Grasshoppers and Elephants: Why Vietnam Fell.* New York: Urizen Books, 1977. An account of the collapse of the South Vietnamese government that focuses on the popular uprisings in the towns and villages against the existing regime.

Wilfred Burchett. *Vietnam: Inside Story of the Guerrilla War.* New York: International Publishers, 1965. A history of the National Liberation Front written by a journalist whose praise for that organization borders on propaganda.

James Cable. *The Geneva Conference of 1954 on Indochina.* New York: St. Martin's Press, 1986. This diplomatic history of the international conference that ended the French phase of the war in Indochina emphasizes the role of Great Britain in orchestrating the French withdrawal.

William H. Chafe. *Never Stop Running: Allard Lowenstein and the Struggle to Save American Liberalism.* New York: BasicBooks, 1993. The biography of the man who instigated the campaign to "dump" President Lyndon B. Johnson in 1968 because of the war in Vietnam.

David Chanoff and Doan Van Toai. *Portrait of the Enemy.* New York: Random House, 1986. An invaluable account of the "other side" of the

270

Vietnam War based on interviews with Vietnamese soldiers, generals, spies, villagers, and others.

Michael Charlton and Anthony Moncrieff. *Many Reasons Why.* New York: Hill and Wang, 1978. Based on BBC radio transcripts, this book consists largely of interviews with key American decision makers between 1945 and 1975, including Gen. Maxwell Taylor, Ambassador Henry Cabot Lodge, and Secretary of State Dean Rusk.

Noam Chomsky. *At War with Asia.* New York: Pantheon Books, 1970. An important polemic that presumes that the American presence in Vietnam is a manifestation of American imperialism and argues for an immediate American military withdrawal from Southeast Asia.

Noam Chomsky. *Rethinking Camelot: JFK, the Vietnam War, and U.S. Political Culture.* Boston: South End Press, 1993. A critical analysis of and commentary on President John F. Kennedy's Vietnam policies.

Mark Clodfelter. *The Limits of Air Power: The American Bombing of North Vietnam.* New York: Free Press, 1989. An examination of the American bombing campaigns of the Vietnam War and a critique of the assumption that bombing would be the key to American victory in the conflict.

William Colby. *Lost Victory.* New York: Contemporary Books, 1989. An account by the director of the CIA during the 1975 fall of South Vietnam that argues that the United States had developed effective tactics for defending South Vietnam only to have U.S. support withdrawn.

Peter Collier and David Horowitz, eds. *Second Thoughts: Former Radicals Look Back at the Sixties.* New York: Madison Books, 1989. A book compiled from talks at a conference of former radical activists of the 1960s; a chapter on Vietnam is critical of the antiwar movement.

Chester L. Cooper. *The Lost Crusade: America in Vietnam.* New York: Dodd and Mead, 1970. A detailed insider's account of American involvement in Vietnam between 1940 and 1970 by a senior diplomat.

William R. Corson. *Consequences of Failure.* New York: Norton, 1974. An examination of the consequences of America's failure in Vietnam on the American military, the government, the middle class, youth, and the economy.

Cecil B. Curry. *Edward Lansdale: The Unquiet American.* Boston: Houghton Mifflin, 1988. A sympathetic portrait of the American military man who pioneered counterinsurgency warfare against Communists in both the Philippines and Vietnam in the 1950s.

Alan Dawson. *Fifty-Five Days: The Fall of South Vietnam.* Englewood Cliffs, NJ: Prentice-Hall, 1977. A journalistic account of the last days of the South Vietnamese regime and the American evacuation from Saigon.

Bui Diem with David Chanoff. *In the Jaws of History.* Boston: Houghton Mifflin, 1987. A chronicle of the wars in Vietnam from the end of the French colonial period to 1975, written by South Vietnam's ambassador to the United States from 1968 to 1972.

Dave Dellinger. *From Yale to Jail: The Life of a Moral Dissenter.* New York: Pantheon Books, 1993. The autobiography of one of the leaders of the antiwar movement during the 1960s, who visited North Vietnam in both 1966 and 1985.

William Duiker. *The Communist Road to Power in Vietnam.* Boulder, CO: Westview Press, 1981. A thorough political history that utilizes Vietnamese, French, and American sources concerning the evolution of Vietnamese communism from its origins in the 1920s to its triumph in 1975.

Donald Duncan. *The New Legions.* New York: Random House, 1967. A denunciation of the American role in Vietnam by a veteran of the Green Berets who served there.

Bernard Edelman, ed. *Dear America: Letters Home from Vietnam.* New York: Pocket Books, 1986. A moving anthology of letters from soldiers, with information provided on their past and present circumstances.

W.D. Ehrhart. *Passing Time: Memoir of a Vietnam Vet Against the War.* Jefferson, NC: McFarland, 1989. A memoir of both the war and the protests against it.

Gloria Emerson. *Winners and Losers.* New York: Random House, 1977. An account of the impact of the war on Americans and Vietnamese citizens based on numerous interviews conducted by a *New York Times* correspondent who was in Vietnam in 1956 and again between 1970 and 1972.

Bernard Fall. *The Two Vietnams: A Political and Military Analysis.* New York: Praeger, 1963. A firsthand account of both North and South Vietnam by a French journalist with extensive experience on both sides of the seventeenth parallel.

Bernard Fall and Marcus Raskin, eds. *The Viet Nam Reader.* New York: Random House, 1965. A collection of documents on the Vietnam War primarily from American and European sources.

Frances Fitzgerald. *Fire in the Lake.* Boston: Little, Brown, 1972. An examination of the Vietnam War that emphasizes the cultural differences and misunderstandings between Vietnamese and American societies.

James A. Freeman. *Hearts of Sorrow: Vietnamese-American Lives.* Stanford, CA: Stanford University Press. A record of the lives of fourteen Vietnamese people during the Vietnam War who subsequently moved to the United States.

Ellen Frey-Wouters and Robert S. Laufer. *Legacy of a War.* Armonk: NY: M.E. Sharpe, 1986. A survey of more than a thousand people, both veterans and nonveterans, that examines how the Vietnam War shaped their lives and opinions.

Ilya V. Gaiduk. *The Soviet Union and the Vietnam War.* Chicago: Ivan R. Dee, 1996. A diplomatic, political, and military history of the role of the Soviet Union in the Vietnam War between 1964 and 1973.

Lloyd C. Gardner. *Approaching Vietnam: From World War II Through Dien-bienphu, 1941–1954.* New York: Norton, 1988. A history of American foreign policy toward Vietnam, from President Franklin D. Roosevelt's plans for international trusteeship for French Indochina to Secretary of State John Foster Dulles's efforts to build the nation of South Vietnam.

Lloyd C. Gardner. *Pay Any Price: Lyndon Johnson and the Wars for Vietnam.* Chicago: Ivan R. Dee, 1995. A history of the Vietnam War that combines international diplomacy, political philosophy, and the psychological makeup of key players, including President Lyndon B. Johnson.

Adam Garfinkle. *Telltale Hearts: The Origins and Impact of the Vietnam Antiwar Movement.* New York: St. Martin's Press, 1995. A study critical of both U.S. policy in Vietnam and the antiwar movement, especially the latter's radical elements, which the author argues alienated most Americans and in effect prolonged the war.

Marvin E. Gettelman, Jane Franklin, Marilyn Young, and H. Bruce Franklin, eds. *Vietnam and America: A Documented History.* New York: Grove Press, 1985. A comprehensive collection of primary documents and historical essays on the Vietnam War, from Ho Chi Minh's 1919 appeal to the United States through the "Great Spring Victory" of North Vietnam in 1975.

James William Gibson. *The Perfect War.* Boston: Atlantic Monthly Press, 1986. An argument that U.S. strategy in Vietnam reflected a misplaced confidence in the ability of the United States to overwhelm the Vietnamese with superior technology and firepower.

Joseph C. Goulden. *Truth Is the First Casualty.* New York: Rand McNally, 1969. A carefully researched examination of the "multi-level deception" of Congress and the American public by the Johnson administration concerning the events in the Gulf of Tonkin that produced the Gulf of Tonkin Resolution.

Bob Greene. *Homecoming.* New York: Putnam, 1989. Accounts of Vietnam veterans' experiences upon returning to America.

Lawrence E. Grinter and Peter M. Dunn, eds. *The American War in Vietnam.* Westport, CT: Greenwood Press, 1987. A collection of essays by scholars and military officials examining what lessons the Vietnam War holds for U.S. foreign policy.

David Halberstam. *The Best and the Brightest.* New York: Random House, 1972. A thoroughly researched series of portraits of American military and political leaders who led the country into the "quagmire" of Vietnam.

Daniel Hallin. *The "Uncensored War": The Media and Vietnam.* New York: Oxford University Press, 1986. An analysis of *New York Times* and television coverage of the Vietnam War between 1961 and 1973.

Eric Hammel. *Khe Sanh: Siege in the Clouds: An Oral History.* New York: Crown Publishers, 1989. A day-to-day account based on oral histories of more than one hundred American soldiers who participated in the

273

1968 battle of Khe Sanh.

Ellen J. Hammer. *A Death in November: America in Vietnam, 1963.* New York: Dutton, 1987. A history of the unraveling relationship between President Ngo Dinh Diem of South Vietnam and American authorities, who were increasingly frustrated with the South Vietnamese war effort, culminating in the military coup that removed Diem from power and ended his life.

Richard Hammer. *The Court Martial of Lt. Calley.* New York: Coward, McCann, and Geoghegan, 1971. An engaging reportorial account of the court martial and conviction of 1st Lt. William Calley for his role in the March 1968 murder of Vietnamese civilians at My Lai.

Norman B. Hannah. *The Key to Failure: Laos and the Vietnam War.* New York: Madison Books, 1987. An examination of the "secret war" in the neighboring neutral country of Laos and of American efforts to recruit the Hmong people into the war effort.

David Harris. *Our War: What We Did in Vietnam and What It Did to Us.* New York: Random House, 1996. A memoir of a leading antiwar activist who argues that America needs to carefully examine, apologize, and offer reparations for what it did in Vietnam.

Thomas R.H. Havens. *Fire Across the Sea: The Vietnam War and Japan, 1965–1975.* Princeton, NJ: Princeton University Press, 1987. A study of the impact of the Vietnam War on Japanese politics, trade, society, and culture.

Tom Hayden. *Reunion.* New York: Random House, 1991. The memoirs of one of the leading radical activists of the 1960s and a critic of the American military presence in Vietnam.

Le Ly Hayslip with Jay Wurts. *When Heaven and Earth Changed Places.* New York: Doubleday, 1989. The autobiography of a Vietnamese woman that describes her family, her encounters with the Vietcong and American soldiers, her move to the United States following her marriage to an American, and her return visit to Vietnam.

Patrick J. Hearnden, ed. *Vietnam: Four American Perspectives.* West Lafayette, IN: Purdue University Press, 1990. Lectures given on the Vietnam War in retrospect by George McGovern, Edward Luttwak, Thomas McCormick, and Gen. William C. Westmoreland.

John Hellman. *American Myth and the Legacy of Vietnam.* New York: Columbia University Press, 1986. An inventive study of the Vietnam War using memoirs, novels, and films written and produced between 1955 and 1980.

Paul Hendrickson. *The Living and the Dead: Robert McNamara and Five Lives of a Lost War.* New York: Knopf, 1996. An indictment of the controversial defense secretary that examines his life in conjunction with those of five individuals who were directly affected by the Vietnam War.

George C. Herring. *America's Longest War: The United States and Vietnam,*

1950–1975. 3rd ed. New York: McGraw Hill, 1996. A study viewed by many as the best brief history of the Vietnam War.

Seymour M. Hersh. *My Lai 4: A Report on the Massacre and Its Aftermath.* New York: Random House, 1970. An account of the My Lai massacre written by the journalist who originally broke the story.

Townsend Hoopes. *The Limits of Intervention.* New York: David McKay, 1969. An insider's history of the decision of the Johnson administration to begin deescalation of the war in Vietnam, written by a Defense Department official.

Richard A. Hunt. *Pacification: The American Struggle for Vietnam's Hearts and Minds.* Boulder, CO: Westview Press, 1995. A history of the evolution and effectiveness of the American pacification programs in Vietnam from 1954 to the conclusion of the war.

Lyndon Baines Johnson. *The Vantage Point: Perspectives on the Presidency, 1963–1969.* New York: Holt, Rinehart and Winston, 1971. The memoirs of the president who presided over the major buildup in Vietnam in 1964 and 1965.

Paul Joseph. *Cracks in the Empire: State Politics in the Vietnam War.* New York: Columbia University Press, 1987. A self-described radical interpretation of the Vietnam War that argues that U.S. involvement in Vietnam was not the result of errors but rather part of a deliberate strategy to thwart social revolutions and maintain world dominance.

Ward Just. *To What End? Report from Vietnam.* Boston: Houghton Mifflin, 1968. A dispassionate report on the war in Vietnam by the *Washington Post* journalist who covered Vietnam in 1966 and 1967.

George McT. Kahin. *Intervention: How America Became Involved in Vietnam.* New York: Knopf, 1986. A history of the development of American involvement in Vietnam between 1945 and 1966 that makes use of declassified documents and that emphasizes the many missed opportunities to avoid military intervention.

Stanley Karnow. *Vietnam: A History.* New York: Viking Press, 1983. A sweeping history of Vietnam from the first Chinese settlements in 208 B.C. to the 1975 fall of South Vietnam; a companion volume to the thirteen-part documentary aired on public television.

Jeffrey P. Kimball. *To Reason Why: The Debate About the Causes of U.S. Involvement in the Vietnam War.* Philadelphia: Temple University Press, 1996. A collection of key primary source documents and scholarly essays regarding the origins of the American military role in Vietnam.

Henry Kissinger. *White House Years.* Boston: Little, Brown, 1979. The memoirs of President Nixon's national security adviser and secretary of state who negotiated the Paris Peace Accords of 1973.

Gabriel Kolko. *Anatomy of a War: Vietnam, the United States, and the Modern Historical Experience.* New York: Pantheon Books, 1986. A controversial history of the war that sympathizes with North Vietnam and documents the impact of the war on South Vietnam.

Andrew F. Krepinevich Jr. *The Army and Vietnam*. Baltimore: Johns Hopkins University Press, 1986. An analysis of American military policy in Vietnam from 1954 to 1973 by a member of the Strategic Plans and Policy Division of the U.S. Army who argues that military leaders used strategies and methods from World War II that were inappropriate in Vietnam.

Jean Lacouture. *Ho Chi Minh: A Political Biography*. New York: Random House, 1968. A biography of the president of North Vietnam that examines his peasant origins, his revolutionary ideology, and his leadership of a movement and later a country at war against the United States.

Anthony Lake, ed. *The Vietnam Legacy: The War, American Society, and the Future of American Foreign Policy*. New York: New York University Press, 1975. Twenty-two essays by scholars and politicians on the effects of the Vietnam War on American society.

Michael Lee Lanning and Dan Cregg. *Inside the VC and the NVA*. New York: Fawcett Columbine, 1992. A brief history of the Vietcong and the North Vietnamese Army written by two American veterans of the Vietnam War.

Edward G. Lansdale. *In the Midst of Wars: An American's Mission to Southeast Asia*. New York: Harper and Row, 1972. The memoirs of a controversial American counterinsurgency expert.

Otto J. Lehrack. *No Shining Armor: The Marines in Vietnam*. Lawrence: University Press of Kansas, 1992. An oral history of the marines and their role in Vietnam, with an emphasis on what it meant to be a "grunt" in Vietnam.

David W. Levy. *The Debate over Vietnam*. Baltimore: Johns Hopkins University Press, 1991. A brief and balanced account of the strategic, moral, and political debates in America over the war in Vietnam.

Guenter Lewy. *America in Vietnam*. New York: Oxford University Press, 1978. A history that examines the charges against U.S. military policy in the war and finds most of them unjustified.

Myra MacPherson. *Long Time Passing: Vietnam and the Haunted Generation*. New York: Doubleday, 1984. Based on five hundred interviews of people who came of age during the Vietnam War, this study argues that both those who served and those who did not were greatly affected by the military draft and the war in Vietnam.

Norman Mailer. *Armies of the Night*. New York: Signet, 1968. A dramatic account of the October 1967 antiwar march on the Pentagon written by an important American novelist who participated in it.

William P. Mahedy. *Out of the Night*. New York: Ballantine Books, 1986. An examination of the emotional and spiritual problems created by the Vietnam War written by a chaplain during the conflict and counselor to Vietnam veterans.

Andrew Martin. *Receptions of War: Vietnam in American Culture*. Norman:

University of Oklahoma Press, 1993. An innovative history of the representations of the Vietnam War in popular culture, including books, films, and television.

John T. McAlister Jr. *Viet Nam: The Origins of Revolution*. New York: Knopf, 1969. A history of the Vietminh and its mass organizing of 1945–1946.

Robert S. McNamara. *In Retrospect: The Tragedy and Lessons of Vietnam*. New York: Times Books, 1995. The controversial memoirs of the secretary of defense under Presidents Kennedy and Johnson, who reveals how his doubts about the Vietnam War grew, even as he publicly supported it.

John Mecklin. *Mission in Torment: An Intimate Account of the U.S. Role in Vietnam*. New York: Doubleday, 1965. A memoir of the public affairs officer of the American Embassy in Saigon from 1962 to 1964.

John M. Newman. *JFK and Vietnam: Deception, Intrigue, and the Struggle for Power*. New York: Warner Books, 1992. A controversial book based on the premise that President Kennedy was preparing to withdraw from Vietnam once he had been safely reelected in 1964.

John B. Nichols and Barrett Tillman. *On Yankee Station*. Annapolis, MD: Naval Institute Press, 1987. An account of U.S. Navy operations in the Vietnam War that is part personal memoir and part military analysis.

Richard M. Nixon. *No More Vietnams*. New York: Arbor House, 1985. The former president's analysis of the Vietnam War and his prescriptions on how to avoid such conflicts in the future.

Don Oberdorfer. *Tet!* New York: Doubleday, 1971. An account of the 1968 Tet Offensive by a reporter on the scene.

James Olson and Randy Roberts. *Where the Domino Fell: America and Vietnam, 1945–1995*. New York: St. Martin's Press, 1996. A general overview of a war that the authors argue was the "wrong war in the wrong place at the wrong time."

Bruce Palmer Jr. *The Twenty-Five-Year War: America's Military Role in Vietnam*. Lexington: University of Kentucky Press, 1984. A senior military officer's history of the war that focuses on the overall strategy rather than the actual fighting.

F. Charles Parker IV. *Vietnam: Strategy for a Stalemate*. An examination of the Vietnam War in the context of the diplomatic relationship between the United States, China, and the Soviet Union, this book concludes that American fears of direct Chinese intervention in Vietnam were largely unfounded.

The Pentagon Papers. Senator Gravel Edition. 5 vols. Boston: Beacon Press, 1971. A large portion of the famous internal Pentagon study of Vietnam that was leaked and published in the *New York Times* and other newspapers.

Douglas Pike. *Viet Cong: The Organization and Techniques of the National*

Liberation Front of South Vietnam. Cambridge, MA: MIT Press, 1966. An exhaustive examination of the strengths and weaknesses of the Vietcong that emphasizes its strengths and argues that the organization was not simply an arm of Hanoi.

John Pilger. *The Last Day: America's Final Hours in Vietnam.* New York: Random House, 1975. An effective instant history of the chaotic end of the American presence in Vietnam.

Robert Pisor. *The End of the Line: The Siege of Khe Sanh.* New York: Norton, 1982. A war correspondent's account of the history, politics, and strategy of this key 1968 battle for control of a village near the border between South and North Vietnam.

John L. Plaster. *SOG: The Secret Wars of America's Commandos in Vietnam.* New York: Simon and Schuster, 1996. An insider's account of the "Studies and Observations Group" (SOG), which took on a variety of covert and dangerous missions in Vietnam, including the rescue of downed American pilots; written by a retired army major who served three tours with SOG.

Norman Podhoretz. *Why We Were in Vietnam.* New York: Simon and Schuster, 1982. A conservative defense of the American commitment to South Vietnam.

Murray Polner. *No Victory Parades: The Return of the Vietnam Veteran.* New York: Holt, Rinehart and Winston, 1971. A brief study of Vietnam veterans based on interviews with two hundred veterans as well as with psychiatrists, social workers, and families.

Gareth Porter. *A Peace Denied: The United States, Vietnam, and the Paris Agreement.* Bloomington: Indiana University Press, 1975. A history of the negotiations and implementation of the 1973 Paris Peace Accords. Based on the fact that President Thieu of South Vietnam was assured by President Nixon of continued American military support, this book contends that the agreement was not necessarily intended to end the war.

Gareth Porter, ed. *Vietnam: A History in Documents.* New York: New American Library, 1981. An important collection of primary sources dealing with Vietnam before and during the years of American military involvement.

Thomas Powers. *The War at Home: Vietnam and the American People, 1964–1968.* New York: Grossman, 1973. This study of the ideas and activities of the antiwar movement contends that President Johnson moved to halt escalation of American involvement in Vietnam in 1968 because of domestic opposition to the war.

John Prados. *The Hidden History of the Vietnam War.* Chicago: Ivan R. Dee, 1995. A history that focuses on covert operations and other little-known facets of the Vietnam War.

William Prochnau. *Once upon a Distant War.* New York: Random House, 1995. A readable general history of the press coverage of the war in Vietnam.

William J. Rust. *Kennedy in Vietnam.* New York: Scribner's, 1985. A history of the Kennedy administration that stresses the ad hoc nature of its decision making regarding Vietnam.

Harrison E. Salisbury. *Behind the Lines—Hanoi.* New York: Harper and Row, 1967. The controversial dispatches of a celebrated *New York Times* reporter who traveled to North Vietnam and toured the countryside during the last weeks of 1966.

Al Santoli, ed. *To Bear Any Burden.* New York: Dutton, 1985. An oral history of the Vietnam War, edited with a generally conservative slant, that includes American, Vietnamese, and Cambodian participants in the conflict.

Jonathan Schell. *The Village of Ben Suc.* New York: Random House, 1967. An account of the destruction by American bombs and bulldozers of a village near Saigon and the removal of its thirty-five hundred people during a U.S. military operation.

R.L. Schreadley. *From the Rivers to the Sea.* Annapolis, MD: Naval Institute Press, 1992. A military history of the role of the U.S. Navy in the war in Vietnam.

Robert Shaplen. *Bitter Victory.* New York: Harper and Row, 1986. The reflections of a veteran reporter who first visited Saigon in 1946, was among the last Americans to leave in 1975, and who returned in 1984 to conclude that the North Vietnamese victory was a "hollow" one for most Vietnamese.

William Shawcross. *Side-Show: Kissinger, Nixon, and the Destruction of Cambodia.* New York: Pocket Books, 1979. A harsh critique of the Nixon administration and its 1970 decision to expand the war into Cambodia.

Neil Sheehan. *A Bright Shining Lie: John Paul Vann and America in Vietnam.* New York: Random House, 1988. This Pulitzer Prize–winning biography of John Paul Vann, a U.S. Army officer who arrived in Vietnam in 1962 and was killed there in 1972, criticizes the American military effort in Vietnam.

Melvin Small. *Johnson, Nixon, and the Doves.* New Brunswick, NJ: Rutgers University Press, 1988. An analysis of the impact of the peace movement on presidential decision making under both Johnson and Nixon.

Frank Snepp. *A Decent Interval: An Insider's Account of Saigon's Indecent End.* New York: Random House, 1977. A veteran CIA official's account of the 1975 demise of South Vietnam.

Ronald H. Spector. *Advice and Support: The Early Years of the U.S. Army in Vietnam, 1941–1960.* New York: Free Press, 1985. An interesting study of the U.S. role in Vietnam from President Roosevelt's opposition to the return of the French in 1945 to the role of the U.S. Army in preparing the South Vietnamese to resist North Vietnam during the 1950s.

Ronald H. Spector. *After Tet: The Bloodiest Year in Vietnam.* New York: Free Press, 1993. A detailed military account of the nine months of the war following President Johnson's announced decision not to seek reelection.

Shelby L. Stanton. *The Rise and Fall of an American Army: U.S. Ground Forces in Vietnam, 1965–1973*. Novato, CA: Presidio Press, 1985. The effort of a Vietnam combat veteran to expose various "myths" of the war, including the idea that the war in Vietnam was in fact a guerrilla war that American officers and troops were ill-equipped to fight.

Harry Summers. *On Strategy: A Critical Analysis of the Vietnam War*. San Francisco: Presidio Press, 1982. An examination of the military strategy in Vietnam by a U.S. Army colonel who argues that the American military professionals, in emphasizing guerrilla warfare, failed to judge the true nature of the war and the enemy.

Maxwell Taylor. *Swords and Plowshares*. New York: Norton, 1972. The memoirs of the general who advocated guerrilla warfare in Southeast Asia and who served as ambassador to South Vietnam.

Robert Thompson. *No Exit from Vietnam*. New York: David McKay, 1969. A British expert on guerrilla warfare analyzes the American military and argues for a continued military commitment on the part of the United States.

Earl H. Tilford Jr. *Crosswinds: The Air Force's Setup in Vietnam*. College Station: Texas A & M University Press, 1993. A careful critique of the air war over Vietnam.

Douglas Valentine. *The Phoenix Program*. New York: William Morrow, 1990. A history of the controversial CIA effort to "neutralize" the Vietcong infrastructure that critics charged was simply a program of assassinations.

Jayne S. Werner and Luu Doan Huynh, eds. *The Vietnam War: Vietnamese and American Perspectives*. Armonk, NY: M.E. Sharpe, 1993. The proceedings of a 1990 conference of twenty-two scholars from the United States and Vietnam, including Tran Van Tra, commander of the People's Liberation Armed Forces of South Vietnam from 1963 to 1975.

William C. Westmoreland. *A Soldier Reports*. New York: Doubleday, 1976. The memoirs of the commander of American forces in Vietnam from 1964 to 1968.

William Appleman Williams et al., eds. *America in Vietnam: A Documentary History*. New York: Doubleday, 1985. This collection of historical essays and primary sources on America in Vietnam seeks to place the war in the wider context of American policy toward Asia.

Marilyn Blatt Young. *The American-Vietnam Wars, 1945–1990*. New York: Harper and Row, 1991. A general history of the Vietnam War written by a former antiwar activist.

Index

TV coverage of war, 242–43
lagged behind public opinion, 251
was favorable, 248
was biased in coverage, 245
Mekong River Delta, 92
military advisers, U.S.
sent to South Vietnam, 71
turnover in, 90
Moss, George, 27, 247
Mutual Security Act, 45
My Lai, 225

National Liberation Front, 71
Communist influence in, 106
protesters' solidarity with, 194, 195
see also Vietcong
National Rifle Association
as model for antiwar movement, 202
New Republic, 62
New York Times, 43, 223
coverage of war by, 250
Ngo Dinh Diem, 51
critique of, 66
early struggles of, 56–57
first elections under, 60
overthrow of, 86, 106
poor leadership of, 91
U.S. backing of, 55
Ngo Dinh Nhu, 77
Nguyen Cao Ky, 105, 112
has no political base, 152
Nguyen Thanh Phuong, 56
Nguyen That Thanh. *see* Ho Chi Minh
Nguyen Van Hinh, 56
Nguyen Van Thieu, 154
Nixon, Richard M., 141, 156
on anarchy in U.S., 160
had opportunity to end war, 153
was committed to war, 198–99, 225
Nixon Doctrine, 145–46, 198

opinion polls. *See* public opinion

Paris Peace Talks, 141, 171
Plan Huy Quat, 114
Podhoretz, Norman, 173
polls. *See* public opinion
Potter, Paul, 108
Provisional Revolutionary
Government of South Vietnam,
195–96
public opinion
on bombing of North Vietnam, 201
on influence of TV news coverage,
248
on U.S. entry into war, 249
on Vietnam War, 211

Pueblo incident, 135

Radford, Arthur W., 36, 44
Rainwater, H.R., 231
refugees
after Geneva Agreement of 1954,
59–60
Tonkinese, settlement of, 67
Republic of Vietnam (South Vietnam)
battle areas of, 90–92
creation, 51
elections in, 60
failure to hold, 106
succeeded despite Vietcong, 126
lack of stability in, 63
politico-religious sects in, 52, 64
reaction to U.S. force expansion,
114–15
repression in, 68–70, 106, 108, 154
Tet offensive has shown
vulnerability of, 133
United States and
aid to
has not brought security to,
65–68
is essential, 84
commitment to, 72
is barrier to peace talks, 152–53
plan in, phases of, 126–30
withdrawal from
support of, 221
con, 228
Vietnamese people do not support,
154
Western objectives in, 63–65
Roberts Board, 207, 218
Rusk, Dean, 71, 101
on strategic importance of South
Vietnam, 73

Saigon, 89, 131
Sanders, Sol W., 85
Shawcross, William, 243
Sihanouk, Prince Norodom, 156, 163
Silent Majority, 149
is a myth, 201
is pitted against protesters, 199
Smith, Walter Bedell, 44
Southeast Asia Treaty Organization
(SEATO), 55, 67
U.S. commitment to South Vietnam
under, 72
Spring Mobilization, 185, 186
Stephens, Melville L., 228
"strategic hamlet" program, 81
Students for a Democratic Society
(SDS), 108, 192